INVISIBLE WOUNDS:
Crime Victims Speak

INVISIBLE WOUNDS:
Crime Victims Speak

Shelley Neiderbach, Ph. D.

THE HAWORTH PRESS
New York • London

The Haworth Press, Inc. 12 West 32 Street, New York, NY 10001
EUROSPAN/Haworth, 3 Henrietta Street, London WC2E 8LU England

Library of Congress Cataloging in Publication Data

Neiderbach, Shelley.
    Invisible wounds.

    Bibliography: p.
    1. Victims of crimes—United States—Interviews. 2. Victims of crimes—United States—Counseling of. I. Title.
HV6250.3.U5N45   1986   362.8'8'0973   86-14831
ISBN 0-86656-460-8
ISBN 0-86656-525-6 (pbk.)

Printed in the United States of America

Epigraph: "Phobiphobia." Copyright 1982, Kate Brandt. Used with permission of the author.

For
PAULINE SWEET, M.D.,
without whom
this would not have come to pass
and
my friends and family
who have been
victims and covictims

We are asked to think that vengeance brutalizes, forgiveness refines. But the opposite can be true. Forgiveness can brutalize. Forgiveness can be pitiless. It forgets the victim. It negates the right of the victim to his own life. It blurs over suffering and death. It drowns the past. It cultivates sensitiveness toward the murderer at the price of insensitiveness toward the victim.

Cynthia Ozick, Author

Public forgiveness and private vengeance suffer from the same vice: They depreciate the victim. Respect for those who suffer requires that no one usurp the victim's exclusive right to forgive his oppressor. Similarly, it requires that the duty to punish must be assumed by everyone other than the victim. That is what is meant by the rule of law.

Aryeh Neier, Professor of Law, New York University

Because the violation of self is invisible it's hard to put your finger on what's wrong here.

Morton Bard and Diane Sangrey, Victimologists

Contents

Acknowledgments

My gratitude and thanks to: Rita Arditti, Bob Arey, Natalie Becker, Hank Campbell, Jean Griffin, Bea Gross, Ron Gross, Jersey City State College Career Development Committee, Dale Kahn, Stuart Marcus, Richard Mayer, Danny Montoya, Michael Montoya, Sharon Montoya, Denise Phillips, Lillian Rodberg, Jack Victor, Fran Zujkowski and, most especially, Susan Iwanowski.

Foreword

In recent years I have been exploring the subject of why victims, despite treatment by competent professionals, still remain psychologically disabled. I have found there are undisclosed, open wounds of victimization kept open by the victims' self-hatred, guilt, and shame. These open wounds retard and prevent the healing process from taking place.

Dr. Neiderbach's concepts, methods, and unique method of presenting the dramatic first-hand account of the victim's personal experience and reaction—with a side-by-side running commentary—is a valuable contribution to the field of victimology.

Mental health professionals, victims, and others interested in understanding and relieving the distress of victims will significantly benefit from reading Dr. Neiderbach's book.

Martin Symonds, M.D.
Assistant Dean of the American Institute
of Psychoanalysis;
Director, Victim Treatment Center
Karen Horney Clinic;
Associate Clinical Professor of Psychiatry
NYU School of Medicine;
Deputy Chief Surgeon
New York City Police Department

Phobiphobia

(with thanks to Robin Morgan's "Phobiphilia")

you don't know how I hate all of you

how I envy all of you

you never have to think twice

about walking to the corner for a newspaper
about shopping for groceries on a Saturday morning
about waiting on the platform for a subway
about taking a long walk on a Sunday afternoon
about running errands on the way home from work
about buying concert tickets a month in advance
about making appointments for job interviews
about being stuck in a traffic jam
about sitting for a haircut
about meeting a friend for lunch

you've never had to walk two blocks

TWO LOUSY GODDAMNED SHORT NEIGHBORHOOD BLOCKS! with

your face steaming like a Chinese dumpling
your eyes wondering if they're wearing someone else's glasses
your gut backflipping like a visceral kaleidoscope
your legs doing their wet spaghetti imitation
your teeth doing a clichéd rattle like plastic castanets
your neck staining like blotted watercolors
your palms itching like cartoon fortunetellers'
your breath exiting in lumps like iceballs
your heart kicking down your chest's door

while a gun is held to the ribs of your brain
and your adrenaline reactor is having a meltdown
and you're programming a mental movieola
with grab-bag mantras   with desperate distractions:

silently singing a Motown medley
remembering the lyrics to ''Bohemian Rhapsody''
dreaming an affair with the lead guitarist
counting backwards from six hundred and seventeen
and the chant   behind pulsing eyebrows   the chant:

I'll be okay I'll be
okay just let me get where
it's safe get me
someplace
where it's
safe   safe   safe   safe   safe   safe
      safe   safe   safe   safe   safe
safe   safe   safe   safe   safe   safe

NOTE

Epigraph: ''Phobiphobia.'' Copyright 1982, Kate Brandt. Used with permission of the author.

Introduction: "A Blow of Redirection"

Twenty-eight years ago I was the victim of a brutal and violent crime—my face was completely smashed in by a mentally retarded assailant wielding a steel bar. "A blow of redirection" is the term used by one of the crime victims speaking out in this book to describe the impact of crime. This term evokes ready identification from one crime victim to another, and it also poses an implicit question. "Redirection"—but toward what goals? This book sheds fresh light on what happens in the struggle for a positive direction.

As both a crime victim myself and a developer/activist in the emerging field of mental health services for crime victims, I have long been troubled and fascinated by the question of the victim's mental health goals and outcomes. The characteristic victim trauma response—rage, guilt, helplessness, and fear—is a given. And evidence is slowly accumulating to indicate that while various types of interventions do indeed help to alleviate and decrease the intensity of these feelings, they do persist over time to some degree. I can bear witness to that myself. But I can also bear witness to the fact that, as is so beautifully iillustrated in this book, out of that ferment, that struggle, can materialize new personality strengths. They travel hand in hand with the victimization-induced characteristics, and it is this play of light and dark that is a hallmark of the victim experience.

This book, emphasizing as it does the full extent of the mental health crisis suffered by victims, comes at a propitious time. The past six years have seen rapid developments in the coalescence of a knowledge base regarding the anatomy and physiology of the mental health response to victimization. Beginning with the formation of an international Scientific Committee on this topic by the World Federation for Mental Health, followed by the work of the President's Task Force on Crime Victims in the United States, the mental health crisis has been underscored and addressed in powerful new initiatives. Among these are the formation of Task Forces on victimization by the American Psychological and Psychiatric Associations, the sponsorship of a Services Research and Evaluation Assessment Colloquium "The Aftermath of Crime: A Mental Health Crisis" by the National Institute of Mental Health, the founding of the Society for Traumatic Stress Studies, and the adoption by the General Assembly of the United Nations of a "Declaration of Basic Principles of Justice for Victims of Crime and Abuse of Power." And now, in this book we hear about the mental health crisis in the voices of crime victims themselves.

1

What are the immediate needs that skillful and sensitive intervention can be helpful in addressing? The crime victims' group intervention outlined in this book functions on many levels: It validates the reality of the experience and sanctions the right to feel as one feels about it; it provides reassurance through the learning that occurs about the "natural and normal" progression of symptoms and stages of resolution; and it meets the need that crime victims experience to talk with those who have gone through it also, and thus is helpful in providing concepts, words, and examples that make it possible to give voice to what one has experienced. These are almost preconditions for the growth of the personality strengths that can emerge. But what is the process through which these strengths emerge?

"Transfiguration" is the word that I have chosen to use to describe what appears to be a process of conversion. The core feelings in the victim trauma response—rage, guilt, helplessness, and fear—are converted, through human support and emotional insight and catharsis, into their polar equivalents. Rage gives way to compassion, guilt finds its expression through a desire to help others—a mission orientation, helplessness is supplanted by keener coping behavior regarding crime prevention, and fear is replaced by, as one of the victims in this book puts it, "finding one's old self and improving on it." And a feeling that underlies the victim trauma response, the sense of one's foreshortened mortality, gradually alternates with redoubled efforts to establish new priorities and to get the most out of life. As I indicated earlier, this process of conversion is an oscillating one, with one feeling predominating at one point in time and the other at another point in time, but transfiguration occurs through time. This is threaded through each crime victim's story in this book.

It is never too late for this process to begin to take place, even if one has been "frozen" or "stuck" for many years. In my own case, it was seventeen years after the mugging itself with the development of a chronic and debilitating respiratory condition related to the damage that was done at the time of the mugging that I first confronted my feelings of rage, helplessness, guilt, and fear. The feelings had, of course, been present over time and had taken a very heavy, but unmeasured, toll on my adaptive capacities, but I had never given them voice—even in my own mind. The rage, once confronted, was palpable and threatened to become overwhelming, but with the assistance of others who were beginning to work in this new field, I began to achieve some insight, some ability to manage the feelings, some transfiguration. For me, a mission orientation has provided the most profound relief. How I wish I could have short-circuited those seventeen years, but what a pleasure it is to see programs such as the one described in this book attempt to provide some more immediate relief, symptom reduction, and human connection.

This book serves another important function—it is one further step in bringing crime victimization "out of the closet." Since most victims are stigmatized by family, friends, and the public, who often blame the victim for his or her own plight, so that they do not have to confront the fact that it could happen to them, victims learn to hide their status, not to speak of what occurred, not to share their feelings. These actions increase a sense of shame and rejection, compounding the victim trauma response. In speaking up, in coming out of the closet, in asserting their identity and feelings, they are making us all stronger. The injury that the victim suffered was human to human, and as this book makes very clear, the remedy is human to human.

Susan E. Salasin
Founding Chair
Scientific Committee
on the Mental Health Service Needs
of Victims of Violence
World Federation for Mental Health

Founding Board Member
Society for Traumatic Stress Studies

Genesis

This study began because I am both a psychotherapist and a crime victim. In 1975, I was mugged[1] for the first time and, though I was then in therapy, the emotional effects were handled as part of ongoing treatment and not given any particular focused attention. In 1980, a second occurrence was, in many ways, a more powerful and life-changing event. This time, I wanted crime-specific therapeutic services, and—I wanted to talk with other crime victims. It was hard for me to believe that I was the only victim struggling with the emotional issues of rage, guilt, and helplessness, and I wanted to know how other people were dealing with the traumas that beset them. I was later to learn that these feelings comprised the cluster of symptoms known to victimologists as Victim Trauma Syndrome (VTS), a generic subset of what the American Psychiatric Association terms "post-traumatic stress disorder, chronic or delayed" (PTSD).[2]

In New York City during the calendar year of 1980, there were, as officially reported,

1,787	murders	(5 a day)
3,986	rapes	(11 a day)
100,550	muggings	(275 a day)
27,358	felonious assaults[3]	(75 a day)
212,748	burglaries	(582 a day)
147,073	grand larcenies	(402 a day)[4]

These numbers reflect only *reported* crimes and in no way convey the psychic impact (setting aside, for a moment, the financial, medical, and social consequences) of a single crime upon a single crime victim. In this respect, statistics obscure and thereby inevitably restrict our view of human events; they reduce to virtual invisibility the true dimensions of crime, individual and societal. What were all of these people experiencing? Though I am myself a psychotherapist and have access to a wide variety of individual and group therapies, I felt this route was somehow insufficient: Only those who had "gone through it, too" might understand the crisis I was experiencing. I therefore scoured New York City for the equivalent of a "Muggees Anonymous" group and failed to uncover one. Ergo, I determined to create such a modality and proceeded to do so.

The road, however, was not very smooth, paved as it was by my ignorance and naiveté. I had approached Victim Services Agency, the single publicly funded service in New York City, to find that, beyond

telephone hotline counseling, no group services were being offered; the
Victim Treatment Service of the Karen Horney Institute could give me six
free one-hour individual therapy sessions (if I could wait three months);
there were group counseling services available for battered women, raped
women, incest survivors, and the families of homicides, but nothing for
the "average street crime victim." Why not?

Theoretical Considerations

A preliminary reading of the tiny library of information about crime
victimization convinced me that group psychotherapeutic services were
not only necessary but mandatory for the mental health of crime victims.
The two noted articulators of VTS, Morton Bard, Ph.D. (with Diane
Sangrey) and Martin Symonds, M.D., both essentially agreed that
victims tend to have similar patterns of response after a crime. If this were
so, then a "universal" treatment plan could undergird and structure
groups that would provide short-term intervention relief. All victims
needed ego reintegration services that would allow for appropriate
ventilation of feelings unacceptable in the nonvictim population, and
acceptance and supportive interpretations by other victims and the
counselor/therapist. As spelled out in American Psychological Association *Diagnostic and Statistical Manual III* (DSM III) "the characteristic
symptoms [of PTSD] involve reexperiencing the traumatic event; numbing of responsiveness to, or reduced involvement with, the external
world; and a variety of autonomic, dysphoric, or cognitive symptoms."[5]

On the basis of this information, coupled with my two crime victim
experiences, I set about developing a counseling plan that would take into
account those symptoms delineated in the literature and other victims'
reports of being unable to find sufficiently supportive and empathic
responses, even from friends and family. In consultation with Richard
Mayer, C.S.W., former counselor at the Karen Horney Victim Treatment
Service, I devised a four-part counseling unit: weekly sessions lasting two
hours or more, to focus on feelings attached to the possibility of
1) remeeting one's assailant(s), 2) fear, 3) anger, and 4) helplessness.
Soon thereafter, Crime Victims' Counseling Services, Inc., was established as the vehicle through which such interventions could be offered;
the first group met in April 1981.

As you might expect, and as the personal accounts that form this book
show, the crime victim's experience encompasses far more than the list
above suggests. The victim must deal with more subtle issues such as:

- Generalized loss of control and derivative feelings that "the system doesn't work," authority does not prevail
- A sense of punishment, by virtue of the crime, for floating unconscious guilt
- A heightened sense that life is irrational—especially for CVCS participants, none of whom knew their assailants prior to the crime
- The need to accept that, indeed, there *was* no reason, that the question "Why me?" does not necessarily have an answer—and the need to invent or create some cause-and-effect rationale in the absence of this rationality, to find a gestalt with which to order the internal chaos a crime generates
- The renunciation of the "Anne Frank Syndrome"—an idealized "people-are-good-at-heart" notion in the face of experiencing the thinness of the veneer of civilization of the assailants
- The acknowledgment that the victim's *own* rage, after the crime, makes him or her feel capable of committing violence, too—that when victims in fact have revenge fantasies, they feel like twins or "doubles" of the perpetrators
- The even more difficult acceptance, after having one's life threatened, of one's mortality—and the consequent grief at its true discovery.
- Loss of trust in individuals, groups, and society.

Gender Differences in Victimization

In the course of leading over two dozen groups of victims of "generic" crime—i.e., male and female victims of non-domestic, non-sexual violence ("average muggees")—some significant differences were observed in the reactions of men and women to the disaster that had befallen them. Most prominent were women's acceptance of the crime events as yet another kind of victimization with which they had to cope. Consequently, their recovery tended to be more rapid and thorough: Since they had all too often in their lives experienced being out of control, having to "take orders" from males in authority, and generally not having great power over their own life choices and responses, women's education-in-living afforded them a more elastic emotional cushion. Men, on the other hand, more often appear to suffer acutely from losing control of their lives, even when the crime event took sixty seconds or less. They were nearly all afflicted with obsessive self-doubt, questioning again and again why they hadn't acted differently, more vigorously, or more successfully in the prevention of the crime or the pursuit of the "alleged perpetrator(s)."

Women are more capable than men of having and expressing desires for violent revenge; in contrast, men tend to want to ask perpetrators questions that are a variation on "why?" and to be given logical, rational answers that leave the emotionally charged issues of fear and loss of control largely untouched.

The commonplace assumption that women are passive during crime situations needs to be reexamined, for it appears to be entirely unwarranted. Women fought back as frequently as men did—which is, in fact, not very often. In general, both sexes neither fought nor fled, but froze and/or complied with the uniformly male assailants who both threatened their lives verbally and brandished (and sometimes employed) deadly weapons in the course of robbery/assault.

Lastly, the women who participated in the counseling groups frequently reported being treated as "hysterical broads" by police, ambulance attendants, assistant district attorneys, and other service providers. Although men exhibited identical expressions of fear and/or rage, women who did so were told they were being "too emotional" while men were lauded for "being able" to express their feelings at all. This form of secondary victimization leads to virtual denial of females' feelings and support for unrealistic vengeance scenarios for men. It tends in both instances to retard recovery by further enraging the victim at a time when experiencing rage to any extent is already felt to be unusual and overwhelming.

To be a crime victim of either gender is to suffer a psychic catastrophe. Crime victims need to reintegrate their fragmented egos and then to integrate the entire event into their private histories. They need not be prisoners of their experience: Victims can confront their rage at the perpetrators, and survive; return to the scene of the crime (street, home, subway, office), and survive; forgive themselves for whatever choice *they* made during the crime regarding the possibilities of fight/flight/or freeze, and survive.

A Further Note

The foregoing topics, and others, were explored by means of written exercises done by all participants during the weekly sessions and then read aloud to the entire group. As you read these statements, note the striking similarities of feelings. These similarities, which did not go unnoticed by the victims, had the immediate, salubrious effect of reducing victim defensiveness and anger at not being emotionally understood. The collective sense of relief was palpable; victims sighed audibly and voiced their individual variations on, "At last—somebody really knows what I'm going through."

The degree of victim isolation cannot be overestimated: Crime victims feel lost not only within themselves but within the human community as well. Therefore, the conversion of the CVCS counseling group into what became a virtual subculture and "intentional family" was swift, predictable, and enthusiastically determined by the participants. This fairly immediate sense of group identity laid the groundwork for the more acute and profound psychological revelations that victims then permitted to surface as the sessions continued.

Victims were especially encouraged to keep a journal or "debrief" into a tape recorder between sessions. They were also encouraged to help begin reducing feelings of powerlessness by volunteering to work with community agencies connected with crime prevention, detection, or victimization.

In an era of increasing crime and decreasing respect for a criminal justice system that seems to protect criminals and ignore victims, it is noteworthy that there are currently—apart from isolated and limited facilities—few civically supported, integrated, readily known and institutionalized efforts to deal exclusively with the psychological trauma incurred by crime victims. Some legal and moral support services exist in and near New York City for those victims who (a) are fortunate enough to have their assailants arrested *and* (b) then choose to go forward with prosecution. This population is quite small, relative to the vast numbers of crime victims whose victimization rarely comes to the notice of the criminal justice system at all.

For most publicly funded victims' services, the object of rendering such services is *not* particularly to promote the psychic welfare of the victim but merely to promote it in the service of converting victims to witnesses, so that prosecution rates can be higher. Indeed, many states refer to comprehensive victims' services as "witness assistance programs," whose central purpose is to aid the victim/witness through the jurisprudential jungle that is the criminal justice system. Psychological counseling, if attended to at all, is generally tacked on as a method of reducing victim/witness nonappearances in court: Counseling services are therefore to benefit the criminal justice system first and the victim second.

It should also be noted that the very term "victim" is *not* in the lexicon of the police or the legal system. "Witness" and "complainant" are used—words that have the effect of distancing the crime victim from a process that actually involved victim and perpetrator in equal measure. "Witness" connotes an onlooker rather than the coerced participant in evil a crime victim actually becomes. "Complainant" suggests (and makes the victim feel like) a querulous nuisance. Neither connotation contains a shred of truth.

Much crime goes unreported and therefore unprosecuted; the Federal Bureau of Investigation[6] estimates that only one in ten street crimes comes to the attention of the police. This bespeaks a vast societal disaffection with police effectiveness, an unwillingness (at the very least) to put faith in the initial stages of the workings of the criminal justice system, and a fairly universal lack of trust that anything will or can be done to seek redress for the victim. Whether or not a crime is reported, the victim must suffer the psychological consequences of the violations of his or her person and/or property with little, if any, connection to or assistance from the criminal justice system. In this vast, unexplored, and systematically ignored segment of the general population, crimes affect the psychological well-being of citizens, their families, and friends. As Bard and Sangrey point out,

> There is nothing more isolating than the pain of violation. It forces victims to question themselves and their world because it destroys two essential beliefs: their sense of trust and their sense of control over their lives. After the crime is over, victims begin to struggle with their reactions to the experience. They are often almost overcome with fear, guilt, and shame. They may feel contaminated and unworthy of help. Their relationships with family and friends can be seriously disrupted, and if they become involved with the police and the courts, they may come to believe that no one understands or cares about what has happened to them.[7]

The central goals of Crime Victims' Counseling Services are to reduce the victim's isolation and alleviate trauma symptoms. These goals are achieved through immediate intervention and by immersing the victim in modified peer group counseling so that he or she can begin ventilating emotional issues.

From April 1981 to April 1982, CVCS logged 1,457 telephone calls. Of these, 521 callers wanted telephone counseling only; 528 wanted or turned out to need referrals to other appropriate agencies such as rape crisis centers, the district attorney's office or the local police precinct; 408 wanted group counseling;[9] and 221 actually registered. The accompanying table shows the major characteristics of the first 100 CVCS participants. Of these, 100 percent completed the series and 71 percent kept in touch

TABLE 1: Statistical Characteristics of First 100 CVCS Participants and the
Crimes Involved

Sex	Female	41
	Male	59
Age	11–20	4
	21–30	19
	31–40	34
	41–50	23
	51–60	11
	61 and up	9
Race	White	83
	Black	9
	Hispanic	6
	Other	2
Class	Upper	0
	Middle middle	43
	Lower middle	54
	Lower	3
Group size	Minimum	5
	Maximum	8
	Average	7
Highest schooling completed	Elementary	0
	Junior high school	6
	High school	62
	College	32
Number of assailants	One	34
	Two	58
	Three	7
	Four or more	1
Assaulted/threatened with gun		49
Assaulted/threatened with knife		46
Assaulted/threatened with other weapon		2
No weapon involved		3

with CVCS afterward. Three percent voluntarily repeated the series. Of this group, only one victim knew the assailants. (See Table 1.)

From the table it can be seen that CVCS services attract mainly middle-class, educated, white adults—in short, the segment of the general population that can normally be expected to seek therapeutic services. But these were, more specifically, those adults who had been victims of violent crimes[10]—pointedly, crimes during which life-threatening episodes predominated. Accordingly, they selected group counseling because of an acute need to deal with crime trauma—those chief manifestations of rage, fear, shame, and powerlessness that rendered them less effective in their lives than before the event and which are called, in victim treatment circles, "victim trauma syndrome" (VTS). While sleeplessness, depression, change in appetite and sexual desire, night fears, distrust, increased drug and alcohol use, and change in relationships are also considered to be part of the range of possible emotional aftereffects of crime, it is the dominance of helplessness, guilt, extreme anger, and terror that drives victims into treatment. It was all these symptoms that the CVCS groups were aimed at relieving.

Findings in the Groups

As a crime victim, CVCS counselor, and participant-observer in the groups, I've been afforded a unique vantage point from which to observe counsellees. While the work of Symonds, Bard and Sangrey, and others is surely authoritative, my work over that year allows me some amplifications:

1. Victims whose lives have been threatened psychologically experience this threat as if it were their actual death. Therefore, they need not only to grieve this symbolic death but to overcome it and begin a psychologically new life. When clients came to CVCS groups, they were indeed severely regressed, as evidenced by sleeping with the light on; increased oral dependencies such as eating, smoking, or drinking; and urinating in bed at night. This "feeling like a baby" which so many clients articulated can be likened to regression to birth, from which the new, post-crime ego can reintegrate and regrow.

2. This symbolic death has the effect of eliminating any notions of immortality that the victim may have held. Generally, humans cherish the childhood myth of living forever, of somehow not having to come to terms with one's own death until the time actually comes. In the post-crime phase, victims must disabuse themselves of the ideal of everlasting life and confront their mortality. This recognition is often devastating to the victim, leaving him or her excessively vulnerable.

3. Part of the sense of acute vulnerability derives from the fact that the death threat has not occurred via accident or even disease such as cancer but through human agency. Such an experience not only leads to distrust of human beings but is generalized into distrust of the world, both the

external world of dependable laws and systems and people who behave humanly *and* the inner world of the self, which cannot be trusted either. Vulnerability engenders the pervasive sense of powerlessness that victims voice so frequently within the group setting. Victims have lost control and thereby have lost autonomy.

4. The assailant is perceived as "The Monster"—that is, the corporeal manifestation of evil, that incarnation of multiple childhood fears resuscitated and focused by the crime. Those who have encountered this monster may seek safety through psychological (and often physical) self-imprisonment. This form of safety is perceived as offering both choice and control. It helps diminish the effects of the essentially unanswerable obsessive question, "Why me???" During a crime, the victim is totally out of control—that is, totally under the control of the assailant(s); the desire to prevent a recurrence of this situation is therefore quite understandable. Victims, however, also find it difficult to acknowledge that crime is not controllable precisely because it is unpredictable, a matter of circumstances and thereby not subject to rational control. It is noteworthy that male crime victims usually have greater difficulty with this concept than females: Males feel disempowerment as a special form of threat to their masculine self-image that underlies feelings of impotence. Rage, depression, and further psychic imprisonment frequently result.

5. Identification with the aggressor is common. This phenomenon is a frequent theme in the literature of psychology. When a crime victim identifies with The Monster, s/he in effect becomes as evil as the assailant—that is, victims (at least in fantasy) can be perpetrators, too. This recognition increases feelings of shame and self-loathing; it convinces victims that they are not much better than the assailants—a double bind that victims find intolerable and which accounts for both the obsessive desire for revenge[11] and the attendant shame of desiring this, for to diminish the perpetrator is to diminish the self that is already in an unstable condition.

6. A symptom spiral occurs. For many crime victims, the event serves to focus emotional difficulties in the past, or ongoing issues in the victim's life. From my tripartite view as crime victim, researcher/activist, and counselor/therapist, I was puzzled by the variations in the order of symptom exhibition: Why did some, for instance, feel anger first and most vividly? Why did others experience it only as a final element of their psychological unraveling?

Again and again, in reading through the group exercises and journals victims were encouraged to keep, and when listening to the revelations within the group meetings, I was struck by the fact that the most tension—and relief—seemed to occur during the final session. A victim would, for example, feel initially at ease in describing helplessness, but at the fourth session s/he would be struggling to confront guilt. Why, if the components of VTS were common to almost all victims, did they not also follow a common time sequence? Through a year's observation of group members and careful analysis of the exercises I had written over the year as a participant/observer in the groups, I discovered that that which one handles worst one handles last. That is, the psychological state of the crime victim will vary over time and will get "worse" as it spirals downward toward that which gives the crime victim the *most* emotional difficulty—feelings of fear, powerlessness, guilt, anger. Over and over again, this proved to be the case. Once one got to the bottom of the spiral, *all* the symptoms would be markedly alleviated as the most difficult one had been exposed and worked through.

The significance of this discovery is that it gives direction for individual therapeutic focus within the group and thereafter. As victims confront and conquer the most vulnerable aspects of their personalities, the sense of emotional mastery and subsequent relief is evident— after that, things begin to spiral upward again, toward regained mental equilibrium.

These findings were garnered by being an active observer within the victim groups. But what was occurring, emotionally, overall? Was being in the group therapeutic? Why? To find out, I decided to interview some of the victims who had completed the CVCS sessions: The text of this study is the result.

The Interviews

All victims who had completed the counseling series by April 1982 were solicited to take part. Interviewees who volunteered to be research subjects were selected to represent some recurrent categories of crime victimization. All are New Yorkers, coming from three different boroughs. Yet they are representative of the kinds of crime victimization that happen over and over, day after day, throughout the United States. As you listen to each voice, you will hear a chorus of thousands of victims not unlike them.

A Note on Format

The taped, edited interviews that form the main body of this study are presented in a double description format. The interviewee's words are always in the left column. You may read them through without referring to any of the citations in the right column. The right column contains quotations from scholarly sources and from written exercises done by other victims during the course of their CVCS sessions. These entries are presented to further amplify and illuminate the issues being discussed. They may be read at the junctures at which they appear; alternatively, you may wish to look at them after all of the interview material has been read.

NOTES

1. "Mugging" is a generic term, meaning robbery plus physical injury in the course of the robbery. It does not appear in any New York State Criminal Code.

2. American Psychiatric Association, Diagnostic and Statistical Manual of Mental Disorders, Third Edition [DSM-III] (Washington, D.C., 1980), pp. 236–38. See also PTSP, acute.

3. Penal Law of the State of New York defines these crimes in the following manner:

*120.10 Assault in the first degree.
(C/FELONY)
A person is guilty of assault in the first degree when:
1. With intent to cause serious physical injury to another person, he causes such injury to such person or to a third person by means of a deadly weapon or a dangerous instrument; or
2. With intent to disfigure another person seriously and permanently, or to destroy, amputate or disable permanently a member or organ of his body, he causes such injury to such person or to a third person; or
3. Under circumstances evincing a depraved indifference to human life, he recklessly engages in conduct which creates a grave risk of death to another person, and thereby causes serious physical injury to another person; or
4. In the course of and in furtherance of the commission or attempted commission of a felony or of immediate flight therefrom, he, or another participant if there be any, causes serious physical injury to a person other than one of the participants.

*140.30 Burglary in the first degree.
(B/FELONY)
A person is guilty of burglary in the first degree when he knowingly enters or remains unlawfully in a dwelling with intent to commit a crime therein, and when, in effecting entry or while in the dwelling or in immediate flight therefrom, he or another participant in the crime:
1. Is armed with explosives or a deadly weapon; or
2. Causes physical injury to any person who is not a participant in the crime; or
3. Uses or threatens the immediate use of a dangerous instrument; or
4. Displays what appears to be a pistol, revolver, rifle, shotgun, machine gun or other firearm; except that in any prosecution under this subdivision, it is an affirmative defense that such pistol, revolver, rifle, shotgun, machine gun or other firearm was not a loaded weapon from which a shot, readily capable of producing death or other serious physical injury, could be discharged. Nothing contained in this subdivision shall constitute a defense to a prosecution for, or preclude a conviction of, burglary in the second degree, burglary in the third degree or any other crime.

*155.40 Grand larceny in the first degree.
(C/FELONY)
A person is guilty of grand larceny in the first degree when he steals property and when the

property, regardless of its nature and value, is obtained by extortion committed by instilling in the victim a fear that the actor or another person will (a) cause physical injury to some person in the future, or (b) cause damage to property, or (c) use or abuse his position as a public servant by engaging in conduct within or related to his official duties, or by failing or refusing to perform an official duty, in such manner as to affect some person adversely.

4. New York City Police Department, 1980 Statistical Report.

5. DSM III, p. 236.

6. Federal Bureau of Investigation Uniform Crime Reports, 1980. By telephone.

7. Morton Bard and Diane Sangrey, *The Crime Victims' Book* (New York: Basic Books, 1979), p. 31.

8. Victim Services Agency, 1982 Annual Report, p. 4.

9. Many victims wanted to come to the CVCS groups but were either afraid to travel, too elderly, had conflicting schedules, or would not go out at night.

10. This is almost identical with figures from The Karen Horney Institute, with the exception of gender. The Director, Jill Stultz, attributes the different 62/38 female/male ratio to the institute's *female* name.

11. In the text, see specifically those citations that begin, "**If the perpetrators walked into this room right now** . . . "

CRIME VICTIMS SPEAK

HOW TO READ THIS BOOK

Writings appearing in this left column, widely spaced in the typeface you are reading, are always and only edited transcripts of audiotaped interviews with crime victims who availed themselves of the group sessions offered by Crime Victims' Counseling Services.

Writings appearing in this right column, in the typeface you are reading, are always and only from books, newspapers, magazines, journals, reports, brochures, and similar sources.

Writings appearing in this right column, in the typeface you are reading, are always and only the author's responses.

Writings appearing in this right column, in the typeface you are reading, are always and only from group exercises and evaluations by members of Crime Victims' Counseling Services group sessions.

One: LYNN

. . . I was coming home at night. I had been with some friends from out of town, and we had gone to a movie. In fact, someone had come with me on the subway, but he got off the stop before I did and so it was near midnight on a Saturday night. The way I'm situated, my house is about two and a half blocks away from the subway exit, and so I got out of the subway and I had about two and a half blocks to go home. I was about halfway between the subway exit and home, when I was aware that there were three men on the opposite side of the street walking toward me. I right away had some feeling that something was happening here. I remember kind of going through my mind, "You know what to do," not real rationally but just kind of the alternatives were really there, and I thought about

Always walk as though you know where you are going. Look around. Acquire a cop's suspicious awareness. Street criminals, especially muggers and purse snatchers, are essentially predators. Spotting victims, stalking them, and then pouncing is all that most of these people do. They develop the instincts of the predator. They can sense vulnerability. They can tell by the way you walk, hold your head, carry a handbag or package, whether you're an easy mark.[1]

Nearly every crime victim reported that s/he got an "Uh-oh" feeling, an intuition that "something was wrong," just before the crime occurred.

19

going back to the subway but
it's one of those that
doesn't have an attendant.
It's just a turnstyle
thing. . . . I might have
been trapped there, and also
the train had just left. It was
like no one would probably be
there. There wasn't anyone
that I had passed on the
street and it's a commercial
couple of blocks, there. It
was deserted, all closed up.
And I thought, "Okay, you can
go on home, it's about the
same distance," and I
thought, "At least if you're
home you're in the house and
you're locked in there, if
you can get in there, but at
least it's not like being
trapped in the subway," so I
decided to go ahead. They
were on the other side of the
street—so I thought, you
know, I can kind of gauge
how this goes by continuing
to mark it. So I did, and
they came across the street
to my side of the street and
one of them was on the sidewalk and the other two were
still crossing the street.
They weren't really that

*Keep away from shrubbery, dark door-
ways, etc.*
*Always walk near the curb. Stay out of all
deserted areas, such as parks, streets,
fields, forests, beaches, subway stations,
schoolyards, playgrounds, steps, etc.
Walk on well lit, populated streets.*[2]

*Behavior that makes you appear asser-
tive:*

- *Looking confident, making eye contact, showing no fear.*
- *Refusing to be intimidated by comments or threats.*
- *Trusting your intuition. If you suspect danger, RUN.*

close to me, at this point—
maybe several car lengths
away, I would say, and the
one that was on the sidewalk
pulled a gun. He told me not
to move, not to run, not to
scream, or he'd kill me. So
I went from the sidewalk to
the street, between the cars,
and the [other] two (meanwhile) came to the sidewalk.
They were kind of going that
way and they kept coming
toward me, and at this point
I just kind of waited . . .
but they were still on the
sidewalk and at this point I
was in the middle of the
street. I don't know. I
can't remember even thinking
what to do. Then—I just
remembered—next they—here
I was in the middle of the
street and they again said
not to move, not to run, or
they would shoot me. So they
came to the street then and
at that point (it was a one-
way street we were on) I
could see down the street a
car coming. I could see the
lights of a car coming, and
at that point they hadn't
touched me or weren't really

- *Not being afraid to be rude, make a scene, or appear paranoid.*
- *Staying alert on the street at all times.*
- *Wearing clothing you can move easily in.*[3]

Nearly all registrants for Crime Victims' Counseling Services group counseling were threatened by assailants with deadly weapons—guns, knives, ice picks, screwdrivers, baseball bats, sticks; in addition, nearly all had their lives threatened orally, as well. It is this life-threatening situation that prompts victims to seek emotional counseling.

If you are threatened while walking on the street, do not hesitate to let loose with screams and run. If an automobile is trailing you, turn and walk in the opposite direction. Walk near the curb. Be on the alert and if a taxicab comes by jump in and protect yourself.[4]

that close to me. . . .
They had threatened to kill
me but they hadn't been
physically very close to me
yet. When I saw the car
coming down the street (they
were probably on one of the
streets, by the cars, and I
was on the other, but we were
all in the street, at this
point, all four of us) . . .
I just ran toward the car as
fast as I could, and they were
running behind me and yelling
at me not to run. The car
came and slowed down, and I
was on the passenger side and
they were on the driver's
side, and I had one hand on
the door handle of the
passenger side and the car
slowed down and then, when I
got there, the car just
speeded away and left. So
they then ran right over to
me, the three of them, and
said, "Why did you think you
could get away with that?
Never do that again.'' [I was
afraid because] I'd never have
that chance again. They were
going to teach me a lesson
and they started pushing me
around. They sort of circled

We have found that the vast majority of people, both men and women, respond similarly to violent crime. The immediate response of an individual who meets with sudden, unexpected violence is momentary shock and disbelief. This first phase is quickly followed by a frozen-frightened response which seems only to permit submissive, compliant and ingratiating behavior to the perceived overwhelming threat to life. The reaction of fear is so

me and pushed me, like from
one to the other, just
playing with me. Slapping
me, not forceful, but just
pushing my head around and
pulling on my hair, [my]
so . . . long hair, and they
were pulling on that, so I
don't really remember them
ever asking me for anything,
like for money or anything
like that. . . . My thought
was that they wanted my money
and that they were either
going to rape me or kill me,
or both. That's what I
thought was going to happen
and it seemed like, at the
first part of it, they were
really enjoying this pushing
around kind of thing. Anyway, they got me down on the
ground through this pushing.
Finally, I kind of backed
away and pushed off of one of
them, and they got me down on
the ground. I remember one
of them pulling at me and one
of my shoes was pulled off,
and again they were not
really like, beating me, but,
like pulling on my clothes,
taunting me, and pulling on
my pants. I remember getting

profound and over-whelming that the victim feels hopeless about getting away. All hope of survival is dependent on appeasing the criminal.[5]

Essentially, the street criminal is a predatory individual who is action-oriented, living in the immediate present, with no constructive memory of the past and little hope about the future. . . . [The] attempt to relate to the criminal is not only ineffective but sometimes dangerous, since he is a predatory individual who is notoriously free of guilt about his behavior.[6]

up, one time, and pulling
away from them and kind of
running down to the next car.
Then they got me down again
and this time I remember
being next to the car, and
seeing underneath the car,
and I saw the lights of
another car coming down the
street. So, at that point, I
just . . . the whole time,
inside of me, I was like . . .
had this thing in my chest
that just knotted up. I was
so determined that this was
just *not* going to happen to
me. It was that I was going
to do whatever I could to get
out of here, whatever I had
to do, I was going to do it.
So when I saw the car lights
[of the second car] down the
street, and I remember, too,
seeing under the car and
seeing those car lights. I
don't know *at all* how I got
up, but I remember running
toward that car, and I had
one shoe on, but how much the
foot with my shoe on it hurt!
It was just like a stinging.
I remember just pounding on
that foot and just running
to the car, and again they

. . . The number of serious crimes in New York City is almost certain to set a record this year, and that the increase has been strongest in middle-income neighborhoods.[7]

ran right behind me and again
they were screaming at me.
Not screaming, yelling at me,
not to run and they were
going to kill me. I got to
the car and there were two
people in it, this time; last
time there had only been one
person, that I remember. I
was on the passenger side
again. This time one of them
had gone on to the driver's
side and two of them had come
behind me, on the passenger
side. The one on the
driver's side is the one
with the gun. I don't know
if the other ones had guns
or not. He told the driver
that he would kill him . . .
[the car] never totally
stopped, but I got to the
passenger side and the car
door opened and the woman
inside helped me open the
door. She was kind of
pulling me in and I got in,
and the car was kind of
going away with the door not
shut, and [the assailants]
were pulling on the door . . .
and we on the inside were
pulling on the door. We kind
of drove away. . . . It was

If the perpetrator of the crime came
into this room right now I . . . would
make sure they didn't have the gun.
Then I'd take a punch or strike them in
some way. I'm not a violent person,
but they violated me and made me feel
very small. It's a feeling that makes me
very angry. In some way I guess striking them would make me feel better. I
don't like the feeling of wanting to get
back at them, but it's a feeling at this
moment I have no control over. I
would really feel satisfied if they were
in prison. This would stop them from
assaulting anyone else.[8]

a man and a woman. They were
pretty young and out on the
town . . . they had drinks
in their hands and they were
all dressed up. They were
really very kind people. She
put her arm around me and he
asked me how I was, and *he*
was going to kill the mother-
fuckers, that was *his* thing.
We got a little further away
and he stopped the car. He
wanted to go back and get
them, and I said I didn't
really want him to do that.
I knew they had a gun and I
just didn't see what we had
to gain by going to search
them out. . . . [The driver]
had seen the gun, so what he
did was, he drove backwards
on this one-way street, about
a block, a block and a half.
[He] knew where they had run
down. We all had seen in
which direction they had gone
and there were some people
down there on the street, and
so he got out and went down
and talked to one or two guys
down the street, but they
didn't seem to be the same
guys, so he went down and
they said some kids went *that*

*The increased fear, suspicion and inse-
curity felt by victims of crime is also
experienced by friends, relatives and
neighbors who help them, according to a
Federal study. The study, made public
Sunday by the National Institute of Justice, the research arm of the Justice
Department, concludes that "friends,
relatives and neighbors suffer hidden
costs of helping victims." On the basis of
New York City data from July 1979 and
September 1981, the researchers found
that 80 percent of those who helped crime
victims suffered some of the same responses: "Feeling nervous or frightened;
increased suspicion of people; feeling
less safe at home or on the street."
However, most supporters did not regret
that the victim had turned to them.*[9]

way, or whatever . . . he
just sort of stood around for
a while, stood outside his car
for a while, and we were
sitting inside and then
finally he said, well, they
wanted to take me to the hospital. I felt that I didn't
need any hospital attention
that, well, I had done some
stuff before with people,
battered women, and had gone
with them to the hospital and
realized some of the things
they went through in some
serious cases, and felt that
I didn't have anything that
looked like I needed any-
thing. I didn't want to go
to the hospital, and so I
was real calm, at that point,
and I hadn't started to cry
or anything. I told them
that it was okay, and that
they could drop me off at the
corner, I could walk home.
And they said, "Don't be crazy,
we're taking you home,"
and they did. They took me
right to the door and waited
and made sure I got in, and
when we went back I got my
shoe. (Also, by the way, it
was sort of torn up, but we

Although no one can predict President Reagan's long-term psychological reaction to being wounded by an attacker's bullet, psychiatrists and psychologists say the emotional consequences of a shooting injury often linger. While they do not know exactly what determines the course or outcome of a victim's emotional recovery, they do say that the duration and the difficulty of that recovery period can be affected by three factors: the symbolic meaning of the crime; the victim's psychological state before the crime and the victim's informal and formal sources of support, such as family and friends.[10]

Nearly half of the supporters reported feeling uncomfortable when talking to the victim about the crime. In most cases, this stemmed from the supporters' increased feeling of vulnerability. But the discomfort also reflected the level of distress of the victim. Supporters of victims with more problems and greater fear of crime and victims who supporters thought were depressed, upset, or talked

got it and I remember later
taking it to the shoe repair,
thinking, well, maybe I
should just throw these shoes
out. I don't know what I did
with it.) Anyway, I got home
and they dropped me off and
left, and I thought later,
"I never got their name,"
or "I don't know anything
about these people that
stopped there that
night." . . . I went up, and
it wasn't until I was in the
house and shut the door—it
was kind of like the incident was over; that is, when
I started to collapse and
cry and was just real upset.
I didn't really sleep all
night. I called a lot of
people. . . . That night
I called the police and then
it wasn't until the next
Thursday that I actually
went in and reported it.
(I was out of town. I left
town that Sunday.) [The
police] didn't send a car
over. . . . They told me to
come in and report it in
person, and I said, well, I
was going to be out of town
and wouldn't be back until

*too much expressed more discomfort than
others.*[11]

*. . . First comes denial, accompanied by
shock and disbelief. Then the victim begins to realize how vulnerable he was,
recognizing that "I could have been
killed." The third stage is often depression marked by apathy, annoyance and
anger over what the victim should have
done to avert the attack. Finally, the
victim begins to reassess his attitudes,
practices and values. He may make
changes ranging from the simple, such as
changing locks, to the symbolic. Such
changes may last a long time.*[12]

Thursday. They said to come
in on Thursday, and that's what
I did. . . . I called
my friends. I called three
friends and I would call one
and talk a while and kind of
calm down a little bit, and
then hang up the phone, and
just as soon as I'd hang up
the phone I realized that I
was still just as upset, and
then I would call someone
else. . . . It really went
through the whole night. I
mean, the first person I
called was maybe about
twelve-thirty
a.m., or something like
that, . . . into three and four
in the morning. One friend
wanted me to come over, and I
thought no way was I going
to go over to anyone's house,
no matter if I called a car
service or anything. There
just was no way that I was
going to do that. Then
another friend set an alarm
and kept calling back to
make sure, just to check on
me and see how things were
going. So there was a lot
of support. I mean, I was
on the phone most of the

* *All but two of the 274 victims in the sample received help from at least one person.*
* *Victims averaged four supporters each.*
* *Victims were in touch with almost two-thirds of supporters within one day of the crime.*
* *More than half the supporters were people the victim knew well and saw often but helpers the victim did not know well also provided significant assistance.[13]*

The acceptance of the victim's behavior without reservation forms the basis of psychological first aid that all victims need to minimize any psychiatric seque-lae from their victimization. By the time anyone meets the victim, the criminal is gone. He has forcibly, through the threat of violence, taken the victim's money and invaded his or her body. Psychological first aid intends to nurture, comfort, and restore the self-respect of the victims for their behavior by giving, not taking.[14]

night, really, and sometimes
I would be off for a half
hour or so and kind of sit
there or pace around or
take a shower. . . . I
packed and I really just did
did little things around the
apartment I didn't really
need to do, necessarily. . . .
I ironed things and I *never*
iron! The next morning I
had to go to Washington, so
I had my stuff all ready. I
hadn't slept really at all,
and I was taking the train
down, and I had my bag and I
had to walk that same street
to go back to get the subway,
and it didn't seem that bad
doing that. It was daylight
and all the stores were open
again and it seemed all
right and I got on the subway. I remember walking down
the street and there were
three men that could have
fit the description of the
three men, because I really
couldn't describe them very
well, other than to say
that they were *not* a few
things—that they were *not*
over two hundred pounds.
There are a few things I

I feel powerless when . . . I ride the subways; when it turns dark; when black males get close to me physically; when someone is very angry or raging; when I replay the mugging in my mind.[15]

could eliminate, but anyway
there were these three men
there and I kind of thought,
you know, these people know
me and *I* don't have any idea
who *they* are. That was the
only time I felt upset again,
going in the morning. . . .
I felt vulnerable at that
point, but then I went, got
the train, and went down to
Washington. I was there
until Wednesday night, three
and a half days. It was a
meeting with other people
from other programs in
education, not people I
know particularly well.
People I meet every year but
I don't really know them
that well and so, at that
point, I didn't really have
anyone to talk to about it,
and I didn't even think about
it all that much. It was
there, but I was just kind
of numb at that point and I
got into my work. I'd come
in at night from the sessions
and do all of the reading
and was very efficient about
doing all those things. . . .
I think [at that point] I
was just numb and I was

I feel powerless when . . . I'm walking alone in a deserted area, or in an empty elevator. I hate being put in any position where I appear to be a weak or frightened person.[16]

functioning, but I wasn't
real alert to anything
around me, particularly.
It seemed like a very pro-
tective environment. I
never went out of the
hotel—was in the hotel the
whole time: The meals were
in the hotel, the conferences
were in the hotel. . . . It
was a *very* safe environment,
plus it wasn't even in New
York. And one night I had
set up to call a friend from
high school who was living
in Washington and go over to
their house and have dinner.
I remember that night going
back, thinking, "Boy, you
were really a dud! You were
the dullest person, tonight,"
and I was just kind of dead
to things around me. I
didn't talk very much. They
just had this baby and they
were really excited, and on
the surface my look was that
I showed my interest, but
inside I knew I wasn't
feeling anything or being
very responsive. . . . I
think I really was in shock—
not numb, not really
depressed. The other thing

Dr. Bard recommends that family members and friends "allow the victim to express his feelings no matter how much it may bother you," because "the person has a need to discharge." He said that there might be an extended period of suffering beginning with a period of one or two weeks of disorganization and dependency. Then there might come a period of six to eight months of fluctuating between feeling better and feeling bad, followed by a reorganization phase of up to a year.[17]

that happened was that
Sunday morning, right before
I left, my parents called
me. I had a sister who was
expecting a baby any day,
and they called because they
wanted to know where I was
going to be so they could get
in touch with me if she
[gave birth]. And that was
typical. I mean, they
usually know when I'm going
out of town and they usually
call or I'll usually call
them. I had thought before,
knowing they were going to
call, "Should I say anything
to them? Should I not?" I
didn't say anything to them.
I don't know how I didn't.
I'm sure they must have
sensed something, because
it was the only conversation
until I went down to
Washington that I had been
able to have with anyone and
not just break down crying.
But I didn't, with them.
You know, "Oh, yeah, I'm
going to Washington, this
and that." . . . I just felt
that they would be so concerned they would want to
come out, and what could

The principles of psychological first aid involve the recognition and sharing of what happened, concern and relief for the safety of the victim, and acceptance without reservation, challenge, or question of the victim's behavior under severe stress. It can and should be done by parents and all helping personnel. Whether the victim is a four-year-old molested child or an 80-year-old rape victim, the procedure is the same. It can be simply stated in three statements.

1. I'm sorry it happened.
2. I'm glad you are all right (alive).
3. You did nothing wrong.

In conclusion, I could do no better than to quote from a letter written to me by a woman who was mugged: "It is not that I wish to wallow in self-pity; it's just that I would have liked someone to have given me the same moral support, and words of comfort and caring that you would give to someone who had just lost a loved one." [18]

they do? I didn't know what
they could do, and they'd be
a thousand miles away [in
Iowa] worried to death about
me . . . so I didn't tell
them. Then, when I came
back from Washington that
Thursday, I went to the police
station, and again I was pretty
matter of fact and in control
about this whole thing. I
walked over there and sat
down and it took about an
hour. I don't think I'd ever
really been in a police
station like that in New
York. I've been in police
stations before, but they
were in Iowa and it's a
different feeling, but it
was exactly what I expected
because it's just like on
TV. . . . You went in there
and you have this big, long
wooden bench and I sat on the
bench. They had a big, high
desk and the people were
behind the desk and I went
up and told them I wanted to
report, that I had been
attacked and they said, "Sit
down, someone will come and
talk with you." Then, from
behind the desk, someone

I feel powerless when . . . I couldn't get
anyone to help me. I feel all alone. I'm
only for myself—no one will help me. I
felt powerless when I went to the
Crime Victims Bureau and they refused to pay my medical bills. Where
are our taxes going? For their salary
but not to help us?[19]

yells, "Come over here!" and
I kind of went over. The
guy who took my report was
also answering the phone and
doing different things, and
they made an order from the
deli and all in the middle of
it he's typing away, he has
his back to me and he's
throwing out these questions
over his shoulder and types
away. End of report. I did
it and then I left, and it
was like I didn't really
expect any more. But on the
other hand I was thinking,
"Boy, this really isn't
right," and I walked out the
door. . . . [They] didn't
even look at me face to face
about it. I know that there
are much worse crimes and
people go through all kinds
of things, and they must see
a lot and maybe they have to
build up their own defenses
about it, and . . . I'm
getting upset, now. The
recall of this seems to be
bothering [me]. [Can] we
stop for a while? . . .
[Lynn weeps and wipes eyes.]
The police hadn't been
responsive to [me]. . . .

I get angry when . . . I feel I've been
taken advantage of. I get very upset
when someone tries to put one over on
me in some way. I don't like to be
made a fool of. When I was robbed, I
was angry because he took advantage
of the fact that I was an unarmed
woman. It makes me mad to think I
have to be so careful when and where I
go, instead of being free to do what I
please. Even the government makes me
angry because they can run your life
without you giving any argument back.
They love to take my paycheck and
spend it freely.[20]

Of all the things, it was
just some kind of human
contact that would have
helped me at that moment.
And, on the other hand,
realizing the self-pro-
tection they must need to do
their job . . . I see it in
myself, sometimes, when I see
my own insensitivities, but—
you know—the whole thing of
walking [away] down the
street when someone has
fainted there. Why do I do
that? You know, and so, why
[did the police] do that to
me? Maybe that's what they
have to do, but when I left
the police station, I hadn't
been upset since that
Sunday. . . . When I got
back [from Washington] that
Wednesday night I was still
okay, but leaving the police
station is when, maybe, the
shock was over and the whole
way home (it was about
twelve blocks) I just cried
the whole way and walked
down the street crying and
thinking how crazy I must
look to people. But I just
thought, "Well, that's what
happened." . . . [The police]

As a witness the survivor is both sought and shunned; the desire to hear his truth is countered by the need to ignore him. Insofar as we feel compelled to defend a comforting view of life, we tend to deny the survivor's voice. . . . The survivor, then, is a disturber of the peace.[21]

I get angry when . . . I am unable to remedy, resolve (involve others) or totally forget an unpleasant experience related to the frightening "victim" status of being robbed and cut down by an automobile, hurt and injured. I get angry when I report to [a] city agency and get negative or placating response.[22]

were essentially indifferent, so when I came home I was really upset. It was a Thursday and it was the middle of the day and I hadn't gone into work and I wanted to stay home. I had the report to write up from [the conference] and so it was the middle of the day. I didn't really know whether I wanted to call someone, because they [probably] weren't home—you know, people are working—and then I was kind of getting into this thing, you know, a little harder to reach out. Interrupting people in the middle of the night somehow seemed better than in the middle of their work. I don't remember what I did. I don't remember if I called people; I know I did by that night. (I don't remember if I did during the day, but at this point I don't remember time periods.) But I know that for a long time after, for weeks after that, I really was upset. I cried all the time, every day, and not even just when I was

Crimes that terrorize take many forms, from aggravated assault to petty thievery. But one crime goes largely unnoticed. It is a crime against which there is no protection. It is committed daily across our nation. It is the painful, wrongful insensitivity of the criminal justice system toward those who are the victims of crime. We complain of a slow-to-react justice system, of overburdened courts, of punishments that fail to respond to the severity of the crime. But the most serious indictment of our criminal justice system is its inhumanity to those who deserve the highest respect and empathy for their courage and tenacity: the victims. The callousness with which the system again victimizes those who have already suffered at the hands of an assailant is tragic.[23]

With plenty of reason, crime victims liken themselves to the patients of a doctor who focuses so much on the technical problem of curing disease that he ignores his patients' feelings. Courts and prosecutors, the victims say, pay attention to the victim only as he may help prosecute the case; otherwise they treat him with indifference. Yet the victim's feelings are

home alone at night. I'd
be at work and I'd be sitting
at my desk doing my writing
and then I would start
crying. . . . Sometimes I
would be [aware of what made
me cry]. Sometimes I'd be
sitting there and, if I had
my hair braided, a braid
would fall off my shoulder
and I'd jump, I'd just jump
for the ceiling! I'd look
at myself and I'd just think,
"You can't even let your hair
move and not be nervous about
it!" and sometimes something
like that would happen that
would start it, or sometimes
it was just a matter of
feeling overwhelmed. It
might not even be related
to the crime, specifically,
but I would just be feeling
overwhelmed, and there were
a lot of times like that the
last six, eight months. . . .
It was not [then] *just* the
crime, but it was also that
all these [other] things that
were happening [in addition]—
parents' illnesses, ends of
relationships, and other kinds
of crises and I thought, "I
can't take this." I remember

*important, and not only because it is
decent to show official concern. Alienated victims contribute in a big way to the
credibility crisis that afflicts criminal justice. Congress, finally aware of the problem, now has a chance to make a gesture
on the victim's behalf.*[24]

**I'm afraid when . . . something hap-
pens all of a sudden, unexpectedly. I
am afraid when I am cornered, someone wants to rape me and I run out of
any kind of excuse. I am afraid someone hides in my car. I am afraid of
someone with me alone in the elevator.
Am I safe? I am afraid to walk on the
street in the night. I am afraid if
anyone follows me. I am afraid someone comes in my apartment and I am
not aware. I am afraid to do laundry
alone.**[25]

*Krupnick and Horowitz (1980) suggest
that "although an assault can be a traumatic and devastating experience, it also
offers opportunities for growth and
change" (p. 46). The victimizing experience may highlight previous problems
and conflicts which serve to delay or
impede recovery. In the context of a
supportive therapeutic environment, they
believe it is possible to assess the victim's
general coping style, level of psycholog-*

that first weekend after the crime had happened: I stayed overnight with a friend of mine. She and her husband had said, "Come on up," and I went up in the afternoon and they had fixed dinner for me and we just sat around and watched TV. Then I spent the night there and I went back on Sunday. . . . The next day, going back, it was . . . realizing that this is the subway, but it was also in the daytime, and I did feel much more comfortable in the daytime. If I had to go someplace it didn't seem to deter me at all [but] at night it really did. I remember I met a friend to go to a movie; it didn't get out too late—it was like one o'clock, and it was in Manhattan, and I thought, "How am I going to get home from here?" He knew what had happened, but he didn't really know that I was still as involved in it as I was. Because he said, "Oh, I'll walk you to the subway," and I said, "There is no way I'm going to get on that subway, it's just impossible."

ical development, and to discover the personal meaning of the assault. Through this discovery, the victim can learn real and fantasied aspects of the assault, leading to effective control and a more positive sense of mastery. They recommend brief therapy "with a focus on understanding the individual's response to the attack," indicating that it has proven effective in helping the victim integrate the trauma and thereby stimulating psychological growth.[26]

I'm afraid when . . . I have to take the subway home after 9:30 at night. That is the time when the subway exit closest to my home closes. Once recently, I decided I would try taking the subway home at night. It would have been the first time. I got to the subway entrance

So I got a cab and I took a
cab home. When I got in the
cab and shut the door, the tears
started just flooding down
and I remember going down
the FDR Drive and looking
out. I was really upset and
yet the cab driver didn't
say anything. But when we
got back he waited until I
got into the building and he
didn't have to say anything.
My feeling was that he was
aware of what was happening
and was concerned about it.
Doing those little extra
things, like waiting until I
got in, . . . it made me feel
much better. Here's the
other side of it: Someone
who I don't know at all, and
he didn't even know what the
problem is, and yet he was
looking after me, is right.
I did take a lot of cabs at
that time, the next few weeks
or months, even. I've been
in New York about eleven
years and probably have not
taken that many cabs, and
yet in the last few months
I've taken more than all the
time I've been here. It just
was something I did to feel

**and I realized there was no way I was
going to be able to go down those
stairs. Instead, I decided to take a cab
and as soon as I was seated in the back
seat the tears started to flow and didn't
stop until I arrived home.**[27]

comfortable, coming home late at night. . . . It was then maybe a few months later and I talked with my friends quite a while, still. Two people were amazingly supportive, and I did end up calling my parents; they had both recently had serious health problems—mother, threat of cancer, and my dad had open heart surgery. So I thought, "You know, they *both* called me, they both let me know what was happening, they told me how *they* were feeling, they really shared it with me even though they knew *I* would worry and they knew I was a thousand miles away and they knew all those things, and I really appreciated it that they did that." It was important to me that they could do that, and I thought I just could not not reciprocate, if there was something happening with me. I really had to share it with them, too. So I called them up that Friday and we talked a long time. They didn't ask a lot of questions; they both just

. . . *Findings suggest that the help seeking that occurs as a result of criminal victimization differs from help seeking behavior in other types of stressful situations, such as illness, depression or changing life circumstances. Crime victims go through a more immediate type of crisis, one of the inherent characteristics of which is reliance on whoever is present. This means that dependence on people with whom the victim has weaker ties (including neighbors, landlords, superintendents or even strangers) may be more common than if the crisis was of a more extended nature, such as an illness.*[28]

All but two of the 274 victims in the sample got some help to deal with their problems from friends, relatives, and neighbors. When victims got all the help they needed, they adjusted better, regardless of the number of helpers they had. . . . The victim's informal support network—their relatives, friends, and neighbors—were best able to provide emotional support and least able to provide technical and legal assistance.[29]

sort of listened and they
both offered to come out,
[even in their poor
health]. . . . They both
said, "We can come, you
know. We can just sit in
the apartment, do whatever you
want to do." They just said
it, and at that point I just
thought, no, because I
partly thought they would be
an extra worry for me. . . .
I just felt, "No, not right now,
and I'll let you know
if that's something I need,
but not right now," and they
said fine. . . . My dad
called me back and he said
he thought about what
happened. I first told him
that I had been assaulted by
three men on the street and
I told him that some people
in a car had really come to my
rescue and that I was okay.
(That, in fact, I really
didn't even lose anything.)
He said he really wanted to
know more about it and know
exactly what had happened;
he wanted to know how I felt
about it. He said he thought
about it a lot and he
realized that it probably

Friends, relatives, and neighbors suffer hidden costs of helping victims: 80 percent of supporters reported experiencing some form of secondary victimization. For some supporters, this meant feeling nervous or frightened, in others, increased suspicion of people, and in others, feeling less safe at home or on the street. These reactions were more common among supporters who lived in the same neighborhood than those who lived elsewhere and among those who felt close to the victim or were relatives than those who did not feel close to the victim.

Nearly half of the supporters reported feeling uncomfortable when talking to the victim about the crime. In most cases, this stemmed from the supporters' increased feeling of vulnerability. But the discomfort also reflected the level of distress of the victim. Supporters of victims with more problems and greater fear of crime and victims who supporters thought were depressed, upset, or talked too much expressed more discomfort than others.[30]

upset me more than I had
expressed, because he knew
that I lived here as long as
I have, and that I've lived
in a variety of neighborhoods,
and work at night and come
home on the train in the
middle of the night, and have
always felt very much in
control of my surroundings
and not threatened by them.
He thought that maybe this
would change my whole view
of myself and my surroundings,
and might kind of shatter
what I had kind of taken for
granted. So we talked about
it quite a bit. Since then,
after that time, they called
all the time, and then I also
talked to all of my sisters
and shared it with them.
All of them. They just
called me all the time—it
felt great. I remember one
morning (it was about two
weeks after it happened) the
doorbell rang about seven in
the morning, and I thought,
"Who's ringing at seven on
a Saturday morning?" A lot
of times I'll just ignore it
but it was a real persistent
ring and I thought, "Okay,

The evidence from supporter interviews was that the effects of crime do not end with the victim. Yet, most supporters did not regret that the victim had turned to them for assistance: one-fifth of the supporters reported they were brought closer to the victim by the experience, and indeed, only two supporters stated that their relationship with the victim was jeopardized because of the incident. Nine in ten supporters viewed their contribution to the victim as important. And the overwhelming majority (97 percent) of supporters did not wish that the victim had gone elsewhere for help.[31]

I'll see who it is.'' It was
[the] UPS man making a
delivery, so I went down
and there was this package—
it was from one of my sisters.
I opened it up and it was
these two stuffed animals,
these Snoopy dolls, and, you
know, there was a note about
[how] she loved me and [that
this was] something for me
to hold, and I just really
felt great. . . . [While the
police didn't respond very
well, other people did.]
People [at work] would see me
upset and just come over and
give me a hug. (Or, even if
I wasn't obviously *real*
upset, they just kind of
sensed maybe I was edgy, or
something; they would come
over or bring me a cup of
tea—they were really great
about it.) I kind of got to
a point where even though I
talked about it with people
for a long time, it got so
that after a while I didn't
know what else to say. The
feelings were still there.
Nothing new had happened,
and what else could I say?
It was like the same thing

During the past ten years, the notion of social networks has increasingly been used to help explain how people deal with a wide variety of problems. Social networks have been defined as the set of friends, relatives, and others with whom the victim exchanges material and personal assistance (such as borrowing money or talking about problems). Research indicates that networks provide the main source of assistance in everyday life and emergencies, and that the lack of a supportive network can lead to physiological and psychological pathology.[32]

First, like grief, victimization has a "normal" and a "pathological" variation, determined mainly by the intensity of the victimizing experience and the strength of the individual's coping behavior. Secondly, the specific symptom picture of grief and pathological grief reac-

was coming out and coming out, and I didn't feel any sense of improvement or any sense of resolve with it. Sometimes it would be a little bit better and I'd go a little longer, but overall I still felt just as rotten, and I thought . . . ["I have to do something about this . . .], and yet I didn't know what to do. Well, even before [that] people told me I had to do something about it—my friends did, my family did, people at work did. They said, "[Lynn], you know, you should really go talk to someone. I'm always here for you to talk to, but I don't know what to say to you and I don't think I can help you. I think you need some other kind of help." A friend of mine who works at the Rape Crisis Center told me about one of the counselors there. So I thought, "Here I'll be in this group and all these other women will have been raped, and I'll call them up and see how they are doing and my whole heart will go

tions is much like that resulting from victimization. In addition, however, the victim often suffers a serious lowering of self-esteem.[33]

If I spoke about my brother's murder, people recoiled. They didn't emphathize, they didn't sympathize, they didn't get angry. They said, "Well, why was he walking down that street?" "What time of night was it?" They acted as if Seth had done something wrong, as if I were now doing something wrong to mourn him, to be angry, to be devastated. The relatives or friends who looked for an explanation for my brother's murder in his behavior victimized our family. The anger that should have been directed at the criminals was mysteriously missing, as though the stabbing were an inconvenient detail to distinguish Seth's death from one caused by an accident or illness. It was as though Seth had done something shameful—and, in a way, he had. His murder had proved that crime might touch anyone. If my brother was not somehow to blame for his death, then no one was safe.[34]

out for them. Maybe that's
what I need, but on the other
hand, maybe that's not for me
right now.'' I just thought
I really need something
that's going to help *me* get
through this, and I really
wanted to keep the focus on
me—as I know that my
tendency, often, is to put
it outside, ignore what's
happening inside. So I
thought, "That isn't what I
need," and then people said,
"Oh, I know this really good
feminist therapist," and this
and that and I thought, "Yeah,
but I really wanted to deal
with the crime." At least
right now. I did not want
to start with a whole psychoanalysis, or a whole in-depth
therapy. I wanted to resolve
this *thing right* now and I
need someone who can help me
focus on what's happening as
a result of this, . . . I
also go to Alanon and I hadn't
at first talked about it.
Some of the individuals were
people that I had even called
the night that it happened,
but as a group I hadn't
really talked about it. One

*Victim counselors primarily see victims
in the third phase of victimization, and
generally get the brunt of a victim's
retroflexive rage. . . . I focus on the
counselor's need to provide a receptive
listening atmosphere to the victim's ventilation of feelings regarding the second
injury. Counselors are taught to be receptive and not defensive, to encourage
victims to express resentment and constipated rage, to assist victims in developing measures to restore their self-respect,
and to reduce the unpleasant, anxiety-
provoking feelings that victims have
about getting even with a criminal who
may be anonymous.[35]*

week I was going to, and yet
other people needed to say
things and I held back.
Finally, it was about three
weeks or so after the crime,
and I shared it and I got
really upset. People were
very supportive and there
were a lot of suggestions;
[someone] said, "Call the
Crime Victims' Counseling
Services. I don't know
anything about it, but they
have this flyer about this
service for crime victims,
and maybe that's what you
need." She [continued], "I
really don't know that much
about it but I've got the
number at home, and the woman
seemed real nice." So I
said, "Well, that sounds
close to what I want," so I
called and started the group
after that. It really did
seem [right] because I knew
I needed to do something—I
wanted something that really
would help me through the
crime things that I was
feeling—the reaction to the
crime, at least to start with.
That, and then see what
happens. So that's what I

Formal assistance agencies had a limited impact on helping crime victims since only one in five victims knew of such agencies. However, three-quarters of those who knew of such agencies went to them for assistance.[36]

Adults need to be able to say, "I can stand on my own two feet. I know what I am doing with my life. This is who I am." Threats to autonomy are felt deeply and painfully in the self, and in a personal crime the victim invariably experiences this threat. Whether the offender is a burglar or a rapist, a pickpocket or a robber, the message to the victim is the same: "You are not your own person. Right now you belong to me. I'm taking

did. . . . I first called
[to register with Crime
Victims' Counseling Services]
probably three weeks or
almost four weeks, I guess,
after it had happened. When
I first called I was still in
a very high emotional state;
I was unusually upset and
really kind of felt desperate.
So when I talked [with you]
it was like the next group
was starting not until
December, which was at that
point maybe a week or two
away. I remember I called
before Thanksgiving, and I
was thinking, "Boy, it seems
like a long way to wait," but
then, on the other hand, oh,
there's Thanksgiving and my
sister had had her baby, so
I was going to go out and see
her and her baby, and I
thought, okay, well, maybe
that's about right. . . . It
was the first time that I was
able to go a few days and be
calm the whole time; that
was probably almost a month
after the crime. . . . [The
central feeling I had was
being upset]. I guess that
it's probably so vague.

over, and there is nothing you can do about it." For some moment of time, however brief, the victim is powerless.[37]

In the fourth and final phase, victims hopefully resolve their unfortunate experience and integrate it into their behavior and lifestyle. There is further development of more efficient defensive-alert patterns, and profound revision of values and attitudes concerning possessions, and sometimes concerning individuals and groups.[38]

Each person has his or her own level of stress tolerance. Something that severely upsets one person may feel quite unim-

Because it was a feeling
that's hard to describe, and
was hard to pinpoint in myself. It was that I didn't
feel any serenity in my
life. I felt very (I don't
know), I was going high speed
and any little thing I would
react to—and usually
negatively, but not always.
I mean, there were some
positive things, too, like I
said about the two Snoopys
that were sent to me by my
sister. It was, like,
normally I wouldn't cry
about that for an hour. It
was really the happiness that
I felt, but you know it just
was a strong emotion. . . .
[I realized I had survived]
and people told me that a
lot, too. People would often say
(when I told them what
happened), "You really
exhibit such a strong desire
to live." I never had been
in a situation where I had to
test that in myself, and I
realized that that's really
true. That feeling that I
had had in my chest was just
absolute determination. I
can't ever remember really

*portant to another. But for every person
there is a point of stress beyond which the
self cannot make the necessary accommo-
dation easily and quickly. Then things get
out of hand. When we lose our ability to
regain our balance, our lives become
seriously disrupted. Being the victim of a
personal crime is extremely stressful,
well beyond the tolerance level for most,
if not all, people. The violation of self
undermines the fundamental sources of
centering and sends the victim into an
emotional tailspin. It takes time and energy and support for victims to regain
their balance.*[39]

*[The] earliest moments of assault . . .
involve a plethora of sympathetic arousal
reactions within the autonomic nervous
system. Reactions within this branch of
the autonomic nervous system have bio-
logical significance in assisting the or-
ganism to reduce the apparent threat by
either fighting or fleeing. When sympathetic arousal occurs, the rate and force
of heart contractions increase; blood
supply to the heart, large muscles and*

feeling that, before. It might, sort of, be what athletes talk about in a race that they're going to win—it was that kind of feeling, when, I guess, my whole thing, that I can control everything. But, in this case . . . I was going to save my life, and so this feeling of being upset [was a] feeling I hadn't really ever felt before. It just kind of made all of the emotional things for me very much on the surface. People could say something to me at work, very routine, and I would overreact very frequently. [It was] excess emotionality; everything was heightened, positive feelings as well as negative feelings. The positive feelings were sort of like the Snoopy dolls coming; . . . more of it was negative, though. I can't remember ever really crying as much as I cried in that period of time. I just felt like I wasn't a thinking person, I was a feeling person, and that I reacted to my surroundings by *feeling*

brain increases with a concomitant constriction of blood vessels to the stomach, intestines and colon. Blood pressure rises and salivation decreases, producing dry mouth sensation. The bronchial passages dilate, permitting the lungs to consume a greater amount of oxygen, thereby increasing the body's rate of metabolism. Dilation of the pupils occurs. Portions of the endocrine system are stimulatd, releasing greater amounts of the hormones adrenaline and noradrenaline into the bloodstream. The liver, which normally stores glycogen, is stimulated to produce the simple sugar glucose from glycogen to provide additional fuel supply for the body's enhanced metabolic rate. Transmission of nerve impulses is facilitated by the production of noradrenaline at the synapse. This is especially required to innervate the smooth muscles of the viscera and blood vessels.[40]

them. Whether it was through
fear or sadness or anxiety,
those were the things that
guided me. It wasn't
thinking or working—you
know, focusing on a task.
Some of [my] emotions were in
the forefront. [My] generally
rational self was kind of put
away, for a while. [I] went
from someone who felt in
control, who could think out
a problem logically, etc., to
someone who was very in touch
with her feelings all of the
time . . . . I was still
functioning, so that rational
part must have been
controlling things. But it
was not conscious. . . . It
was a very strong feeling,
that distrust of self. It
was, I think, partly what I
said about my father's
questioning—that I thought I
was on top of things, that I
could handle any situation
that I encountered and
that . . . my instincts
weren't as good as I thought
they were, or that . . . [I]
shouldn't have gotten [my]
self into trouble. I guess
that's it. And also I felt

It is useful to distinguish between supporting the victim's feelings and agreeing with his or her perceptions. The feeling that the victim is expressing when he or she makes an attribution is the wish to get back into control. The other person can reflect and support that feeling ("You're really upset about this. That's a natural reaction.") without being drawn into a discussion of the validity of the attribution. Victims need to find a reason in whatever way they can, and those who want to help them should support that effort as reparative.[41]

One of the major themes running through interviews with assault victims is the intensification of feelings of vulnerability and helplessness. This reaction, identified as one of the most common in post-traumatic stress disorders (Lazarus,

that I did the right thing
at that moment. I didn't
really ever feel guilty
about it. I don't think I
ever really felt that. It
was more that I felt that
because I, right at *that*
moment, not at the moment of
the crime, at the moment
afterwards—reacting so
emotionally to things, that I
didn't trust that my instincts
would take care of me like I
had trusted before. That's
what I didn't trust. I
didn't trust, for example,
that I would be riding on the
subway and there might be
three men standing there—
that I wouldn't do something
crazy to them. You know,
totally inappropriately. Or
walking down the street. In
the past I *did* feel my
instincts were pretty good, in
terms of things that I should
be cautious about, and all of
a sudden I thought, "You know,
I'm just sort of burnt out,"
that I don't trust that those
instincts [are] going to get
me through, any more. I'm
going to either react to
everyone or to no one, and

1966), can serve as the catalyst for revision of one's self-concept, leading to a loss of self-esteem. The victim of an assault has experienced subjugation to another person, and this can lead to feelings of humiliation and shame that threaten one's sense of independence. This threat becomes especially salient in individuals with developmental or characterological concerns about dependency. The failure to prevent an attack can be interpreted as an indication that the self is not strong and in control.[42]

that's how I felt like I
didn't trust myself any more,
and I didn't know if I would
get it back. I was afraid
that I wouldn't get it back,
that I wouldn't ever, really,
be able to be sure of myself
in those kinds of situations,
again. . . . [Four months
after the Crime Victims'
Counseling Services group,
my sense of "getting it back"
is] changing—I feel there are
times when I still
doubt it, but at first I was
so cautious that it bothered
me—that I felt that I was
always going to be obsessed
with every step outside my
apartment. But at this
point I feel that it's not
an obsession, that it's a
keenness that I've developed,
and that I feel good about it.
I feel that I've just become
more alert, [though] I always
thought I was pretty keenly
aware of my surroundings,
prior, but now I feel even
more so, and I feel positive
about it at this point. I'm
more cautious. Not that I
restrict myself, I'm just
cautious. . . . and, still,

I'm afraid when . . . I enter or leave a subway station—day and especially at night; when I'm waiting for a subway; when I'm riding on a subway; when I see faces that remind me of what I think my two assailants looked like; when I'm in my apartment alone at night; when I sleep on my back; when I hear black males speak; when I project how and when I'll have to travel to and from home to get things done; when someone calls and it's the wrong number; when I take a shower; often, generally, when I'm alone; when I remember certain dreams; when I replay the incident in my mind; when I walk the streets (especially at night) and I see "suspicious" looking men; when strangers come closer to me than that public zone of comfort allows; when my cats perk their ears; when I enter my apartment at night after being out; sometimes even when I leave my apartment during daylight; when my back is turned in an unprotected position; when I feel nothing; when the light is out at night.[43]

I'll sometimes doubt it in
myself. I'll still some-
times have feelings that I'm
overreacting, or my instincts
aren't quite there yet.
But, generally, I feel that
they're coming back and I
feel that not only have I
developed what I had before,
but I've developed newer
ones, and kind of refined
them to where it's even
better. . . . [I] was afraid
to go out or return at night,
[I] couldn't trust [my]self
or trust the environment.
Since I've moved [which was
arranged *before* the crime] I
feel really somewhat less
comfortable with this neighborhood at night, and I
don't know if it's just the
reality of the neighborhood,
which I do think is a big
part of it. It's more down-
town, it's more deserted at
night, and so that's just a
reality of the neighborhood—it's
new to me and I think
it's also a reaction to the
crime. I just still don't
feel comfortable with going
out at night. Somehow, not
going out—it's coming *back*

at night that I have a
problem with—[that's when
the crime happened]. So a
few times I have not done
things because I knew I'd
have to come back. Friends
have been very good about
that saying, "Oh, well, just
stay over," but then it's
like not only does it take the
whole night but it takes half
the next day, and I really
don't have that much time,
so that we could go to a
movie, something very simple,
or sometimes I won't, or
I'll say, "Let's go to the
three o'clock," which I
didn't used to go to. I've
made those changes. It's
made some shifts in [my]
daily life—I wouldn't say
really substantial, but
subtle ones. It's not that
they happen every time, but it
does, now and then. . . .
[My feelings were] sort of
mixed, [after] the very
first session. Part of it,
I remember telling my story
and I got upset again,
telling my story. I remember
I started crying and, as I
said, I had just gotten

I'm afraid when . . . it becomes dark,
when it's time to go to sleep, when I
hear a noise I can't readily identify. It
seems lately I'm afraid a great deal of
the time. I'm also afraid when walking
alone and see more than one person
walking together. This can be day time
or night time, but while dark I don't
walk alone. I'm afraid of being in a
position where I have to protect myself
and not confident I could put up a good
fight. I sometimes am afraid that I'm
losing my sanity and also that I'm
becoming the type of person I don't
like and one that others won't like,
either.[44]

back from Thanksgiving
vacation and I was thinking
that oh, this is over with.
It was like a realization
that, "No, there's really a
lot here and you're still
feeling a lot about this, and
you haven't resolved it.
You've just been in a
situation where you have had
a lot of support, these last
few days, and with your
family, and so forth, and
that was nice, but it doesn't
mean that the feelings still
aren't there." That was a
realization that I didn't
particularly like. I would
have preferred it to be gone,
but on the other hand, I
did feel good that I was
involved in something that
was helping me deal with it,
and that I felt very good
about that. The group seemed
to be something that I could
relate to, that the types of
activities seemed to be something that made sense to me.
I do remember that first session,
after we shared our
stories and we did a writing
exercise. Then we kind of
got into generally talking

Negative feelings about the self are diffi-cult to communicate, especially in a cul-ture that values winners with bright, optimistic smiles. A crime victim who is feeling ashamed and guilty may find it extremely difficult to share these feelings with others. The inability to talk about negative feelings can, in turn, make them seem even more important, setting up a cycle of anxiety in which the victim is increasingly preoccupied with emotions he or she cannot confess. The victim may feel isolated and alienated from others.[45]

about criminals and those
that have consciences and
those that don't, and we
talked about that quite a
bit. [Another] person that
was in the group . . . wanted
to keep on about it, but I
had mixed feelings. I
definitely came back [for
the other CVCS sessions]
because I felt that it was
still helping me more than
anything else that I had
been involved with, and it
was very specifically
focusing on the crime, which
is really what I wanted. I
felt that fifteen minutes
talking about criminals was
all right, given the two
hours for other things. I
felt it contributed to what
I needed to do. . . . I
remember the last session
very well. We kind of shared
where we all were, at that
point, and I was feeling
very good, by the last
session. I mean, not that
everything was resolved, but
I felt that I could see in
myself the changes that had
happened, that I was really
doing better, and that I was

If the perpetrator of the crime came into this room right now I . . . would want to kill him for what he did to me. I would shake him until I could kill him with all my strength—how dare he take away from me what I have worked for, struggled for? How dare he destroy my library card, union drug card? What did he do with my personal possessions that mean so much to me? I would want him to pay for his crime. I feel his potential can be rape, robbery, that he is a dangerous, non-caring, an animal let loose in society.[46]

really kind of finding that
old self and improving on
it. I really felt much
better than I had in months,
even before the crime, and I
think it was also associated
with the move. I had moved
right before that last
session, so I think, with
those things together, it
made me feel much better.
In fact, I just hadn't felt
that good in a long time,
and talking about it that
night, I remember, also
helped. It was good to be
able to share it, because
we wrote one night about
fear (not the last night,
but an earlier one) and I
remember writing the way I
feel about coming home at
night and things related
directly to the crime. Then
I remember writing about fear
of moving and fear of the new
neighborhood, and fear of the
new apartment and the
neighbors and the new
building, and I just kind of
became paralyzed because I
hadn't realized consciously
that I was afraid of it.
[The CVCS session] helped

I'm afraid when . . . I am walking alone and someone is walking close behind. When a young black man is walking toward me with no one else around (or behind me). Sudden or loud noises or movements. I'm alone in a subway train. In an enclosed area with a strange man (elevator, etc.).[47]

bring it out and it also . . .
made me think, you know, if
you're really afraid and you
are now more aware of that,
what are you going to do and
how are you going to make
this move? Something that
you can deal with. I became
more active in trying to confront my feelings, and I
don't think I would've been
aware if we hadn't done that
writing exercise. They
would have still *been* there,
and so I talked with people
about it and people took it
very seriously. So by that
last meeting the move had
been resolved, and a lot of
fears. I realized they were
real, but that they can be
resolved and that people
helped me. So by the time
of that last meeting I
realized the move had been
resolved and the crime in *its*
way was being resolved, and
that, in fact, where I was
at that point (as opposed to
where I was before) was
better. So at the last
meeting there was another
person in the group who was
not at that point at all,

*The need that victims experience for men-
tal health services has been well demonstrated. In a recent survey of victims
regarding their most distressing problems following victimization, mental
health and emotional problems were
rated as more serious than lost property,
lost income, bodily injury, or lost time at
work. Yet only one in five victims thought
there might be good mental health services available to them, and only one in
10 actually sought such services.[48]*

and I remember he was saying
that it was really good to
hear from me. I remember he
was saying he still was
having nightmares and the
light was still on—those
things, yeah. I thought I
left with thinking that for
me the timing was perfect, it
really was. It started at
the right time and it ended
at a very good time, and I
don't know if it created the
cycle or if I contributed to
it, but it matched, somehow.
It met my needs, oh,
definitely! . . . I think
that [sharing my feelings
in the sessions] was important to me. It helped me to
talk about it with people
that I didn't really know
that well, or didn't know at
all. To hear other people's
experience brought down those
barriers of "me only," and so
there was a lot of comfort.
Beforehand I had sort of
thought, you know, "You're
going to hear about all this
from other people and it's
just going to make you more
paranoid, hearing about all
of these other crimes. And

I'm afraid when . . . everything
around me is much too silent, when
doors, windows and floors creak.
When I hear strange noises even if I
think I know what that noise is. I sleep
with the light on. When someone
stands too close and just is there, especially if there's space around that person. I worry when someone stares at
me too long, and when I have nightmares. I think one day I'll have to live
alone again, that if it would happen
again *this* time, I may not mentally
survive. That this time I would snap.
(But I'm not as afraid as I was when it
first happened, when I suspected everyone and anything.)[49]

you're going to worry about this block and this subway station,'' but it didn't happen that way—it kind of made me realize that it could be any block and it put a better perspective on it for me. It made me realize that it can be *any* block. It's really not just the one block. That was valuable. [The written exercises in the sessions were] the most surprising to me, because I usually (in other group things I'm in, where they have us write something) it's always the thing I dislike the most. I usually resent doing that kind of thing. I just don't like it, and yet I found that it was something that was valuable for me. In another instance I remember we talked about powerlessness and anger and fear. There must have been one more . . . ''If the assailant''—that was the very first one. All of them really helped me to kind of think through those feelings, think through the specifics. The one on power-

The most common problems (affecting three-quarters of the sample) from which crime victims suffered, were psychological problems including fear, anxiety, nervousness, self-blame, anger, shame, and difficulty sleeping. Emotional problems affected victims of property crime (burglary) as well as victims of violent or personal crimes (robbery and assault). Almost all victims reported some type of problem as a result of being victimized.[50]

I feel powerless when . . . I'm overwhelmed with too many things to do and too many pressures. I feel powerless when I'm tired or really exhausted. I feel powerless when I am indecisive and I can't act; when my thoughts are cloudy and I'm confused. I generally feel that I have power although often not enough. I lose power when I'm intimidated, when I'm outnumbered, and when I'm unprepared. I lose power when the other person has a weapon. But I always retain some

lessness I remember. I hadn't
even really considered that
one, and it was the little
thing, too, like powerlessness
over losing something. I
remember we talked about not
being able to find your keys,
or whatever. It is and it
was very good for me, all
those written exercises. I
liked the one about fear—I
wrote down these things that
I hadn't really known would
come out and that was good,
but then, in the sharing of
them—hearing other people's
contributions—was like
sometimes they would trigger
new things. Oh, yeah, I
feel that was good. It
expanded what would be
meaningful to me. Some of
theirs I didn't relate to, but
some I would. Also, it
was the whole thing. It
involved understanding, that
we *all* experience fear or
powerlessness or anger or
what we would do to the
assailants. I remember the
differences—that *I* still
haven't really ever felt
that I would kill him
[the assailant with the gun].

power—the power to respond and to
act and to choose not to. I often feel I
do have power over others—some ability to control others, when in reality I
know I am powerless over other people's lives and decisions. I believe I
have power over myself in most situations, but I feel powerless when I'm
exhausted, afraid, overwhelmed with
things to do, overwhelmed emotionally, and insecure.[51]

[Probably because I] didn't
ever get a good look at
them. . . . [An important
part of the sharing was that
I felt understood by the
other victims. Absolutely.]
And [my] understanding of what
they went through aided [me]
in understanding [my]self.
Yes. *Yes!* Identification
was useful for putting [my]
own life in perspective;
definitely. . . . I
remember one thing right off
the top of my head, while we
were talking about, oh,
things we were doing, like
leaving the lights on at
night. I don't remember
another example, but for me
it was all of a sudden all
this contact with my family,
my parents, brothers, sisters.
Then I remember your talking
about how often it's the
behavior changes, in that
you're going to regress to
sort of a more infantile
stage, or a state where you
might have been protected by
parents, for example. Maybe
that partly accounted for
part of the reason why my
relationship with my parents

Victim-blaming is a very common occurrence in the aftermath of a personal crime. It provides a readymade answer to the question "Why me?" It's a cruel answer, and it is almost always unwarranted by the facts, but it can be terribly seductive. Practically everyone has been exposed to enough popularized psychology to know about concepts such as unconscious motivation. Under the influence of their need to attribute, both victims and their loved ones are ripe to decide that the victim has been somehow unwittingly responsible for his or her own injury. Victims who accept the blame may be further violated by their confusion and guilt as they struggle to uncover the alleged unconscious impulses that made them arrange for the crime to happen.[52]

and my family, all of a
sudden, became much more
important than it had been in
quite a while. And leaving
the light on was, you know,
that "night-light-when-you're-
a-kid" kind of thing. I
remember a couple of times
thinking, "That makes a lot
of sense!" and it just kind
of cleaned up some muddy
thoughts. Also, it wasn't
just your responding to
things that I had said, or
other people had said, but I
thought that the sharing of
your experiences was significant, too. I remember the
thing about the clarinet,
with your nephew, and not
to mention the ones that you
personally went through,
too, but I remember that one
'cause it just happened that
week and you were talking
about it. It brought out,
well, this is kind of an ongoing thing. It's not just
one incident. But you could
clean it up and move on with
your life, it's part of what
is your life on an ongoing
basis, and it's trying to
develop the resources within

The sharing of my own reactions during
and after the two muggings I survived
was, I think, critical in my understanding
of what victims experienced emotionally.
Moreover, the empathy I was thus able to
extend to group members was clearly a
benefit—as was their ability to identify
with me as a "covictim." While it would
be foolish to insist that professional victim counselors submit themselves to a
crime as a part of their training, it does
imply that crime victims can be useful
peer counselors and perhaps become
trained themselves.[53]

yourself to live it and to
be able to function, even
when these things happen. I
remember you were telling
about how you dealt with the
nephew and the things he had
said, and so it was all
right—that's another way.
It wasn't just the reflecting
on things that the group had
said, but it was also your
participation that I thought
was significant. . . . I
don't know [if the groups
would have been the same or
better without a counselor];
I really don't know. It
seems like without a counselor
there would be some value in
it, but it might take longer
because for a group of people
who don't know each other, and
don't have any structure,
you might need some leadership.
It might take longer till you
really got to what people were
feeling. At least for me,
with that crime-related thing,
the feelings are so much
"right there" that you want
to get to them quickly. It's
different for, say, Alanon,
where really it's a part of
your life sort of forever. I

If the perpetrator of the crime came into this room right now I . . . would like to beat him up. Still. It's six years now and the rage hasn't left. Because he's still (I think) (not knowing otherwise) on the loose—has not been arrested. Sometimes when I wash my hair I feel the scars on my head, feel the concave places on my skull where the gunbutt hit—it *always* reminds me of that night. I can't forget the *sound* of the metal hitting my skull again and again, and how black and blue my hands were for weeks, having used them to ward off blows. If the perpetrator walked in now I'd pick up the metal lectern, and try to kill him with it—tack him to the wall or floor and continue to beat him with it, until he stopped fighting. THEN I would call the police and have him REarrested, and prosecute like crazy. It's six years—but the feelings are like yesterday's—fresh and sharp and murderous.[54]

didn't see the crime victims
group as something that would
be ongoing forever. I saw it
as something needed for these
circumstances, for the crisis.
And because of that, then
there aren't people that
serve that transition, like,
say, in Alanon, where there
are people that try to bring
in the new people and kind of
lead it. There isn't that
sort of thing, so I think
that if you just brought people
together on December first,
any number of people that all
had called this number and
this was where the meeting
was, there would be some-
thing that would come out
of it, but it would be pretty
unpredictable each time. . . .
When I heard other people's
responses it was, ''Yeah, that
makes a lot of sense,'' but I feel
that, too. And I hadn't
even put that down! [It gave
me an angle I] might not otherwise have had, so it was worth
listening to them. Sometimes
I would kind of remember it,
and go home and write down
some of those same feelings
and include the new ones from

the other person, too, because it was like, "Yeah, that really makes sense for me, too, I just hadn't thought of it, or hadn't even realized it in myself." It was clarifying, back and forth, and to be able to share—it really focused. When we usually met, at the beginning, it was more general, it wasn't as focused as the written exercises were. So the written exercises focused our discussion afterwards, also. Say it was "fear." If we hadn't picked a topic, or if you hadn't picked a topic, and if we weren't talking specifically about that, then we wouldn't have had the same kind of discussion, I think, if we had continued with just our general discussion. So I thought that was valuable, to really try to focus on certain aspects that aren't typically experienced. . . . I didn't [keep the journal] a lot because most of the time I wanted to do it and just didn't do it, but I did a few times and I found it

There really is no substitute for compassionate outreach to victims. Concern must be indicated. At the same time, the key, at least initially, is to be a good listener, to be able to sit through some of the very painful feelings of a person in distress. I don't think just anybody can do it. Training and experience are needed to be able to deal well with victims. There are really three levels here. One is better public education so that less stigma is associated with victimization. The second is a good compassionate outreach program. And then, there needs to be a competent, experienced person who is willing to listen and bear some of the grief.[55]

valuable. It wasn't so much
like a sharing (as if I had
called someone). It wasn't
so much as clarifying as it
was cleansing, for me—
letting it out, putting it
down on paper. I might have
numbered things, or just even
organized them into para-
graphs; it crystallized
things a little bit for me.
It was also a time for
reflection. I did, a couple
of times, when I came back
from the meetings. I would
kind of write down what I
learned, or what I was
feeling, and that helped me
to use it as a part of a
reflective process. . . .
[Now, four months after the
CVCS session] I'm still
affected by it. It's something that is part of how I
am reacting to my environment—when I come home at
night, or if I'll come home
at night, and my cautiousness
on subways and my reactions
to people. The other part—
being kind of totally
obsessed with it, that *is*
gone, in terms of a day-to-
day living. I'm not having

Salasin: The President's Commission on Mental Health did not make a single reference to crime victims, although improved mental health services for criminals were recommended. Given the dramatic incidence of crime nationally, and the cycle of social isolation, withdrawal, and depression that accompanies victimization, there are large numbers of persons at risk for serious mental health problems who have no constituency in the mental health community. Do you personally see this as a responsibility for the mental health system to address?

Sharfstein: Yes. I find that these kinds of victims do not have a strong lobbying group to gain the attention of a key policy force such as the President's Commission on Mental Health. The Commission did hold a number of public hearings around the country, but I am not aware that anyone came forward to represent victims and talk about the need for accessible services.[56]

nightmares like I did, not
never (though it might even
be a few weeks or a month,
but every once and a
while). . . . Yes, I
definitely would [say that
I've largely recovered]. I
feel very much so. I just
feel not only recovered, but
better than before. . . .
[I don't know how much of my
recovery] was directed by
the cycle of the sessions,
or how much would have been
my own cycle in spite of the
sessions; even so, the two
really coincided for me. It
just really fit, at a time
when I may have myself just
blocked it, not dealing with
it any more, like after that
Thanksgiving holiday. If I
had been left to my own
resources, I may have just
gone on to this point and *not*
talked about it, just left it,
when obviously there was still
a lot that I was feeling. So
I think it helped me to keep
expressing it, and keep
working through those
feelings, when on my own I
don't think I've would have
(at that point, after Thanks-

Yet if you work, as I have, in either the general medical or psychiatric area of an inner-city emergency room, victims are your "bread and butter." You are continuously dealing, first with the acute psychological consequences of victimization, and then with the more chronic, debilitating aspects. Anyone who has organized an emergency service in a New York City hospital has had to take this into account in terms of planning.[57]

giving). I think I would
have said, "This is enough,"
and just kind of left it,
[buried it]. So I think
going through the groups
substantially changed how I
resolved those feelings. I
think one reason [I would
recommend the CVCS groups]
is for the same reason that
I chose to go to it, as
opposed to other things. I
would recommend it to people
because it really focuses on
the crime and your feelings
about the crime. I don't
know of anything else and I
couldn't find anything else
that really does that. I
think we tend to often deal
with the other things and
not really focus on that, and
kind of overlook the real
substantial impact that it
does have on our lives. So I
would really recommend it to
people, even people who
didn't seem all that
incapacitated by [being a
crime victim]. I would still
recommend it to them, because
to many people I probably
seemed okay. I would do that.
So that's one thing, because

As has been well demonstrated in the literature, victims feel a tremendous amount of guilt about their own victimization. Shame and stigma are associated with being a victim. I think this is a primary deterrent to victims reaching out to anybody, be it a friend, minister, or mental health professional. The solution to this is better public education, better public understanding of the whole process of victimization and the need for services.[58]

If the world doesn't make sense, people can't do anything with confidence. They are thrown back into helplessness— shattered by the sight of the lightning. Victims of personal crime need to find some way of pulling themselves together. They go through a mental process to reorganize and understand the world that has become chaotic. This process helps to reintegrate the violated self, reducing the dissonance caused by its fragmentation. . . . A victim wants to be able to say, "I understand this thing, and I am no longer frightened by it."[59]

it really focused on the crime—but then, the other is because it worked *for me*. I think it really contributed to my being able to talk about it, to my being able to think things through. Being involved with other people who had been through similar things [was], I think, significant for me. Boy, I don't think [CVCS] should be changed at all. . . . You know, [some]thing that has occurred to me through this whole thing is that (and it came out because of the other people, in a way that I never had perceived before), trying to discover for myself what are the things that are really important and to put my time into that. And the things that are *not* really number one, even if they are a close number two, they are *not* a number one, and *don't do them!* I'm really taking that very seriously, and I think that the crime pushed me into acting on them. I kind of thought about it before, but never acted on it, and I've kind of gotten

I think I'm more informed about what happened to me. For the first time, I got support from people who really could understand what I went through.[60]

In the normal course of a crisis reaction, the recoil phase will eventually give way to the final phase—reorganization. The violated self becomes reorganized over time as the victim assimilates the painful experience. Feelings of fear and rage diminish in intensity, and the victim begins to have emotional energy left over to invest in other experiences. The victim's level of activity becomes more even and balanced as the need to deny the victimization ebbs. Victims think less about the crime and become less interested in talking about it, but when it does come up, the conversation is less emotionally tinged and much less upsetting. Gradually victims are able to put the experience

to where work is really
important to me and people
say, "How have you've been
[handling your] relationships?"
and other things. I want the rest
of my life to be as *un*stressful as
possible, and so, if my free
activity is working on with [my]
organization and helping them
and fund raising and stuff, that's
really creating more stress, then
don't do it. You know, I really
am cleaning up those things
in a way that I never took
seriously before.

into perspective and commit their energies to other things.[61]

NOTES

1. Nicholas Pileggi, "How to Stay Out of Trouble," *New York Magazine* (February 8, 1982), p. 20.
2. New York Women Against Rape, flyer.
3. Safety and Fitness Exchange, brochure.
4. Crime Victims' Counseling Services (hereinafter CVCS), crime prevention instruction sheet.
5. Martin Symonds, "Victims of Senseless Violence," *Psychiatric Worldview* (Lederle Laboratories), (Jan./March, 1977), p. 1.
6. *Ibid.*, p. 2.
7. *The New York Times*, November 22, 1980.
8. CVCS group exercise.
9. *The New York Times*, March 23, 1982.
10. *The New York Times*, April 6, 1981.
11. Kenneth Friedman, *et al.*, *Victims and Helpers: Reactions to Crime* (New York: Victim Services Agency, 1982), p. 25.
12. *The New York Times*, April 6, 1981.
13. Friedman, p. 138.
14. Symonds, "Victims of Senseless Violence," p. 2.
15. CVCS group exercise.
16. CVCS group exericse.
17. *The New York Times*, April 6, 1981.
18. Symonds, "Victims of Senseless Violence," p. 3.
19. CVCS group exercise.
20. CVCS group exercise.
21. Terence des Pres, *Survivors* (New York: Pocket Books, 1976), pp. 43–44.
22. CVCS group exercise.
23. John Heinz, "Op-Ed Page," *The New York Times*, July 20, 1982.
24. Editorial, *The New York Times*, September 23, 1982.
25. CVCS group exercise.

26. Richard Spates, "The Mental Health Needs of Victims: A Review of the Literature With Recommendations for Research," American Psychological Association Task Force on Violent Crimes (1982), p. 8.

27. CVCS group exercise.

28. Friedman, p. 144.

29. *Ibid.*, p. 5.

30. *Ibid.*, p. 14.

31. *Ibid.*, p. 5.

32. *Ibid.*, p. 3.

33. Spates, p. 6.

34. J.L. Barkas, *Victims* (New York: Scribners, 1978), p. xi.

35. Martin Symonds, "The 'Second Injury' to Victims," *Evaluation and Change* (Special Issue, 1980), p. 38.

36. Friedman, p. 15.

37. Morton Bard and Diane Sangrey, *The Crime Victim's Book* (New York: Basic Books, 1979), p. 15.

38. Symonds, "The 'Second Injury,'" p. 37.

39. Bard and Sangrey, p. 16.

40. Spates, p. 9.

41. Bard and Sangrey, pp. 62–63.

42. Janice L. Krupnick and Mardi J. Horowitz, "Victims of Violence: Psychological Responses, Treatment Implications," *Evaluation and Change* (Special Issue, 1980), p. 45.

43. CVCS group exercise.

44. CVCS group exercise.

45. Bard and Sangrey, p. 86.

46. CVCS group exercise.

47. CVCS group exercise.

48. Susan Salasin, "Caring for Victims: An Interview with Steven Sharfstein," *Evaluation and Change* (Special Issue, 1980), p. 18.

49. CVCS group exercise.

50. Friedman, p. 5.

51. CVCS group exercise.

52. Bard and Sangrey, p. 65.

53. Author's notion.

54. Author's group exercise.

55. Sharftstein, quoted in Salasin, "Caring for Victims," pp. 19–20.

56. *Ibid.*, p. 19.

57. *Ibid.*

58. *Ibid.*

59. Bard and Sangrey, p. 53.

60. CVCS self evaluation.

61. Bard and Sangrey, p. 46.

HOW TO READ THIS BOOK

Writings appearing in this left column, widely spaced in the typeface you are reading, are always and only edited transcripts of audiotaped interviews with crime victims who availed themselves of the group sessions offered by Crime Victims' Counseling Services.

Writings appearing in this right column, in the typeface you are reading, are always and only from books, newspapers, magazines, journals, reports, brochures, and similar sources.

Writings appearing in this right column, in the typeface you are reading, are always and only the author's responses.

Writings appearing in this right column, in the typeface you are reading, are always and only from group exercises and evaluations by members of Crime Victims' Counseling Services group sessions.

Two: DANNY

It was November eighteenth, at a quarter of ten in the evening, and I was walking south on Central Park West. My idea was to take an IND train down to West Fourth Street and transfer to a D train and take it into Brooklyn, where I live. I'm not very familiar with the IND line, so at about Ninety-third or Ninety-second [Street], I walked down into what I thought was an entrance for the IND, and I discovered that it was an exit only. So I backed out, and I continued south until I got to Eighty-seventh [Street] and Central Park West. I saw another subway, what I thought again was an entrance, and walked down near the bottom. I realized that it was another exit and it was gated off by an iron gate, so I turned around to come back upstairs (back onto the streets) and as I turned

Harvel Wilder worked nights. Taking his big magnum revolver, he headed into Manhattan in search of "people who had money." From the time he was 15 years old, he made hundreds of dollars a night prowling the city streets from Times Square to the upper reaches of Park Avenue, robbing everyone from "men with attache cases" to clerks in small shops. "There was about four of us," he recalled, "and we'd snatch six or seven people till we felt we had enough—till we was satisfied." Most New Yorkers live with a vague, uneasy fear of their city, and it is men like Harvel Wilder they conjure up in their imagination when they walk a deserted street or stand on an empty subway platform.[1]

around two men were already
on their way down. They
checkmated me, one on one
side and the other on the
other side, and I was against
the wall of the stairs. One
said, "We have a gun, this is
a stick-up; we're going to
blow your head off. Don't
try anything and no one will
get hurt. Close your eyes."
So I cooperated. I closed
my eyes but not all the way,
and they lifted everything
I had. All the cash, all the
personal effects, valuables,
watch, blank checks, credit
cards, driver's license,
everything. Briefcase; and
after they took everything
they told me to turn around
and walk the few remaining
stairs down to where the
platform is, which I did. I
had slowly turned around and
peeked around that one area
that follows the stairway,
and I realized that at that
point in time they had run
away. I slowly came back
upstairs onto the street. . . .
[Then] I went to a pay phone.
Oh, I forgot to tell you that
they were very generous.

. . . . I have collected many clinical examples of frozen fright where the individual has confused the listener with surface pleasantries, ingratiating, extremely cooperative, and seemingly friendly behavior. Though this behavior is deeply rooted in profound fright, it is confusing both to the victim and to the criminal. Later on when the victim reviews his behavior under peaceful conditions, he plays down the ingratiating aspects of his behavior under stress because he is ashamed of it, and thus lays down the seeds of guilt. The appeasing, ingratiating, compliant behavior of a victim of violence during the phase of frozen fright often leads to the false conclusion that the victim produced or participated in the criminal act.[2]

They left me with twenty-five cents and two [subway] tokens. I made a call to a very close friend; explained to him what had happened, and he calmed me down. . . . I reported the crime that night after I got back home and they gave me a claim number. . . . About four or five days later, I got a call from a detective, and he told me that he was checking out a person who had allegedly tried to cash a check of mine for $275. The bank, of course, did not cash the check; [the bank officer said] if he did find anything he would contact me, and he also asked whether I would be able to prosecute, and I told him I would be. That was approximately three weeks ago, and I have not heard anything from them. [I've had no other contact with the criminal justice system]. . . . My family does not live in New York; my parents live in Milwaukee. I did not and don't intend to tell them. It would serve no purpose at this point,

Personal possessions can take on symbolic significance as expressions of self. The way a person dresses, his or her car, home, and furnishings are all outward manifestations of inner identity. We surround ourselves with extensions of ourselves that have emotional value because they express who we are. Logically, then, the theft or destruction of a person's possessions can be experienced as a violation of self.[3]

It is important for the victim to be truthful even about facts that are embarrassing or things that make the victim look bad. The police will not conduct the best investigation if they doubt the victim's credibility. When victims exaggerate their losses—falsifying claims of property value in order to collect higher insurance payments, for example—they may reinforce police cynicism and contribute to an indifferent investigative effort.[4]

they would only worry. I did tell my sister (who lives in Phoenix), and she responded with a great deal of concern and support and warmth. . . . Oh, I have a big family in Milwaukee, [but no one locally to whom I can go]. [People at work responded to me] with a great deal of warmth and sensitivity, uniformly. At least with the people I worked with. People who I didn't work directly with made cute jokes about it, which I didn't appreciate; perhaps it was their only way of saying, ''I'm sorry it happened to you.'' But the people who I work closely with were very sensitive. A couple of people came up to me and gave me a hug without even my asking, and they wanted to know if there was anything they could do, and they wanted to know if I felt like talking about it. I gave them a fairly good idea what happened and how I felt in the aftermath—feelings of fear, paranoia, and anger. [I went to work] the next day; I came in late, but I

The special care of loved ones can do a great deal to help a victim who is feeling guilty and ashamed. But the victim will also have to deal with the reactions of strangers, people outside the warm circle of family and friends. In a society that stigmatizes crime victims, these reactions can be difficult to handle.[5]

Feelings of guilt and shame are common, normal reactions to the violation of self that occurs in a personal crime. . . . A sensitive friend or relative should keep an eye out for this kind of confusion. Those who are close to the victim can also help if they are tolerant of the victim's need to express negative self-evaluations. If the loved one can just listen, without becoming argumentative or alarmed, the victim will often discharge these feelings and move beyond them.[6]

went in the next day. . . . While the crime was in progress [I was] terrified, just terrified. I knew that there was a very good chance that I was at best going to get badly beaten, if not killed. I was just simply terrified for three to five minutes, and then after they left there was a certain amount of shock, but there was also a very overwhelming relief—relief from the stark reality of great bodily harm. [They'd] moved closer in toward me, asking me in very rough tones, "Okay, where is the money? Where are the valuables?" and they didn't seem threatening at that time. They started to move in and get ready to get very rough, or take desperate measures. I know that my first instinct—when I saw them and they cornered me— was to fight. I squashed that immediately, once they told me they had a gun and they were going to blow my head off. Well, I felt threatened the whole time, but shortly after they

Dr. Morton Bard, a professor of psychology who is director of the Center for Social Research at the Graduate Center of the City University of New York, said that the emotional effects of gunshot wounds differed from those of wounds inflicted by other weapons. "If someone comes at you with a fist or a knife or a chair, you can try to ward it off," he said. "That lack of control if the weapon is a bullet exacerbates the victim's sense of powerlessness."[7]

Certainly one does not have to survive the concentration camps in order to arrive at awareness of life's imminent

cornered me and I realized that I wasn't going to try and fight, that that would be crazy, they came in closer—before they actually started putting their hands all over my body to take what they really wanted to take. . . . When they started to frisk [me, it felt] terrible. They didn't rough me up in any way; in fact, there was a strange warmth—not warmth, but they were gentle, even the way they took off my watch. Probably because they didn't want to ruin it, but instead of ripping it off they were very gentle in how they took it off. And they did that with everything they lifted from my person. Just very gently took things out. . . . ["Intimate?"] That's a hard thing for me to respond to because, maybe, of the way I think and feel about intimacy. When I said, "warmth," before, the word "warmth," and then I quickly tried to modify that, maybe I didn't feel intimate, [but controlled by] someone who is controlling my life

value. It can come abruptly, with the shock of death-encounter, or gradually after passing through a period of protracted death-threat, and sometimes in a moment of character-changing revelation. Dostoevsky is a wonderful example. As a young man he was arrested for mildly revolutionary activities, condemned to death, and taken to the place of execution; his sentence was commuted to imprisonment only after the ritual of execution had been carried up to the actual point of shooting. He genuinely thought he would die, and later that same day he wrote an extraordinary letter to his brother:

> *Brother, I'm not depressed and haven't lost spirit. Life everywhere is life, life is in ourselves and not in the external. . . . This idea has entered into my flesh and blood. Yes, it's true! That head which created, lived by the highest life of art, which acknowledged and had come to know the highest demands of the spirit, that head has been cut from my shoulders. . . . But my heart is left me, and the same flesh and blood which likewise can love and suffer and desire and remember, and this is, after all, life. On voit le soleil! (Mochulsky, 141).[8]*

and everything. I felt
totally vulnerable and totally
powerless. It's hard for me
to respond to that
question. . . . Before
calling Crime Victims' Counseling Services, I felt
scared, and at the same time
I felt very hopeful that I
would get a certain kind of
response, but I was scared.
I knew that I was beginning
to feel certain feelings as
a result of the crime—the
fear, the paranoia, the anger.
There was a certain amount of
guilt, and I knew that there
were other feelings that I
couldn't label that I was
feeling, or they were
beginning to surface, and I knew
that I probably would
have a very difficult time
if I tried to deal with all
these feelings by myself. I
realized that I needed some
kind of support system outside of myself and my
friends. So, after approximately four or five days, I
called CVCS. [Once I] made
the appointment to come down
to the group meeting, I felt
very hopeful and I was looking

With her rage building, Mazabras got off the bus at 72d Street and went to her bank to inform them that her checkbook was inside the stolen billfold. She then visited the stores she has credit cards with and informed them of the theft. Then she told police, who took her to the scene of the crime, but the bandits, of course, were long gone. So Mazabras, her dignity bruised and her confidence in mankind a bit shattered, went home and wrote an open letter to the stylishly dressed man: "Yesterday while boarding the bus on 60th Street and Third Avenue in the throng that followed here you stood, wearing beautiful and stylish clothes, a red scarf with the grandiose air of a gigolo. Smoothly like a snake, you stole my billfold. And after I was on the bus you sent me a beautiful smile, feeling so victorious. For all the bucks I had, I hope you enjoyed them. Because I value my beautiful life, my dignity and my cool. Your act of stealing from innocent by-standers is simply the work of a coward. I am deaf born, beautiful and have had a hell of a hard time making a living. To think you are free to take my meal while I continue looking and doing all kind of

forward to it. . . . I had
a great deal of anxiety. The
anxiety is directly related
to the fear. Anxiety that
the same thing could happen . . .
people who I think sound like
the assailants. I get very
anxious. Or if I see people
who I think are suspicious, I
get very anxious and all that
anxiety, I think, is just
nothing but fear. I've been
walking around with a lot of
fear. . . . The fear, to me,
manifests itself in many
different ways. One way is
anxiety, and that seems to
be the most prevalent way
right now; the other way is,
I think, that the fear
manifests itself with the
anger and the guilt. I think
that's all traceable to
fear. . . . [I] keep thinking
about what's happened; I did
that for the first two weeks.
Subsequently, I haven't been
doing that too much, but there
was a little "videotape" that
I would play in my head for
minutes at a time. Maybe a
hundred to two hundred times
a day, I'd play it over and
over and over, usually when I

work, you son of a bastard, you dare rob me of my dignity. My rage is so great I wanted the public aware of how fast you and others act. You can go to my bank and try to remove my money. They have been alerted. You can go to all the stores and buy all the red scarves you want. They are waiting for you. You also can use my keys, my lock has been changed. But the day you will be caught, you had better count your blessings, because that is the day I really will count mine."
  Sincerely,
  Suzanne Mazabras[9]

I'm afraid most mornings going on the subway. I'm afraid of people that stare even mildly at me. I'm afraid when I do new things. I'm afraid on weekends when I should be doing something constructive—taking courses. I was so frozen afraid last week that I could not move.[10]

was at home alone but it could happen anywhere. But usually it happened when I was alone. . . .These "instant replays" *have* receded; today I almost never do it. It's much better today, which is a little over a month. . . . Most of the time, many times, "the videotape" happened exactly as I thought I remembered it. Frequently there were the modifications—like me being shot, knifed, beaten, a combination. A couple of times the table was turned and I got control, or somebody else from the outside interceded (not necessarily on my behalf, but they foiled the crime). For the most part, it was I who got shot, knifed, or beaten or a combination, and I wasn't found until the next morning. It was a very deserted area and, had something like that had happened, my guess is I wouldn't have been found until the next morning. . . . When I did the "instant replays," I was fantasizing what else *might* have

I feel powerless when . . . my self-respect and control are taken away by any weapon that could endanger my life. When fighting back can cause the loss of my life. I have a need to stand up for myself in life, not to be anyone's victim. I work for my money. I earn it and it is my right to do with it as I wish. I cannot bear being a victim of any crime emotionally. I hate feeling powerless. It is a betrayal of all I have fought for to be an independent person and I have fought hard to be mature! My reaction is to fight back by at times completely forgetting anything that has happened to me. It has been that unbearable! The power of forgetting to a great degree is helping me to survive. I absolutely hate with all my being—being rendered helpless and powerless due to the crime! For myself personally to regain power is to love in myself what is beyond possession—[accept] my own soul. For those who have

happened, and then I was often flooded with this over-whelming relief that I really came out of it physically unscathed. There was that relief, that enormous sense of relief, that something terrible could have happened, easily could have happened, but didn't. [But I'm] still afraid to go out or return home. I'm very careful about how long I stay in the city before coming back to Brooklyn. I'd feel fairly comfortable knowing that I would maybe return at ten or eleven in the evening. Now, I'm very conscious, and I try very hard to get back by seven or eight o'clock. . . . The crime occurred at about ten o'clock, quarter of ten, so if I get home before, it's not going to happen again, "then I'm saved." I use the subways fairly exclusively, rather than taxis, private car, or walking, though I walk in the city as much as I can. I like to walk. But my primary mode of transport is the subway, so that I have

rendered me powerless—I do not feel they deserve the life God put them on this earth for![11]

to reenter the situation
daily. I have no other
option right now; subways are
it. When I went to work
the next day, and had to get
on the train again, it was the
morning. It was very crowded
and that was somewhat consoling. It was somewhat
helpful that I was very,
very anxious. My eyes were
just scanning back and forth,
looking for suspicious
characters, waiting for something to happen. . . . Just
entering the station, I did
that as quickly as I could.
I tried to muster up as much
courage as I could, and I
swelled my chest and
straightened my back and got
the meanest look on my face
I could come up with. I don't
suspect that I was too intimidating (the way I was really
feeling) but it all happened
in a couple of minutes. [I'm
almost six feet, two inches
tall]—not your garden-variety
victim. Well, maybe I am.
That's the whole point. The
point is that I don't look
like your easiest victim.
I don't. I tried to look

REEL 263105 CUT_____
TAPE# 48332 VTR 3/1/82
AIR TBA ACTION 9 MMM
CRIME VICTIMS' COUNSELING
SERVICES

tougher or at least not
approachable. I didn't want
to be approached by any-
body. . . . I can't remember
the last time I felt so
powerless or out of con-
trol. Absolutely, totally.
The degree, on a scale of one
to ten, when it happened, was
a ten-plus. Today it depends
on the kind of mood I'm in
and where I am. Right now,
at this very moment, in my
apartment and it's daylight,
it's about seven. I would
walk outside and it can still
be daylight and I can be with
you, and maybe two other
people, and it would be a
six. When the crime occurred,
physically and emotionally I
felt that I was at the total
mercy of two other people.
They could have done anything
they would have wanted to.
Physically, I felt totally
fatigued and weak, totally
out of control. I urinated—
I wet my pants, which I'm
not ashamed to say. I was
that scared, which also
emphasizes how much out of
control I felt and was. It
was just total; it permeated

Hello, my name is Danny and I'm a crime victim—I was mugged. Have you been a crime victim, too? Have you been robbed or raped? Has a burglar intruded into your home and into your life? I'm over six feet tall, but I know what it feels like to be afraid, nervous, depressed, angry and helpless in the face of crime. I had nightmares and even went to sleep with the lights on! Then I called Crime Victims' Counseling Services and I got free group counseling to help me cope with the emotional aftereffects of the crime. I found that I didn't have to be alone with my feelings—the other crime victims and counselors understood just what I was going through. They really helped. Don't let crime destroy your life. New groups are forming each month at Crime Victims' Counseling Services. Call 212 875-5862 or write us at GPO Box 3003, Brooklyn, New York 11202.[12]

my entire being, physically
and emotionally. . . . After
the first session of the CVCS
group, I felt assured. I
felt again hopeful that whatever negative feelings were
beginning to surface, or
whatever problems I was having
as a result of the crime that
I knew I couldn't deal with
well on my own would be dealt
with in the group. I had a
real chance to heal that way,
to recover more quickly. I
felt very confident in the
way that it was approached
and how it was run, and the
opportunity I had to deal
with my feelings. It gave me
a real chance to look at my
feelings in a nonthreatening
environment, and I found it
very, very helpful. There
was a noticeable decline in
anxiety, of fear in riding
the subway system. It's
still measurably fearful and
probably will be, for some
time to come, but I don't feel
as angry any more, and I don't
feel as guilty any more. All
those feelings are still
there to some significant
degree, but a good part of

Dr. Bard recommends that family members and friends "allow the victim to express his feelings no matter how much it may bother you," because "the person has a need to discharge." He said that there might be an extended period of suffering beginning with a period of one or two weeks of disorganization and dependency. Then there might come a period of six to eight months of fluctuating between feeling better and feeling bad, followed by a reorganization phase of up to a year.[13]

the edge of them has been dealt with and are removed. Some of that has to do with the passage of time, but a lot had to do with the sessions. What I found most useful about the sessions again was that I was given many opportunities to deal with some very tricky feelings, with the help and guidance of somebody trained to do that and it was in a nonthreatening environment. I don't mean nonthreatening in the sense I wasn't worried about a crime; I wasn't worried about anything happening to me while I was there. What I mean by non-threatening is that somebody was there to tell me that what I had gone through was terrible, even though I was very fortunate. Like the rest of the group, I found out it was normal for me to go through the feelings I was going through; it was normal for me to feel confusion on top of that. And the give and take, the dialogue in dealing with the feelings and various exercises in

Salasin: One of the most intriguing issues in the treatment of victims is the differentiation between the short- and long-term effects of victimization. The existing treatments that do appear to have merit are all principally short-term treatment models. No one yet seems to quite understand the common delayed effects, and their severity over time. I can see that if a compelling case were made, financing might be available for short-term care, but it would still leave open the whole issue of longer-term services. Do you have any reflections on this?
Shaftstein: I find this a problem for mental health services across the board. It is much easier to find funding for short-term care than for long-term care, for group care than for individual care. The fact is that in the area of victimization, short-term, responsive services that are

dealing with the feelings, were extremely useful for me to get in touch—with more clarity—about those feelings, and then to deal with them. Hearing the others in the group made me feel that I wasn't alone in my feelings, wasn't as big a jerk as I thought I'd been. I felt that the counselor, and I'm very serious about this, I felt the counselor—her identification was complete and it was sensitive. She was able to articulate from her own experience, as well as from her own training, a lot of the things that I was feeling but couldn't label or articulate myself. That kind of identification really helped me in dealing with the feelings that I had, especially the feelings that I didn't want to look at, that I traditionally don't like to look at for my own reasons or excuses. The anger, the guilt, and the fear. Basically, the fear; I didn't want to really look at the fear, and I knew I had to if I wanted to get past a

crisis-oriented and that include compassionate outreach are probably the most cost-effective kinds of services. In the short haul, this is what we should be aiming for in our programs and their financing. However, there is a group of casualties who, even with good, short-term, acute intervention, will become longer-term problems for the mental health system. We have to take care of them as well. For example, there is a role for longer-term psychotherapy when a longer-term working through of problems is needed. Very often, victimization brings to the surface some long-standing problems of personality development that have to be dealt with at that point—in fact the opportunity for growth presents itself with the victimization. More costly and longer-term therapy must have some means of support, as well.[14]

certain point in recovery from the thing. I was able to do that within the context of the group and with the counselor's aid. Once I heard that identification communicated the way it was, it became very helpful. I could actually connect that feeling and talk about it, and talking about it with the others took the edge off the pain. Just being able to speak and talk about what I was feeling, and know the others were listening and understood, was very helpful for me. Even though the other people had been victimized by different sorts of crime, the identification of the feelings was there. It was pretty uniform. The written exercises made me able to take an inventory of how I was feeling, and once I was able to take that inventory and sort out the feelings, I could actually deal with each feeling and each issue. There were many things that I didn't realize that were bothering me as a result of the crime that sur-

Although violence invariably will be experienced as stressful by most, if not all, victims, its impact will vary depending on a number of factors, such as pre-existing neurotic and developmental problems, and sets of personal or cultural meanings and attitudes regarding the event. Most persons will be able to dose themselves with the painful reality of the attack, and gradually integrate into their lives the traumatic ideas and feelings provoked by the assault. Some, however, will develop a stress response syndrome that is characterized by phases of ideational denial and emotional numbing. Where these phases appear to be overly intense or prolonged, some psychological interaction between the current meanings of the event and previously existing ideas is interfering with the natural psychological healing process, and professional help may be needed.[15]

I get angry when . . . my instincts are threatened—when I feel I might lose what I have or not get what I want; when my cats get too vocal; when I make mistakes with a talk I feel I should perform better; when I hear about other victims of crime; when I hear or see other people victimized or intimidated; when I hear/see people (especially black males) act tough or talk with a lot of jive; when people are rude and loud; when I can't sleep; when I get a headache; when I'm aware of how I avoid tasks or things I need to do; when I focus too long on what material possessions and money I lost from the mugging; when I focus

faced because of the sessions
in general, and because of
the feedback and the give
and take, in particular the
exercises. [For instance],
I didn't think I felt any
guilt, at first. I didn't
think I felt any shame, at
first, but going to the
sessions and sharing the
feelings, talking about the
feelings, identifying them, I
realize now that there was
an appreciable degree of
guilt and shame as a result
of the crime, and that talking with others and with the
counselor reduced those
feelings. . . . I stopped
keeping a journal—that could
be my own laziness. I found
it useful and I found it use-
less, but in terms of dealing
with most of the feelings
that I had after the crime,
it was the least helpful. It
wasn't that it wasn't helpful—it was a good idea and I
think it has a lot of use,
'cause I tend to block things
out and, if I record them, at
least that will trigger off a
thought or a feeling that I
had hours ago or many days

too long on the time and energy I have
had to expend to restore whatever
normalcy/comfortability in my life
since the mugging; when people don't
respond more tenderly or dramati-
cally, i.e., with more warmth and concern (on my terms) when I tell them
about the mugging.[16]

ago. . . . I'm still not as
integrated now as I was to
the level before the crime
[six weeks ago], but as a
result of the sessions I
realize that it's going to take
some time, and I'm not real
concerned about that. As I
was saying, I feel that I have
readjusted to some level of
daily routine. I'm still
anxious, I'm still scared—not
as frequently. I still have
trouble sleeping and I still
sleep with the light on, and
I'm still very much aware of
feeling these feelings of
anxiety. They're just not as
strong or as intense or as
frequent. I would uncondi-
tionally recommend the groups
to other crime victims,
because for me it gave me that
link back to readjusting to
some degree of normalcy in
life. It gave me a real
meaningful opportunity to
deal with the aftermath of the
crime, which would have taken
me much longer—I'm convinced
maybe never. I'm serious.
The complications emotionally
were significant for me,
anyway, and I know a

I felt much better knowing I wasn't alone in my fears and feelings. I also felt a bit of relief knowing that worse things could have happened to me than what did.[17]

lot of people victimized by far
more serious crimes than I was.
I had my life threatened, that's
pretty serious, but I came out
of it physically okay. What
I'm trying to say is that it
was an enormous help in terms
of support system, in terms
of people saying, "Yes, we
know what you went through,
here's why you are feeling
the way you are, here's what
you can do to get yourself
put back together emotionally
a little bit faster,"
reassuring me that I can feel
my feelings, they're acceptable. It's okay to feel
that way. It's nothing to
be ashamed of. Mainly the
support, that's what was very
helpful to me. Knowing
that there is help out there,
that's extremely important to
me. I was lucky I saw your ad
in the *Park Slope Shopper*. I
thought about evaluating the
groups for the last session,
and the only recommendation
that I would have (and maybe
it's just not feasible at
this point in time) but we
met in a classroom. Number
one, it has glaring

Extremely competent presentation with plenty of opportunity for victims to share their reactions and feelings and receive excellent feedback. Top-notch, and I'm a critical person.[18]

fluorescent lights, it has
hard chairs, it has sort of
a starkness about it.
Ideally, I would hope that a
situation like that could be
in an environment where
there are easy chairs in a
small room, gently decorated
with a fireplace, coffee—
that's very conducive to
warmth and support, as
opposed to a starkly
decorated or undecorated
classroom. Dealing with something a little warmer and more
comfortable would lend itself
to the whole idea behind
it. . . . I'm very glad to
do this follow-up interview
and I want to participate as
much as I can, be as helpful
as I can, 'cause I think the
whole idea behind it is
extremely helpful to anybody
who's undergone that kind of
experience. Just to reiterate
the whole idea behind the
sessions, I think it would be
wonderful if the exposure
were there. Everybody either
has been a victim of a crime
or knows somebody who's been
a victim of a crime. It's
not an unusual thing. What

*Another role for victim programs sug-
gested by the research would be to develop ways to help supporters in their
efforts to help victims. Interviews with
those helpers who provided assistance to
victims showed that supporters suffer
many of the same aftereffects of victimization as the victim—increased fear of
crime, increased suspicion about other
people and general anxiety. If victim
programs could give advice and emotional support to potential helpers to
prepare them for helping victims, it
would benefit both victims and supporters
and perhaps partially contain the ripple
effect of crime. Supporter programs
might involve education about the impact
of crime on its victims, as well as the
impact that helping has on the helper,
tips on providing psychological first aid
to crime victims, mutual support groups,
and suggestions for community and individual crime prevention activities. En-*

we don't have today, as far
as I know, is any kind of
service outside of private
therapy, which can be very
expensive and most people
can't afford. We don't have
the kind of service that
deals with the issues and the
feelings that can be just as
dangerous to a person as the
crime itself, if those issues
and feelings are not
addressed. I think a lot of
men (I think I can speak for
a lot of men, at least from
my generation, and I'd be
happy to say I'm thirty-eight
years old) grew up in this
culture feeling that they are
in control, they are invulnerable—it's the macho
syndrome. There were some
residuals in me that way,
although I did not feel I had
tremendous control even
before the crime. The point
I'm trying to make is that
there are so many people out
there who are victimized who
don't want to look at the
feelings that they feel;
they feel that they are unacceptable, it's not right
for a man to feel fear, or

gaging in anti-crime activities could help both victim and supporter develop a sense of control over their environment by introducing ways to reduce vulnerability to crime.[19]

The evaluation I made on my feelings here reflect a certain kind of stability I feel in these areas, with continued improvement.[20]

guilt, or shame, and those
become displaced if they are
not addressed. This service
affords people that kind of
opportunity so that their
recovery from the crime, the
aftermath, is very helpful.
Immeasurably helpful. So
that's what I want to say—
that it's been an enormous
help to me.

I'm just glad I went to the meetings, and that there are groups like this that can help crime victims.[21]

NOTES

1. *The New York Times*, November 17, 1981.
2. Symonds, "Victims of Senseless Violence," p. 2.
3. Bard and Sangrey, p. 12.
4. *Ibid.*, p. 113.
5. *Ibid.*, p. 89.
6. *Ibid.*, p. 88.
7. *The New York Times*, April 6, 1981.
8. Des Pres, pp. 197–198.
9. *The New York Daily News*, May 5, 1981.
10. CVCS group exercise.
11. CVCS group exercise.
12. CVCS Public Service Announcement for WOR-TV, acted by Danny.
13. *The New York Times*, April 6, 1981.
14. Salasin, "Caring for Victims," p. 20.
15. Krupnick and Horowitz, p. 43.
16. Danny's CVCS group exercise.
17. CVCS group evaluation.
18. CVCS group evaluation.
19. Friedman, p. 16.
20. CVCS self evaluation
21. CVCS group evaluation.

HOW TO READ THIS BOOK

Writings appearing in this left column, widely spaced in the typeface you are reading, are always and only edited transcripts of audiotaped interviews with crime victims who availed themselves of the group sessions offered by Crime Victims' Counseling Services.

Writings appearing in this right column, in the typeface you are reading, are always and only from books, newspapers, magazines, journals, reports, brochures, and similar sources.

Writings appearing in this right column, in the typeface you are reading, are always and only the author's responses.

Writings appearing in this right column, in the typeface you are reading, are always and only from group exercises and evaluations by members of Crime Victims' Counseling Services group sessions.

Three: NANA

It was about two-fifteen in the afternoon of October twelfth, 1981. I was rushing into my apartment building. I was supposed to get a phone call and I was walking into my building. I think, at the very last second, I saw a man walking towards me. It made me a little nervous and I think that was the first time I saw him. I took a step into the building and he was behind me, and then I really was nervous. There's no doorman; there's an outside door that's usually always open and then, about five more feet, there is a locked door. He had entered this passageway right behind me, and that made me very nervous. I had a sense that I was in trouble, and I've been in trouble before, and always had a sense. (And always, when I did have this sense, it always happened that I was in

The two biggest threats to New York City as a place to live or work are crime and unemployed youth, a coalition of the city's business and civic leaders has decided. The group, called the New York Partnership and formed under the leadership of David Rockefeller, already had an agenda of New York City problems. But the members have decided that before anything else they devise can succeed in improving the city as a place to work or live, the streets and subways must be made safe.[1]

Whether you're carrying packages or not, vestibules, lobbies, and stairwells in buildings without doormen or tenant patrols are areas where you are most vulnerable to attack. They are out of sight of most police anticrime patrols and of passersby. Tenants of buildings without doormen should develop their own security procedures and stick to them.[2]

trouble.) He said to me, "Where is St. Luke's?" and my suspicions were confirmed. I knew immediately that, it was like, "Do you have a match?" It's the same thing. Especially since St. Luke's is right behind him. I mean, you couldn't miss it. I knew, at that point, that I was in trouble, for sure, and my instinct was to get out of the building. So I tried to get past him, to point to [St. Luke's Hospital], but I guess he realized what I was doing—trying to run past him and out of the building. [I] used the gesture as a means of bypassing him, but it didn't work and I was immediately thrown into the corner, and within a second I had a knife right in my neck. He was holding me [from behind], his arm wrapped around in front, with the knife [in his other hand] right here under my neck. He said, "Give me your money," and at that point I had about twenty-six dollars. I was coming into the building and I was in a rush.

Many stickup men and burglars get into apartment buildings because tenants are simply hesitant to challenge them. Police advise that New Yorkers not feel shy about shutting a door in a stranger's face. Good manners must at times give way to good sense. . . . It's safer to question such strangers from behind a closed door than to challenge them face to face in the lobby. It is also important to get the confrontation over with as quickly as possible so that another tenant doesn't stumble into the trap. "Crooks don't all look like crooks," counsels one anticrime detective, "and we've come to the sad point where it's better to be rude and safe than polite and sorry."[3]

The fear is apparent everywhere: in the faces of women who have taken to walking in the middle of Georgetown streets at night to avoid potential assailants who might be lurking in parked cars; in the dinner table conversations of neighbors, who passionately recount the chilling details of the latest rape or mugging; in arguments between wives and husbands over whether to keep a gun at their bedside. . . . Residents of Cleveland Park have formed a neighborhood association to discuss ways of combating burglaries. Some Georgetown women rush home after work in order to walk their dogs before darkness. In other neighborhoods, some mothers warn children returning home from school: "If you see anything unusual, don't go in the house. Just run away."[4]

If the perpetrator of the crime came into this room right now I . . . think I would kill him. If I could get his knife I would cut him into a million little pieces. I would then leave the pieces at the bus stop. Maybe the people who ran away would see him.[5]

I had two wallets in
my hand. One is a long
wallet—it looks like a
checkbook, and a little
change purse. I gave them up
immediately and he gave them
back. He said, "Just the
money." So in the meantime,
the purse with the money
fell. It's a little leather
purse. It fell on the ground
and I was never so afraid in
my life. (I've been in
robbery situations before,
once where the robbery was
in progress; I reacted then
in anger, not in fear.) At
this point, though, it was
just sheer fear. . . . I've
had three incidents in the
last ten years where I've
been robbed. Two months
before this, I had a rape attempt
in the park, as I was running.
This is only two months
before. I was still a nervous
wreck from that. I didn't go
for any counseling after that,
but I was aware that such
counseling existed in New York
City—I knew there were rape
hotlines and stuff like that,
but, see, I wasn't raped. I
felt violated [by an attempted

Seeking the safest way to deal with such people, Dr. Symonds interviewed dozens of violent criminals who themselves had been victims of crimes. These criminal-victims were never hurt because they knew what to do: They readily gave up whatever was demanded and without protest; they made no effort to contact the other criminal (not even, "Look—I'm a brother criminal"). All emphasized how dangerous any conversation can be— even saying, "Take it easy" can cause criminals to explode into serious violence.[6]

In the second phase victims develop what I have called "frozen fright," which is terror-induced, pseudo-calm, detached behavior. The victim experiences a traumatic psychological infantilism, in which all recently learned behavior evaporates and only adaptive patterns from early childhood predominate. In later retrospective reflection by the victim and others, this behavior appears to include ingratiating, appeasing, compliant, even cooperative and voluntary acts, which confuses everyone including the victim.[7]

Thousands of New Yorkers have had their lives shaken by violent crime, according to police statistics. And whether they have suffered through the murder of a husband or they themselves have survived an attack by knife-wielding robber or a purse snatcher, the victims say in interviews that they have found their lives changed. Some say fear and caution are now a part of their daily routine. For others, there is anger at a criminal justice system they believe has failed them. Still others say there is disappointment in their own cherished beliefs about people and a city they once loved.[8]

rape]. I got out of it all right, but I was still nervous from this instance. My only reaction was fear. I thought I was going to be dead, when I had the knife in my neck. So when he said, "Just the money," I pointed to the floor and I said, "It's in there," and as soon as that knife came away from my neck (he had to lower the knife to pick up the money) my instinct was to get out again. My instinct during the whole time was to escape, and when the knife came away from me I grabbed it with my hands, I grabbed the knife, and tried to get past him again . . . to get out of the building. I just thought, "I'm going to be dead and I just have to get out of here," so I grabbed the knife. I wound up with—I didn't even know it at the time—I had a slice here and a slice here. I didn't get by him, though I grabbed the blade. I guess I didn't know what I was doing, but my instinct was to get away, escape. He was a big guy. I'm strong, but I guess

I'm afraid when . . . I'm alone more than with others. Since I was mugged I'm afraid more now then ever before. Maybe the muggers will come back and finish off what they started. I panic inside and am very terrified of this thought. I'm afraid of the dark now and never really was since I was a child. I run home quickly before night falls (about 6 p.m.). I fear I might not get home safe and will die. I'm afraid when I approach my building, walk up the steps, open the door and look around to see no one is around. I'm relieved when I'm alone and yet fearful to be alone. I feel my heart pounding and my body trembling at times. I'm afraid to enter the elevator or to even climb the three flights of stairs to the fourth floor where I live. I'm afraid someone is waiting to get me. I see no one is around and then I open my door with fear, afraid someone just might be inside. I'm relieved to see no one is. I slam the door shut quickly and lock my locks. I've made it safe again, home. But the next thought always is, "I will be going out soon. How will I cope?" Will I always be afraid and never find complete freedom from my fears? This thought panics me and my heart pounds heavy and I breathe heavy and I feel panic and fainting.[9]

I wasn't strong enough. I'm
five feet, three-and-a-half
inches, and weigh about a
hundred and twenty-two. I'd
say [he was] six feet, and not
heavy, and not thin, probably
one hundred and seventy
pounds, and so I couldn't get
by. The next thing I knew I
was being beaten. I thought
I was being stabbed. It
looked like stabbing motions,
and at that point I started
screaming as loud as I
possibly could, just screaming
and just trying to get
away. . . . [Like] at the
rape attempt in the park I
started screaming *immediately*,
but there was no weapon then.
When I had the knife in my
throat, I didn't even consider screaming because I
knew any move and I was going
to be dead. But at the point
where I could get away and
the knife was no longer in
my throat, I was screaming.
My instinct was just to scream
as loud as I possibly
could, and hope that someone
would hear and come by. I
wasn't even thinking about
that at the time, and I

*There are other individuals whose re-
sponse to sudden, unexpected violence is
not frozen fright but anger. Even though
their behavior is rooted in profound
fright, the victims recall only being angry. They screamed, hit, or yelled. They
said to the criminal: "Get the hell away.
What are you doing? Leave me alone, I'll
call the police." Some have attacked the
criminal with their purse, their hands, or
thrown things at him. What happens to
the victim depends on circumstances and
on the mental health of the criminal.
While some back down and even run
away, more often the criminal feels frustrated and angry. This results in a violent
attack on the victim to beat him or her
into submission and compliance. A
woman said to a criminal who was robbing her store: "I'll never forget your
face." He shot her in the head and
blinded her.*[10]

screamed really hard. When
I listened to my own screaming, it was freaky. I scream
very, very horrible in
life-threatening situations.
I was just being beaten and
then my mind just . . . I
just felt it really wasn't
happening. I continued to
scream, but at some point,
I guess, it just became so
horrible that I felt it was
just a bad dream and at that
point someone had come to the
door and he [the assailant]
took off. I guess that was
soon after, because I
remember then being outside
the building, just running
around saying, ''This is a
fuckin' nightmare, you know?
This isn't happening,'' and I
started to swear and just be
a little crazy. I was
bleeding all over the place.
I wasn't hit in the face,
that's what I couldn't
believe. Afterwards, too.
I knew there was a knife in
my face, but you couldn't
even tell . . . [I was
bleeding from] my lip, my
hands were bleeding profusely,
and my head. I had a huge

. . . the immediate response to the event . . . consists of shock, disbelief, and denial. In this phase there is a temporary paralysis of action and a denial of sensory impressions. When denial is overwhelmed by reality, victims enter the second phase.[11]

If the perpetrator of the crime came into this room right now I . . . would fucking bite his NUTS off!! I'd take his head and bash it into the tile floor! Maybe then, I'd feel better. I want blood!!! I'd probably scream a lot. I feel HATE, HATE, HATE! Because these people changed me, and they're probably out right now hurting other people and laughing about it. These fucks don't have the right to breathe! There is no justification for hurting other lives. They need to be put to sleep, like rabid dogs! Only I'd wish them painful, degrading, ugly death and time to re-live each time they've hurt someone and have to suffer eternally.[12]

cut in my head. I don't
know how I got it, if he hit
me with the blunt end of the
knife, or . . . he might have
thrown me into the doorknob,
because the woman [who had
come to the door] said I was
being thrown around. . . . A
few people heard my screams,
but only one person reacted.
My super [later] said that
the super across the way
heard screaming, but it
sounded so distant that he
didn't bother to check it
out. My next door neighbor
heard screams, looked out
the window, but didn't see
anything. I was in the
building [and unseen] and
[so he] didn't do anything.
There was a man in the parking lot across the way, the
doctor's parking. I don't
know why *he* didn't respond.
He's in a booth. I mean,
he's not the type that would
just overlook it. I
remember going over to him.
They wanted me to go to the
hospital. First, I went
upstairs [in my building]
and then I came down, and I
still wouldn't go right to

*Essentially, the second injury is the vic-
tim's perceived rejection by—and lack of
expected support from—the community,
agencies, and society in general, as well
as family or friends. This second injury
often follows any sudden, unexpected
helplessness. For example, whenever
anyone is suddenly hospitalized for injuries or illness, certain consistent emotional responses emerge. After the initial
shock and disbelief, the person becomes
frightened, and his or her past feelings of
security, safety, and invulnerability are
shattered. In addition, the person's idealized image of himself or herself as a
self-sufficient, autonomous individual is*

the hospital. I went over
to him and asked if he
didn't hear my screams. I
just couldn't *believe* it,
that he didn't. I was in
shock and I just walked over,
bleeding all over him, and
they're trying to bring me
to the hospital and I just
wanted to know, didn't he
hear my screams??? . . .
When this woman arrived on
the scene after hearing my
screams, the assailant
escaped at that point, fled
with my money. . . . I
went outside. I don't know
how I wound up outside, but
I remember I was outside,
walking around saying,
"Well, this isn't happening,
this is a nightmare," and she
wanted to take me right away
to St. Luke's emergency
entrance, which is two blocks
away. I said I had to go
upstairs first because I had
my roommate's van and I had
it doubleparked, so I didn't
want to get a ticket. So I
just needed to go upstairs
first, and this poor guy
hadn't been up yet, that day.
He comes out of the room and

damaged. These feelings of fright that occur even in the most resourceful individuals lead to clinging behavior toward hospital personnel, particularly toward the treating physician. This in turn heightens the person's sensitivity to the interpersonal distance of others, and may cause him or her to experience the ordinary professional conduct of the physician as indifferent, impersonal, and unfeeling. It is only after some time, when the person is fully recovered and on his or her own two feet that the physician's professional attitude can be placed in proper perspective. If hospitalization is prolonged, or the disability is persistent or painful, even the most healthy individual will respond with and retain feelings of depression and constipated impotent rage.[13]

I feel powerless when I look back at what happened to me in that deserted hallway. When I was held up at gunpoint by a complete stranger. I tried my best not to resist knowing that the trigger of the gun was cocked and put to my aorta. I feel powerless when I think of our court system and see how inept it really is. When I was on jury duty I experienced this ineptitude. A murder was committed in 1977 and yet the criminals were brought to trial in 1981. The man was found guilty of

sees me covered wtih blood and acting a little crazy.

I knew he was going to park his van and I had him call my boyfriend, and then I walked to the hospital with them, my roommate and the woman. So this whole sequence lasted five or ten minutes, by the time I got to the hospital. It took six hours at St. Luke's Emergency Room, if you can call it an emergency room. It was two hours before they sewed my hand, five stitches here, four here, and even though the wound in the head was much bigger, just four stitches here [pointing]. . . . As it turned out, this medical treatment was fifty dollars, which I could afford. I mean, if it was any more, I couldn't. I have no hospitalization. . . . I found out about the Crime Victims' Compensation Board through this very nice woman at the hospital, who gave me some forms to fill out. I got a case number, and I finally sent it in. . . . [My roommate] called the

murder and yet had been free for four years.[14]

For years, Illinois police have carried cards informing suspects of their constitutional rights. Now police are adding a card to let victims know they may be entitled to compensation. Patricia Goldman, director of the Illinois Crime Victims Compensation Program, said the cards had been sent to the 25,801 law enforcement officers in the state. To qualify for compensation, a person must be the victim of violent crime or the relative of a slain victim. The crime must have been reported within 72 hours and the

police while I was on my way
to the hospital, and they
came to the hospital and
interviewed me while I was
waiting for treatment.
Detectives came, I'd say,
within fifteen minutes or
something, maybe. I'm not
sure. It might have been
longer. They were all
right. They took the
information. They weren't
particularly interested. I'd
just say they were okay. . . .
The next day a woman called
me up, a woman detective,
and wanted me to come down
and look at pictures, which
I did. I knew, to this day,
I wouldn't know the guy if I
fell over him. It was too
fast. I think he had on just
dark clothes, and he was
black and tallish, but that's
all. I'm not even sure if
he had facial—I think he had
some kind of facial hair—
sideburns and a beard, but
to this day I don't think I
would ever know him unless
he told me. . . . The only
other [agency I had contact
with] was the Victims'
Compensation Board. I filled

victim must cooperate with authorities. The maximum compensation a victim may receive was raised this year to $15,000 from $10,000.[15]

Victims' misperception of both the behavior and attitudes of police and other emergency personnel is often heightened by the emotional insulation that all such professionals develop in order to function without distress in crisis work. Yet persons who have just been subjected to a terrifying experience such as victimization want someone to nurture and comfort them. Many emergency personnel do nurture and comfort victims, and are remembered in a positive manner for doing so. Some emergency personnel, on the other hand, provide for the victim in an excessively detached, impersonal manner, and are remembered negatively by the victim. In the latter case, the experience offers victims a scapegoat for their bottled-up feelings of anger and resentment that couldn't be expressed to the now-anonymous criminal; without fear of retaliation they freely express these feelings to recognizable figures of authority such as the police.[16]

If the perpetrator of the crime came into this room right now I . . . wouldn't even know it. This is one of the things that continue to bother me. I feel that I am recognizable and yet they are not. I sometimes feel I could be walking down a street or waiting on a platform

out all the forms and then
[I'm very bad about mailing
things in on time, so I let
it go for a while) I was
talking to a friend of mine,
a policeman, and I was
telling him about the forms
and everything, and I said,
"Do I have any chance of
realizing some money at
least for the hospital? Pay?
Weeks of work that I lost?"
And he said, "Well, do you
have money in the bank?"
And I said, "Yes, but I don't
have a lot, but some," and
that I had written it down,
and he said I shouldn't have
done that. So I lost interest
in sending it in, and then
this woman kept calling me up
to find out why I wasn't
sending it in. She called a
few times, and finally I did
send it in this one day.
So far, no money. . . . I'm
one of a large family, so I
got very mixed responses
[after the crime]. For the
most part, everybody was
just happy that I was alive.
A lot of them live in suburbia
and don't know why I'm living
in the city, anyway, so their

right next to one of them and not even
know it. I feel it may be one of the
reasons I have become so suspicious of
people around me. I find myself feeling
very uncomfortable when someone
stands too close. Comments on the
street which I used to be able to dismiss
or even confront in my own mind, I
now find intimidating. I'm still very
jumpy. Someone will approach me and
just walk by me on the street and I'll
react with a start. I feel threatened. If
I were able to recognize the men, I
don't know how I would react upon
seeing them. I wish I could remember
what they look like, if only to report
it.[17]

*And yes, I also know I am fortunate to
have escaped with my life. Frankly,
though, I am rather tired of learning my
lesson. I am tired of phrases like "It was
your own fault." In eight years in New*

immediate response was, "Well, now, at least, you'll move out of the city," and one sister went so far as to tell me that I had a death wish for not moving out of the city! I couldn't believe she said it. I was hurt that she said it. Another sister spent a lot of time trying to talk me into [moving out of Manhattan], but at the same time she came down immediately for me, from Nyack. The next morning she went with me to the police station to look at pictures and took me to her house, and I stayed there for a few days while I was recuperating. I [then] went up to Rhode Island to get out of the city, mainly because I didn't want to go back to St. Luke's to have the stitches taken out. My sister's a doctor, and she could do it. I don't tell my parents when things like this happen, just because they have enough to worry about and I don't like them to know. I mean, in all four times when I was

York, two apartments I have lived in have been robbed. I have been held up for cash in the subway. All my children have been mugged at least once.[18]

Family and friends can be most helpful in this phase by being nurturing and comforting, allowing the victim to find his or her own recuperative rhythm, and thus supporting the struggle. Gerald Caplan suggests that the best help is active: "The sufferer will be given opportunities for rest from his wrestling with his problem; but he will also be stimulated and encouraged to 'wake up' after his rest periods and return again to his consideration of the problem." Again, the helper needs to pay close attention to the victim's own expression of needs.[19]

The important people in the victim's life—family and close friends—also need to explain the crime because they identify with and are threatened by the victim's pain. Their attribution may take the form of self-blame or of blaming others, depending on the situation and the personality of the loved one. The other person's need to attribute has the same source as the victim's: It is a way to restore order

assaulted or robbed, whatever, I never told my parents.
As it turned out, they
found out when somebody
called, thinking I was at my
parents' house. They called
me there and spilled the
beans and not only about
that but the attempted rape
in the park. So of course
my parents were very upset,
but at least they didn't try
to talk me into moving. They
knew I wouldn't move out of
the city. Well, everybody
was really good afterwards,
but I *did* get that reaction—
like, you're crazy to go on
living in the city. . . .
Then, the death-wish episode.
It's very strange, because
it's a sister that I'm very
close to and that I spent a
lot of time with. I don't
remember if I did respond to
that [remark]. I think I was
just hurt and didn't say
anything. And I'm not even
sure if I brought it up
with her since. I've said
it to other people—you know,
that that was her
reaction and that it
bothered me. . . . My

*to a disordered universe. It is intolerable
to feel that there is nothing you can do to
prevent loved ones from being hurt. This
is especially true if the victim is seen as a
person in need of special protection—a
child or an elderly parent, for example.
Those who love the vulnerable ones may
feel that they have failed them in some
way because they have not kept them
safe.*[20]

"Blaming-the-victim" experiences were
reported within group sessions with
astonishing frequency—indeed, the phenomenon was nearly universal. Victims
had particular difficulty in handling this
"punishment" by family and friends at
the very time they wanted comfort and
understanding.[21]

friends were very good, also. Everybody was just glad that I didn't die and some of them said that I was right to do what I did. Some people, of course, thought I just should have . . . thought I wouldn't have been hurt if I had just given up the money, and that was it, not tried to get away. I got that reaction from some people; they think I wouldn't have come up with the injuries if I had stayed still. I feel I'm not sorry that I did what I did. I think my biggest feeling is wondering what would have happened if he would, in fact, have just gone away. I mean, I'd really love to know if it was possible to do it, but my instincts said ESCAPE. I would like to know, and I will never know. It's a little weird to think of when I didn't get away and I wondered why he didn't stab me, even. I don't know. Maybe the knife was knocked down or something. Or maybe he was the biggest

Clinical researchers on crime victims agree that a key ingredient in the passage to a new integration and stability after the crime is other people. Ochberg (1979) says that treatment for the first phase of crisis, which can be either rage or resignation, or alternating rage and resignation, is ventilation and others rallying around the victim. The need for support is so great that Bard and Sangrey . . . note, "If a victim does not get proper support during the impact phase, his or her defenses may come back together in a dysfunctional way that will cause considerable difficulty later." Symonds . . . thinks that a lot of anger expressed at officials, especially the police, is anger over lack of support generally from the people the victim knows. He quotes . . . one victim: "What hurt me most was the complete indifference and lack of consideration for my feelings in my hour of need by people I know and work with."[22]

Most violent criminals are unsophisticated individuals who are grossly deficient in imagery. They rarely fantasize about what they will do; they just do it. Though their acts can be viewed as cruel and sadistic, the vast majority of criminals are not sadists. They achieve no pleasure from absolute control and humiliation of another human being nor do they experience gratification from a victim's suffering. Criminals, especially violent criminals, are basically indifferent, unrelated and unresponsive to anyone else but themselves. They are notoriously free of guilt about their behavior but do have fear of being caught. If there is any feeling a criminal has about his behavior it may be shame. It is the shame of being caught, exposed, and losing "the respect" of his peers, but no feelings about the victim's plight at all.[23]

creep of all. It's a weird
kind of thing, but I *do*
think about it. . . .
People at work were sup-
portive. They would call up
and see how I was for the two
weeks that I didn't come in
to work. They helped once I
did come back. I realized
I wasn't able to, when I had
the wounds on my hands.
I'm a barmaid, and I couldn't
carry up the ice buckets,
but everybody helped me do
that. So I got *physical*
help from people at work,
as well as emotional support.
They were both very
important to me. . . . While
the crime was in progress,
my overall feeling was that
I was going to die and it
was the greatest fear I've
ever known. It was just a
sick kind of fear and then,
at the same time, I was to
do whatever I could to get
out of the situation. I
was feeling for my life.
After the assailant left,
the feeling was, "I just
can't believe it. It's
just not real." I think
it was too awful to think

**If the perpetrator of the crime came
into this room right now I . . . would
want to know why he beat me. I would
want to have him arrested so that he
couldn't do it to other people but even
more I wish it were possible to have
him experience the same fear situation
in the hopes he would never do it
again.**[24]

*During the past ten years the notion of
social networks has become common in
social work, crisis intervention, medical
sociology, and numerous other fields.
The concept of the network was developed as a research tool with which to
examine the numerous social ties in
which individuals participate in contemporary life. Instead of examining people
in different groups, on the job and at
home, for instance, the individual's social life is traced through the ties the
person has to all the people he knows and
the ties those people have to each other.
Sketching these ties out, with lines con-
necting all the people who know each
other, the lines form a net-like pattern,
hence the term network. The concept of
the network has been crucial to the
reinterpretation of urban life. Almost as a
backlash against the image of life in
contemporary, industrial, urban society
as alienating, isolating, and unfulfilling,
many researchers . . . have demonstrated
that friendship, support, and intimacy
are available by means of networks.*[25]

about. I might have been
dead. It drove me crazy.
I found out about Crime
Victims' Counseling Services
from my boyfriend. He heard
it on the radio, and ever
since it happened I'd been
extremely nervous. He
always wanted me to get some
kind of counseling. And so
the woman at the hospital—
I don't know who she was,
a nurse, some woman in the
hospital—was very supportive when I came in. I
don't know who she was and
she soon went off duty for
the day, soon after I got
in. But she was just so
nice—she hugged me. I
mean, a complete stranger,
and I could feel such support from her. She gave me
some numbers to call, like
the Karen Horney Clinic,
things like that, but not
CVCS. I didn't call the
Karen Horney number. I
forget why I didn't call.
Like I said, I'm bad about
mailing and good at putting
things off . . . I don't
remember exactly when I
called CVCS, I just know

Crime Victims' Counseling Services offers:

- *Group counseling: a series of four free sessions each month for victims of any crime, reported or unreported. After the initial four sessions, participants may join ongoing groups.*
- *Referral service to individual counselors and therapists, through the CVCS Clearinghouse.*
- *24-hour hotline to get in touch with CVCS.*
- *Self-help networking program.[26]*

One of the crucial responses to crime is to seek help from formal organizations or from one's network of friends, relatives, neighbors and acquaintances. In a survey of 1,106 adults in Chicago, researchers attempted to sort out the characteristics of those who do not seek help, those who seek help from their networks and those who go to formal agencies. . . . A number of distinctive groups were distinguished: Self-reliant non-seekers who had strong informal networks and appeared to be comforted by the mere availability of people to assist them, reluctant non-seekers who had the lowest self-esteem and the least effective coping responses and were the most vulnerable, help-seekers who used only informal supports, and help-seekers who used only agencies. Those who sought only agency support were distinguished from those who used informal supports by higher levels of role strain and more stress, but also by less adequate informal supports and reticence about problems. Those who used both informal and organized supports differed from those who used only informal assistance in the number stressful events they had to deal with. Brown . . . concludes,

that I'd been extremely
nervous and when walking
down the street . . . when
people were walking too
close behind me, I got
really upset. Even today,
when I was coming out of
my door, somebody was coming
down the stairs and my heart
was jumping, because when I
opened the door I didn't
expect them to be there.
I'm just very jumpy ever
since it happened. In
elevators, or in confined
spaces, or walking down the
street alone. And some-
body—usually young black
people—walking towards
me. . . . After I registered
for CVCS, I felt relieved
that I'd be able to talk to
somebody about it, because I
was extremely nervous and
maybe CVCS would help. That
was about ten weeks after it
happened. I was still anxious
in subways. Like I said, in
confined spaces, when I'd be
out walking alone, or even
with others at night, I was
just more anxious. I realized
that anything can happen at
any time, you know. It was

*"While others have suggested that pro-
fessionals are contacted only after informal associates fail to provide assistance,
it seems more likely that these respondents were simply reluctant to keep asking informal associates for assistance."*[27]

**I'm afraid when . . . I am walking
alone and someone is walking close
behind. . . . When a young black man
is walking towards me with no one else
around (or behind me). . . . Sudden or
loud noises or movements. . . . I'm
alone in a subway train.. . . . In an
enclosed area with a strange man (elevator, etc.). . . . Running in the park
(or anywhere) and have to pass a man
who isn't running.**[28]

**I'm afraid when . . . I have to go in or
out of my apartment. I'm always worried that someone will again be waiting
in the hall for me. It has only been this
past week that I've started going in and
out by myself, and it's only during the
daytime. I think coming home is even
worse than going out. I'm always
afraid that someone is waiting to get
into the house with me or get me in the**

the afternoon and you
wouldn't think that at two
o'clock in the afternoon anything like that could happen.
I guess I was more anxious
in a lot of different
situations. For example,
I'm just not at ease when
I know my sister and my
niece are coming to my
house. I'm anxious that if
I don't ring the bell back
soon enough (because that's
what happened to me), it
could happen to them. When
I walk out my door I have to
look both ways before I go
anywhere. I'm still much
more cautious. Some of
that is realistic caution,
but things I was never
anxious about before get
to me now. I probably
wouldn't ever go in that
elevator to the train. I
probably wouldn't go in
that at night, any more,
since this happened to
me. . . . I guess, with
me, I'm probably more anxious
than careful. I have a fear
of being out late on my own
now, whereas I didn't before.
And I've been living in New

hall. **Until I get my three locks open,
my heart is in my mouth. I can get
killed in the hall till I get the locks
opened.**[29]

1. Only list your last name and ini-
   tials on the mailbox and phone
   directories.
2. Get to know what neighbors you
   can buzz if there's trouble.
3. If someone has broken into your
   home DON'T GO IN; call the
   police.
4. If someone enters your home late
   at night, don't move, pretend you
   are asleep.
5. Get to know your community,
   where there are police phone
   boxes, etc.[30]

**I get angry when . . . I realize that we
the innocent average people will always
have to live in fear. We live locked in
our homes, three locks on doors, windows shut tight "no air," reluctant to**

York ten years, in this apartment. Longer than that. So I'm accustomed to moving around a lot in New York. I used to walk home in that neighborhood where I was assaulted at two o'clock *in the morning*! You know, from five or six blocks from work, at night, and that didn't faze me in the least. Ten or eleven o'clock at night, if I was hungry, I would just go out to Broadway. I wouldn't do that now. I'm fearful of something happening, I guess. Somewhat. . . . I do mistrust strangers, yes. It's probably, for the most part, distrust when I'm out and I'm alone. Usually I distrust young blacks. I mean, I'm not prejudiced. I've never been prejudiced, but every time something has happened to me it's by a young black and it's sort of *conditioning*. I hate to have that feeling, but I do. It isn't only blacks now, when I'm running in the park. It took me a long time to run in the park alone again, but I'm doing it, and when I

go out alone at night while the others live brazenly free to come and go as they wish—fearing nothing—what should they fear? The courts are on their side, constantly protecting and advising them of THEIR rights. What about us? What about our rights? You must dig extensively to find out. I get angry when I realize how hard we must work for the things we desire in life and how easy it is for someone to take it away.[31]

I'm afraid when . . . I see black kids hanging out—in groups and individually—crossing streets with the light— bicycles and skaters running the light. Sometimes I am almost paranoid about jsut getting to the other side—when I let myself project into what might happen if the two come back for revenge.[32]

have to pass *any* man when I'm
running just in the park, for
some reason my heart pounds.
Once I ran past a guy, a
business guy carrying an
attache case, a white man,
young. Well, my heart was
practically beating out of
my body when I ran past him.
I have a mortal distrust of
men when I'm alone, these
days. I didn't have it
before. Well, not at all.
I'm a woman living in a
crazy society. There's some
distrust, but it's much
greater now. . . . [I'm
sometimes] afraid to go out
or come home. Even today,
I peek out my door before
I leave. Before I came to
work this morning, I came out,
I came down the stairs, my
heart was pounding so. In
order not to be surprised I
looked out the door, but
right after it happened to
me I wouldn't go out the
door without looking out the
peephole. I don't always do
that, but I did it today
because a few times, when
I'd come out my door [since
this has happened to me],

I'm afraid when . . . I enter my
apartment building alone—there are
too many good hiding places between
the front porch and my apartment (on
the fifth floor) where a robber, burglar, rapist, murderer, whatever,
could be lurking.[33]

I'm afraid when . . . I leave my apartment. When I enter my apartment—

I've been surprised by
people. One time I had to
go back in and close the
door and stand there till I
stopped shaking before I
could go on. In the
beginning I was afraid to
go out. I still did it, but
I was nervous about it. . . .
I *do* keep thinking about it,
but not so much, probably,
now as . . . a few times
when you think about what
happened, it's almost too
hard to think about. It
happened a lot, especially
in the rape attempt. I
used to get these flashes
of turning around and seeing
this body hurling itself at
me and I'd just get the
shivers. It seems so
horrible, and I guess [I do] a lot
of thinking about when I
tried to escape and couldn't,
how I wound up in pretty bad
shape. But I really thought
I was going to be dead. So
I think about that. Maybe
being dead. . . . It was
good talking about it [in
the CVCS groups] and having
some things confirmed, like
that secondary victimization

will it have been violated again? When
I go to sleep, because will I be rudely
awakened by an intruder? I constantly
feel that maybe they will try something
else. I cannot quell those thoughts with
a reassuring "it-can't-get-worse." I
think it might if I drop my guard for
just a second. I fear my anger.[34]

*Most women have never been given the
information and skills they need to protect themselves from rape. We may be
given vague warnings about strangers or
told to resist without being taught how.
Everyone is capable of learning some
skills to protect herself. The first element
of successful rape avoidance is attitude.
Research studies show that attackers select victims whom they perceive as helpless and vulnerable. A calm and confident attitude can deter crime in many
cases.*

- *Be aware of your environment at all
  times.*
- *Trust your instincts when they tell
  you danger is near.*
- *Don't ever be afraid or embar-
  rassed to make a scene or draw
  attention to yourself if someone is
  threatening you.*
- *Be especially alert when you are
  sick, tired or have taken alcohol or
  drugs of any kind.*
- *Have a positive mental attitude: I
  can succeed; I am strong and powerful.*

thing that my sister said—
you know, "You have a death
wish"—knowing that was
wrong on her part and *I*
wasn't the one. It was a
secondary victimization.
Also, it was a little strange
because I go there with my
story and I hear some other
very horrible stories, too,
and I almost felt like Wow!
I came out a lot better than
these other people. *I* didn't
have a gun to my head for an
hour and a half. One guy
had brass knuckles, he said.
I felt it was useful to
listen to other victims
talk, to *be* with other
victims. *I* found that
supportive, and supportive
for them, also, to know that
they have a lot of the same
feelings. . . . I went to
all four. It was quite
worthwhile. It was helpful
just to talk about it and
to know that other people
were going through the same
thing, and that eventually
I will get over the nervousness and that, yes, I was
right in doing what I did.
The support that *I* wasn't

• *Be aware of your rights: I have a right to say "No"; I do not have to follow another person's orders; I have a right to be where I want without harassment.*
• *Be aware of the dangerous places in your life. Think about your options at home, on the street, at work, at play. Where could you go for help? Would someone be near enough to hear your scream?*
• *Be alert in badly lit areas, in elevators, with groups of people you don't know well. Don't be afraid to change your plans or your direction if you sense danger. Being rude is better than getting raped.*
• *If you are attacked, try not to panic. Try to breathe deeply and think about your options. Women have deterred rapists by screaming, fighting, talking their way out, trickery, or doing or saying something disgusting or crazy.*

The best-prepared person is the one who has thought about and rehearsed many different strategies. Indeed, she is less likely to be attacked because of her attitude on the street and about herself. To fight back, a person must be trained by experts.[35]

I think it was really nice that people cared enough to devote their own time to helping people in these situations. It was good to have the feeling of support from others.[36]

Crime Victims' Counseling Services, Inc., helps anyone who is a crime victim. It is a not-for-profit, tax-exempt organization whose major purpose is to provide free group counseling for crime victims who are experiencing the emotional aftereffects of crime. Victims are the most

the crazy one *really* helped. It was helpful just to talk with other people that underwent the same sort of things, and to realize all the simlarities and the feelings. I just found that helpful. And that the counselor's interpretations were useful. I thought she picked up on things well. When either I said something, or [Eddie] said something, or anybody, since she had also been in the same situation herself in the past, she was very articulate about it now. Her empathy, based on being a crime victim herself, was excellent—in addition to her professional expertise. . . . I had a hard time writing. If I ever had to make a living on it I'd starve, but I found it helpful because I guess it just forced me, a little, to think more about how I felt, to make it concrete. It was interesting and helpful to hear people read their exercises aloud. I just remember *knowing*, in

affected but the least considered people involved in a criminal incident. The judicial system devotes 94 percent of its human resources and budget to crime and the criminal. The victim gets little, if any, help or service. Almost everyone who has ever been robbed, mugged, burglarized, or raped goes through an emotional crisis. In fact, criminal violence can short-circuit a person's life. Crime victims suffer post-crime trauma and shock with varying degrees of fear, guilt, helplessness, anger, memory impairment, a tendency to avoid activity, and painfully recurrent, intrusive recollections or dreams.[37]

Ordinary acts of competence and kindness can help to restore the victim's faith in humanity during this crucial period. When the police are responsive to the victim's needs—when they arrive quickly, listen carefully, and appear to be concerned—the victim will often feel significantly comforted and reassured.[38]

Rape crisis centers often suggest to victims that they keep a diary in which they write down everything they can remember about the rape and what happened afterwards. Some victims use a cassette tape recorder instead of a diary. This technique may be helpful to any crime victim in crisis. It is a good way to ventilate feelings. It will often serve to jog the victim's memory and to help him or her keep the facts straight. The record can be a crucial refresher for the victim who testifies in court since hearings and trials are sometimes delayed for months after the crime. Keeping a record will also allow the victim to see how his or her feelings change as the crisis resolves,

the first session, what
[Philip] . . . I just *knew*
what he was going to
respond to . . . I found
some of the self-defense
and prevention information
helpful. Some things I
hadn't known and I think
everybody should know. I
passed it around to some
people. . . . It's four
months after the crime,
now—I think I'm less
nervous. Still more nervous
than before it happened, and
I think probably more
depressed (not that I'm
depressed every day, but
when I think about that,
about what happened and when
I think that it's not going
to be any better—you know,
with Reagan in office and
the economy the way it is,
just knowing that the
incidents may happen again).
I don't have a good feeling
about . . . life, in general.
I feel powerless more readily,
these days. Just at
different times, thinking
about, you know, what a crazy
person is, what he could do
to you. . . . I feel that

which can be especially helpful in the discouraging days when it seems that things will never be all right again.[39]

WHAT IS EFFECTIVE RESISTANCE?
Resistance is not: *freezing with fear; screaming helplessly; struggling half-heartedly; slugging it out with an attacker. Resistance* is *a learned skill that anyone can use successfully. Here are some tips that can help you if you are ever attacked.*

1. *Start breathing deeply. This will help you remain calm.*
2. *Assess your options. Can you run? Are there people nearby or an open store or building to run to?*
3. *Make a scene. Yell NO, STOP, or FIRE in a loud, powerful voice. (Practice yelling into a pillow at home. A loud yell does* not *come naturally to most women.)*
4. *If all else fails, you may decide to strike your attacker. Do so with all your might; a halfhearted attempt is worse than nothing.*[40]

I feel powerless when . . . I feel that I'm not in control of my destiny. When I want support and there isn't any to be gotten, and I feel estranged from my peers, be it at work or with friends. I feel powerless when I feel vulnerable, unprotected, indecisive, confused, and alone. When I see no change or solution.[41]

Crime Victims' Counseling
Services has helped a lot,
oh, yes! Just feeling that
support, and knowing people
like you is terrific. And
to realize that there's a
need for this sort of thing
for crime victims. It's not
something that you just get
over right away, or ever.
You need that support. You
don't need people saying,
"You know, you should have
done this and you should
have done that." This
support of—that you did
what you could—that was
very helpful, because I did
get that reaction, like I
said, from other people.
Almost like questioning my
sanity: "Why the hell did
you resist? If you wound up
dead it would have been your
fault." I would recommend
the CVCS group to other
victims, of course. Because
you're very vulnerable. When
you talk to people it hasn't
happened to, they just can't
understand what you feel,
really. They can have
sympathy, but they really
don't know where it's coming

The sessions were very helpful. They enabled me to deal with feelings of fear, anger, guilt and insecurity subsequent to the crime. The psychological atmosphere fostered was warm, accepting and totally non-threatening, which encouraged trust in coming to grips with the feelings that began to surface. This also permitted me to focus on related problems, which was an enormous relief. This experience created a support system that addressed a great deal of my anxiety. I feel very fortunate that it was available. The aftermath of the crime, I am certain, would have lingered much longer had it not been for these sessions. There were practical suggestions, as well, that were very useful. Thank *you* very much.[42]

from because it hasn't
happened to them. Not that
I wish it on anybody. It's just
that you know where they're
coming from. And where you've
been. They're different places.

NOTES

1. *The New York Times*, January 4, 1981.
2. Pileggi, p. 22.
3. *Ibid.*
4. *The New York Times*, December 14, 1981.
5. CVCS group exercise.
6. Arthur S. Freese, "If You're a Crime Victim," *Modern Maturity* (April/May 1981), p. 89.
7. Symonds, "The 'Second Injury,'" p. 36.
8. *The New York Times*, May 5, 1981.
9. CVCS group exercise.
10. Symonds, "Victims of Senseless Violence," p. 2.
11. Symonds, "The 'Second Injury,'" p. 36.
12. CVCS group exercise.
13. Symonds, "The 'Second Injury,'" p. 37.
14. CVCS group exercise.
15. *The New York Times*, November 23, 1980.
16. Symonds, "The 'Second Injury,'" p. 37.
17. CVCS group exercise.
18. *The New York Times*, November 12, 1980.
19. Bard and Sangrey, p. 40.
20. *Ibid.*, p. 63.
21. Author's observation in CVCS groups.
22. Friedman, p. 28.
23. Symonds, "Victims of Senseless Violence," p. 2.
24. CVCS group exercise.
25. Friedman, p. 25.
26. CVCS, brochure.
27. Friedman, pp. 22–23.
28. CVCS group exercise.
29. CVCS group exercise.
30. New York Women Against Rape, flyer.
31. CVCS group exercise.
32. CVCS group exercise.
33. CVCS group exercise.
34. CVCS group exercise.
35. The New York City Advisory Task Force on Rape, "What You Should Know About Rape: A Guidebook for Women in New York City" (1981), pp. 2–3.
36. CVCS group evaluation.
37. CVCS, brochure.
38. Bard and Sangrey, p. 117.
39. *Ibid.*, p. 114.
40. Safety and Fitness Exchange, brochure.
41. CVCS group exercise.
42. CVCS group evaluation.

HOW TO READ THIS BOOK

Writings appearing in this left column, widely spaced in the typeface you are reading, are always and only edited transcripts of audiotaped interviews with crime victims who availed themselves of the group sessions offered by Crime Victims' Counseling Services.

Writings appearing in this right column, in the typeface you are reading, are always and only from books, newspapers, magazines, journals, reports, brochures, and similar sources.

Writings appearing in this right column, in the typeface you are reading, are always and only the author's responses.

Writings appearing in this right column, in the typeface you are reading, are always and only from group exercises and evaluations by members of Crime Victims' Counseling Services group sessions.

Four: HAL

I was approached on a quiet street by two teenage black boys, coming from either side. They closed in on me and one of them stuck a metal thing (which I felt was a gun, but I couldn't see because it was under my chin) in my neck. All I could see was that it was black and metal and cold, and the other one started moving his hands over me and said, "Give me your money." And when I had given him my money, which I keep separate from anything else, he suddenly decided he liked the jacket I was wearing. It was a nice, leather jacket with a matching hood that I had just for a short time. I didn't like the idea, but I let him unzip it from me and take it. . . . In mid-winter, naturally, that's why I was wearing it. And just as they took off with

The street is so dark and deserted that you almost don't spot the three young men leaning motionlessly against a parked car about midway along the block. When you left the dinner party, your host suggested you walk up West Eighty-ninth Street to West End Avenue to get a cab. Now you wonder. As you approach, one of the three youths saunters on ahead of you, the other two silently shove off the fender and begin to tag along behind. Are you about to be held up? Are you being paranoid? Are you going to get killed? What do you do?[1]

My former purse was one of those big mooshy Sportsac things you can put everything into. It was stolen from me in Central Park. The reason I took that purse to the park in the first place was so I could use it as a headrest while I read the paper and watched my son ride his bike. My purse was taken from behind me when I sat up to concentrate for a moment on an article about, would you believe it, defense preparedness. That is the funny part. My purse had in it everything that is important to me in a material way, everything. Credit cards. The fam-

127

my coat, suddenly the place
was surrounded with people.
But during that moment [of
the crime] there was not
a soul that I could see.
When I turned around I discovered that a motorist had
turned his headlights full
on us and we were in, like,
a spotlight. [Later] he
told me he had observed what
was taking place and had
deliberately shined his
headlights on us to prevent
any possible harm, and I'm
grateful to the fact that
the man remained there. [I
was not physically hurt in
any way.] He asked if I
needed any help. He
probably would have taken
me to the station, but I
was so confused I didn't know
where I was at. [I'm sure]
the lights had something to
do with my not being hurt.
That is, the lights provoked
other people into coming out
and seeing that something
was wrong, which is why all
of a sudden I was surrounded
by everybody in the project.
[I didn't] make any screams
for help, or raise my voice,

*ily Blue Cross card. Tubes, compacts,
and vials of makeup. Driver's license.
Pills. Check register and checks. Keys to
my home. Also—in the wallet—73 cents,
the button that fell off my winter coat last
year, and a 13-cent stamp that I had
carried around for quite a while. I could
mention the ways in which my activities
have been constrained since my purse
was stolen. How it is not that easy to get
the locks changed when the locksmith will
not accept the checks he knows are now
bad. How I look a fright without my eye
shadow. Why a purse-snatching is a violation and an outrage. But yes, I know.
There are lessons to be learned here.
Smart people do not go to the park with
their checks. No one should look upon
her purse as a portable filing cabinet.
The intelligent woman strews her belongings about her person, in order to confuse those not on her side. . . . Each time
these things have happened, we have
considered ourselves fortunate that the
incident was no worse. After all, we
could have been killed. We have scolded
ourselves. Stay alert at all times. Be
careful in crowds. Do not trust people.
That is the unfunny part. It makes me
crazy, if you want to know, to have to
conclude the story about my former purse
with the realization that I am fortuante
not to have had a knife in my back. To
just count my blessings, and be thankful
for my good luck.[2]*

*Whatever the situation, if the worst
does happen, police suggest the victim*

I just yelled, "No," at one point, just as they were taking the jacket. But by that time there was no point. My feeling was that to resist, with a gun in my neck, I wasn't interested. When the gun was passed and it was on the way away from me, it was the first time I let out any sound. . . . They didn't take anything else, like my watch, my rings, or anything like that. No, they didn't even look. They knew what they wanted. . . . This was in a housing project. I wasn't aware of [the guard] until it was over. He came by and offered to take me to a phone booth, where I could notify the police. He even offered me a coin if I didn't have any, which I thought was very nice. And the lady who was using that phone—as soon as she understood that I was in immediate need, she got off the phone, and let me make my call to the police. Within five minutes they were there—they drove up. Apparently, the Eighty-

remain as calm as possible. Do not try to engage the holdup man in conversation, and never chide him after he has robbed you and is making his getaway. A Columbia University student was shot and killed by a young mugger who was angered because he felt his victim had "insulted" him. Victims should try to remember as much about the culprit as they can. Notice any details that might aid you in describing the perpetrator and his mannerisms. Make a conscious effort to remember. When trying to determine the criminal's age, height, weight, hair color, and complexion, make comparisons between the suspect and yourself or people you know. Notice the type and color of the clothing worn, but concentrate on physical features, since criminals usually change their clothes immediately after committing a robbery; reversible jackets are pulled inside out, and hats are taken off or put on. Dial 911 as soon as possible, and tell the operator you are reporting a robbery. Identify yourself and your location. Tell the operator whether the stickup men were armed and, if so, with what. Tell as much as you know about the direction of their escape.[3]

fourth Precinct must be
around the corner—it seemed
it was right behind the
projects. They took it as
very matter of fact. Just
took me into the car, and
took me to the station, and
asked what had happened. I
recorded the crime, filled
out a form of some sort.
Then they were going to
take me upstairs to identify
photos, but at that point
(when filling out my form)
I had put down my age, which
is sixty-three. So I was
out of their jurisdiction,
and I had to get in touch
with this group called
"SCRU"—Senior Citizens
Robbery Unit, and I would
have to wait for them to
call me. [Then] they let me
call the gallery where I was
supposed to meet [my wife]
and I was also supposed to
go there to meet a group of
people—we were going to go
to the movies. So I called
and they came and got me,
and brought a coat. I told
them what had happened and
also, aside from the fact
that I no longer had the

This reaction of seeming indifference of the police that the victim experiences is due to a common misinterpretation by the police of the concept of professionalism. In their zeal to be neutral, and since it is a crime in the past with the criminal gone, they aggressively question the victim as to the details of the crime. This behavior rejects implied expectations of comfort to the victim, as well as rejects the victim's implied criticism that the police have failed to do their job of protecting him from crime. One woman who was the victim of a mugging told me that when the radio car responded the patrolmen sat in the car and she had to lean on the ledge of the open window of the car and talk to them. In addition, these men said: "You aren't the only one who has been mugged. We get plenty of other calls." Such behavior or comments are hardly comforting to the victim and make her feel worse.[4]

The proceeds from police auctions of unclaimed stolen property should be returned to robbery and burglary victims whose goods were never recovered instead of going into the Police Department's Pension Fund, a Queens lawmaker said yesterday. State Senator Gary Ackerman (D-Flushing) said the pro-

money for it, I no longer had the will to go to a movie. My only family is [my wife], and she was immediately, of course, involved. The first thing [my friends] wanted to know was, was I hurt. That was the first question, and my answer was quite obvious: I was not hurt. Everybody, including me, didn't realize my relief—or that I had possibly escaped had not clicked in my mind. Any fears that I had weren't there until the kids left. . . . About three or four days later I got a call from Mr. Nomentario, saying that he was coming by with his partner to show me some of the photos. And they did come by and I did look at photos. None of them were the particular kids that I had seen, which is entirely likely, but I was able to identify features that looked similar. I'm an artist and I gave them, mainly, the eyes, face shape, hair, basic haircut. The general concept of the

ceeds of the police auctions, like one held last week for jewelry and other valuables, is now going into the fund for police retirees. "The city estimates," Ackerman said, "that it receives $1.3 million a year from these auctions, with all of it going to the Police Pension Fund. That money should go to crime victims and not to the police. I'm not trying to deny our dedicated police officers their well-earned retirements, but those golden years shouldn't be financed out of the heartache of crime victims." Ackerman said he has introduced a bill to set up registries of stolen property and crime victims, to try to match victims with unclaimed booty. His proposal, he added, calls for the proceeds from the auction of any remaining stolen property to be returned proportionally, less any recovery for insurance, to those victims whose goods were not found. "Obviously, the police pension money which is now provided by the auctions would have to be replaced with general revenues," Ackerman noted. "But this burden, under my bill, would result in a much fairer system than the current one where the burden falls solely on crime victims."[5]

young kids—I don't know
kids' ages too well—but
one looked about sixteen and
one looked about fourteen.
The one with the gun had to
reach up to put the gun to
my neck, so he couldn't've
been too old. Fourteen
would've been the most. . . .
The funny thing is, I'm a
trusting soul, for a New
Yorker, and my first reaction
was I was walking from a
friend's house and I saw
these two boys coming to me
(and I like to be unprej-
udiced), and I like to feel
that they were going to
ask me a question. And all
of a sudden, I became aware
that this was a time to run
away. I should have gone
the other way—I felt this
just at the point where it
was too late to go, when I
realized that they were
closing in. I didn't know
what they were going to do.
I didn't know, but there
was a point in which it
was too late. I was
entrapped already, but there
was a point before they
actually closed in when I

I'm afraid . . . when I pass a group
of people together, especially if they
are teenagers—and black. This can be
day or evening—but most severely in
the evening or at night. I also am
afraid when I'm trying to sleep, because my mind raves on with continued
repeats of what happened—and what I
should have done—or could have done.
Or omitted when talking to the police.
Yet I want to sleep all the time. My
initial reaction was to be afraid to leave
my house today. I started out on an
errand into Manhattan—and put it off
for tomorrow. I did make a phone call
and put myself in a position where I
must go tomorrow—I can't back out
again. This is all too new to me.[6]

*The probability of being a victim of a
violent crime almost tripled between
1960 and 1976. Through 1978, the occurrence of violent crimes continued to
rise. Nationally, murder increased by*

knew that it was not a normal scene. If someone was going to ask a question, they would have asked me it then. They got a little too close. The next thing I knew they were on top of me and they weren't very big, but that gun scared me. I know nothing about guns except that they can work very fast. . . . When the police from the SCRU unit came with the photographs, they were very pleasant, they were delightful—we had a very interesting talk about the whole situation, but I had no further contact with the criminal justice system. Nothing after that. The perpetrators have not been apprehended. I'm supposed to contact [the police] in case I saw one of the kids and wanted to identify them, but as far as I know, I have not seen them. . . . Somewhere along the line, I was directed to Victim Services Agency, and I'm trying to remember where. I think I called. I must have looked it up,

two percent, forcible rape by seven percent, robbery was up three percent, and aggravated assault seven percent. Crime is on the increase in every geographic region, in cities as well as rural areas. Violent crime in the first six months of 1979 jumped 13 percent over the same period in 1978, with suburbs and Southern states experiencing the greatest increases. But the concern with crime is even greater than statistics would indicate. Crime has a major psychological impact upon people, for the impact of violent crime goes beyond any ordinary fear of injury based upon current statistics. This concern with crime, and especially violent crime, for example, is much more pervasive than concern about home and traffic accidents, which actually kill and injure more people each year.[7]

In the rush to begin solving a crime, a victim's humanity is lost in the paperwork. Evidence is collected, testimony is recorded, the process moves forward—but no clues are given the victim about how, why or when it works. The system bends over backward to avoid trampling on the accused's constitutional rights. He is provided with legal counsel, is advised of his rights throughout the proceedings, is given free medical care if needed while incarcerated.[8]

or they gave me a piece of paper and it said something on it, I don't remember. I'm trying to remember the sequence. I think I did call and they gave me the . . . No, I had been told about SCRU—oh, that's it! They told me about the Victim Services Agency and they told me about SCRU. Victim Services didn't apply to me, as again it was because of my age, which I thought was very weird. I was very put out and I remember saying, ''You mean nothing's going to be done about it for the next few days, until they get in touch with me?'' I couldn't believe that there was going to be no action at all until they got to me, until they got around to it. Later, the two detectives just explained that there isn't a thing you can do—they [the assailants] go into hiding for a few days. And that's the point where they can't be found. It's later on when they come out and start boasting about their prowess that they

Older people are particularly vulnerable to street crimes. They have been singled out as easy marks by bands of young street toughs, most of whom are under the mistaken impression that the elderly and retired have money and valuables hidden in their apartments. The victimization of old people in Coney Island got so bad that the local precinct had to set up a special escort service using a police van to shuttle people from their apartment buildings to nearby supermarkets so they could do their shopping without getting mugged. Officials at senior-citizens' centers should be alert to any youngsters hanging around outside. When elderly women carry their pocketbooks, they should keep their keys and cash in a dress or coat pocket. Police caution old people to stay away from areas where there are city schools and from large groups of youngsters. Sergeant Michael DeRienzo of the Manhattan Senior Citizen Robbery Unit tells of one technique used by an elderly woman when a crowd of teenagers couldn't be avoided. She'd march right up to one youth and say, "How's your mother? Tell her I was asking for her."[9]

might possibly be caught—
I have to take their word
that they might possibly be
caught. I never saw anyone
from the District Attorney's
office, or any representative
beyond the SCRU people. . . .
While [the crime] was going
on there was nothing in my
mind except somehow it was
right to comply and do it
as smoothly as possible. I
didn't talk NO words. I
somehow didn't think there
was any point. I have an
idea that words would have
loused it up. Besides, I
was totally numb. There
was an undercurrent of
consciousness of what was
going on the surface.
Absolutely numb. Just after
the assailants left, that's
when it hit me, when I
realized that they were
leaving and that I was
basically okay. I was very
confused. I didn't even
know which direction I was
facing. And I remember my
first impulse was to start
walking the way I was
continuing to walk. I
didn't have a coat. It was

. . . the 20-year-old convict talked about his life on and off the streets. He made it clear that while the city feared him, he had very little fear of the city or the massive system it had set up to deter, try and punish him. "I use to always think I could beat it," he said, "and I always did. I always beat it." But with his next breath, he admitted: "Well, I didn't really beat it. I mean, they gave me so much." Mr. Wilder was a very active robber, but not a particularly cunning one. While his police record shows that he was arrested 11 times and convicted five times and had six dismissals, he admitted that several times he had been caught in the act of robbing a store or stealing a car. But if it was sometimes difficult to avoid the police, Mr. Wilder said, it was easier to avoid prison. He never complained that the police harassed him or that the evidence against him was poor. Instead, he expressed amazement that he was allowed to walk out of the courtroom aain and again. Sometimes I'd get in the bullpen," he said, referring to Rikers Island, "and think, 'They got me now'—and then they wouldn't. I'd go to court and they'd say, 'Well, the lawyer's not here and such and such not here.' So they'd let me go, give me a date to come back to court and I never come back—till I got busted again." In five years of muggings, robberies and car thefts, he served less than a year on Rikers Island, although the New York City Police Department had classified him as a "career criminal." He was sentenced to his first "hard time" only last summer, and even as he counts down the days in Coxsackie, Mr. Wilder says he feels he was "lucky." A spokesman for the Manhattan District Attorney's office said that without a detailed court record there was no way of determining just how and why Mr. Wilder was released so often. The records of the six dismissed cases, she said, were sealed, and while Mr. Wilder did receive

cold out, but my first
impulse was to continue on
the way I had planned, as
if nothing had happened, and
then suddenly I realized,
"What am I doing???" I was in
a kind of shock at that point;
I didn't feel the cold. I
felt very tense muscles,
stiff, and I just didn't feel
I could bend, at that point.
Like I turned into a solid
mass, like Lot's wife.
After I was inside, when I
made my first contact with
someone who was not an assailant, I started to feel
again. Well, it was very
gradual. The only thing,
intellectually, I was glad
that they were there, and
part of me was wondering
where the hell they were
until then. When I was there
being mugged, there was an
absolute blank of people,
just for that period of
time. Where were they??? I
guess I'll never know the
answer to that—I was just a
lonely person walking down
the street. The kids must
have timed it that way,
knowing their habitat.

sentences of 20 to 30 days in some other cases, the office's records did not show the final disposition of the cases.[10]

Immediately after the crime, during the impact phase of the crisis reaction, the victim falls apart inside. His or her sense of personal intactness and integrity has been shattered. The self responds to violation by becoming disorganized. Victims often feel as if they are in shock. Some victims become numb and disoriented. They move about aimlessly or feel physically immobilized. Physiological disturbances such as the inability to sleep or to eat are common. Disbelief is a frequent reaction: "This just can't be happening to me." . . . The impact phase is often marked by feelings of vulnerability and helplessness. Victims are sometimes filled with a profound sense of loneliness, a feeling that they are alone and bereft. They may become quite childlike and dependent, unable to make even the simplest decisions.[11]

If, for instance, you suspect that you are being followed, either by one man or sandwiched between a group of potential muggers there is a basic defensive move suggested by the police: Potential victims should quickly change direction. As soon as he becomes suspicious, the man head-

That guard is supposed to be walking around all the time, but for that moment he was somewhere else. They must have known where he was. There was no one around. In fact, there *was* another guard for another project—another apartment project—that walked over at that moment, just per chance, with two people. Right after the event, all the guards, all the people, everybody turned up. It was a party. It made me feel a little warmer and there were some young kids also—teenage boys and girls who started talking to me and trying to get me to identify the kids, 'cause they seemed to think they would know them by the description of the clothes. Several of them seemed to think they knew who it was. I didn't have enough wit to ask for their names and addresses, under the circumstances, but I *would* expect the police to do some research on the subject, themselves. . . . When I

ing toward West End Avenue in search of a cab should cross to the other side of Eighty-ninth Street and start walking back toward Riverside Drive. If the three youths keep walking toward West End, there is no harm. But if the three turn around and again follow, his suspicions have been confirmed and he should bolt from the group and start yelling for help. The noise is bound to light windows along the darkened street no matter how late the hour, and most muggers will take off after the first outcry in search of a more docile victim.[12]

Informal assistance may be preferable to the victim in particular situations. For example, informal supports may be best-suited to provide practical aid, such as the temporary use of an automobile for victims of auto theft. Treatment of serious injuries, on the other hand, usually requires the competence of professionals and formal organizations. Formal organizations may be essential for certain types of victims who do not have well-developed social networks.[13]

While the public cannot change the entire legal system, there is one aspect that they can substantially influence. That is the police. The police are usually the first individuals the victim meets and

met [my wife] an hour or a little more or a little less later, I was a mess. I was just *very* tense, and I was just beginning to feel my fright. I mean, it didn't manifest in any way, particularly. All I know is that I didn't sleep that night and that's not my way. I slept through a revolution. . . . [My] friends, once they found out, responded very warmly and concerned, and congratulatory about the fact that I had complied instead of trying to resist or argue. *I* don't like losing the things, but it's preferable to getting hurt. . . . I don't think I might have attempted to fight them off if I were younger—knowing me. I've always been on the pacifist side of anything. At forty, I was very involved in yoga, very deeply, and [resisting] would not have been a part of me. . . . I did mention it [to people at work], of course, and again the first question was, "Were you hurt?" And

most of the time they meet the victim after the crime has been committed and the criminal gone. Police attitudes can be quite crucial in reducing the acute psychological trauma of victims and also help prevent the debilitating secondary trauma which most victims undergo. From personal experience I know the police are sensitive to criticism and resent anyone telling them how to do police work but police officials have a high regard for professionals in their particular specialties. They are receptive to ideas which will improve their ability to be of help to the public. If we in the helping professions support the concept of victims needing psychological help, the police, who are in a unique position to administer psychological first aid, will turn to us for help in how to do it.[14]

. . . victims and their friends and family may have some or all of the following reactions. Each person is different—there is no standard reaction. The only sure thing is that there will be some kind of reaction.

Anger
Helplessness
Guilt (whose fault is that?)
Worthlessness
Crying spells
Uncleanness
Fear of being alone
Isolation and feeling different
Nightmares; inability to sleep
Fear of men, crowds, night . . .
Mistrust
Depression
Loss of sexual interest
Moodiness[15]

If the perpetrator of the crime came into this room right now I . . . would kill them slowly. I would beat them first. I would kick them and rape them. I would hurt them like they hurt me. Not like they hurt me—worse. I

after that it was, they've just been through something similar. The shop had been burglarized and a little while before that, they had an armed robbery in the store while customers were there. They understood the whole situation very well, and they said exactly what everyone else said: "It's just good that you didn't get hurt." . . . About twenty-four hours went by between the crime and calling Crime Victims' Counseling Services. I think I was fortunate to get the information so quickly. I wasn't quite sure it would do me any good, but I didn't see any harm. I do believe that self-help groups are the only answer, in any case. [Before I entered the group] I was still a little frightened about going out to a night event, but I figured I would get my courage together and go in. As a matter of fact, [my wife] went with me the first time. It was twenty-

would like their family to suffer like my family has. I honestly feel good that I am able to state this. I do not feel like a hypocrite. They SHOULD suffer. It's okay to feel this way. Even though I do not think I would commit murder, it is good just to fantasize about it.[16]

[He] reports that the person who experiences victimization without adequate emotional support runs a high risk of suffering long-term disability, and even those persons who "weather the crisis very well may nonetheless suffer devastation in their family and social relationships" . . . He cites the research . . . which indicates that of 12 crime-related problems, the most common one reported by victims was mental or emotional suffering. This problem was ranked highest among the problems felt to be "very serious" in nature by the same victims. Victims also experienced a sense of helplessness, with only one victim in five (who had mental or emotional problems) believing there might be a helpful service available in the community. Only one in ten sought out such a service.[17]

four hours after the crime—
nearly to the minute. . . .
A few days afterwards, or
a week afterwards, I still
felt that sense of powerlessness. I had the feeling,
"What can you do about it?
Is there anything you can
do? Was there any other
choice?" I played *that* over
and over again, "Was there
any other choice?" Each
time I came up with,
"Nothing." Every time I
had those thoughts I
remembered the feeling of
the gun. I've never for-
gotten it. I don't think
I will ever forget it. All
I have to do is remember
the feeling of the cold
steel in my neck, and there's
only one answer. That
sense of powerlessness was
entirely appropriate to the
situation; I was totally over-
powered by the weapon. Not
by themselves or their
persons or by their sizes,
which I could've dealt with
on another level. By the
weapon. That I could have
died. I still haven't gotten
over it, totally. When I see

I feel powerless when . . . I am
trying to relax a little, especially when
I am lying down on my bed. I hardly
ever sit down because I cannot sit still.
I keep looking around the room and
see all the work I have to do so I get up
again and do what I can. In other
words, I can do something about my
body, but I cannot quiet my mind and
control my thoughts, until I become
weary and tired mentally and I fall
asleep. When I awake I count my
blessings and not my bruises.[18]

I feel powerless when . . . I am unable
to control the outcome of a situation.
When it's late, dark, and I'm in bed I
feel my safety is not in my hands and
all I can do is impatiently wait for sleep
to come and hope I see the morning.[19]

a group coming towards me,
I try to avoid it. A group
of *anybody*. But, in
particular, black kids.
And I've always prided myself on having no prejudice.
It's been idiotic, and I
don't want to, but I still
can't help it—it's an
emotional response. I see
black kids and I will not
go near them if I can avoid
them. Kids of that age.
On the street. In the subway. I just hope that they
don't come near me. Any
place. It's any place. I
start to get hot and cold
until I pass them. I still
try and keep as far to the
other side of the street as
possible. I feel really
vulnerable around New York
male youth. On an emotional
level. I'm not talking about
intellectually. Intellectually, I will argue with myself
that it's all nonsense. While
I'm doing it. . . . I didn't
sleep at all [the night of
the crime]. In fact, it was
several nights before I got
back to my normal pattern.
All I have to do is start

Sometimes a phobic reaction brings some latent fear to the surface. Racist feelings are common in cases where the criminal is of one race and the victim of another. If the criminal is black, for example, and the victim is white, the victim may become afraid of all black people. The society is racist, and everyone in it is affected by racism. No one is free of its taint, though many people struggle to overcome it. Victims who have tried to maintain unprejudiced attitudes toward people of other races can be deeply troubled when their racism surfaces in a phobic reaction. A woman whose apartment had been burglarized was asked to describe the person she imagined the burglar to be.

I just assumed he was a young, black man. It never occurred to me that he might be a Puerto Rican, for example. I also think that maybe I didn't dwell on it because I am very conscious of my prejudices. I think they're pretty mild compared to many people's, and I think I deliberately didn't want to put labels on this guy, so I didn't think about it too much. I really didn't want to say, "Oh, this was just some . . . whatever . . . some . . . nigger (uncomfortable laughter) breaking into my place." I'm aware of those feelings and that's what people think, immediately. The whole business about he committed a crime, so he must be black. That kind of prejudice makes me angry so I think I was fighting it unconsciously.[20]

running "that record" and I
lose sleep—just repeating
the feelings of that
incident. Any part of it,
or something triggers it.
If I watch a film that has
something of that in
it . . . I tend not to
watch those films any more,
at all. I never did like
them. Now, I won't look at
them. Even this interview
in a way is setting off
some of these things, but
levity is helping. . . .
[The crime] has really
changed my life. Even to
this day, I resist going
out at night, which is
something I've never had
trouble with before. I've
stopped going to meetings
which I had been going to,
and when it comes to going
to the theatre (which is all
mostly at night) we haven't
been going as much as we had
been. Part of the reason is
that I'm waiting for when
the darkness comes later.
I told myself when it
starts getting light I will
be able to start going to
more things, and maybe by

In the postacute phase, the dramatic events of the crime are continually replayed by the victim. Those who fought back and weren't hurt seem to have a minimum amount of psychological trauma. They feel exhilarated and potent. Those who fought back and were hurt still feel supported by society. They easily find sympathetic responses, though some have felt annoyed by police reactions. They felt the police were defensive. It took the tone: "You didn't let me do my job. Next time you let the police protect you." In general, victims who fight back seem to have greater social acceptance than the victims who have followed society's rules and have complied with the criminal.[21]

I'm afraid when . . . I see young blacks or Puerto Ricans between the age of 16 and 25 on the streets where I work or in the hallways of buildings I enter. Also, when I see one loitering around street corners or buildings where I work. I will not walk on the same corner where I was assaulted. Also, more apprehension about responding to someone who needs first aid.[22]

next year it will have eased
off. I have problems during
the daylight, as I go to
work, or use the trains,
only when I meet these groups.
And I'm very well aware of
anything that's going on.
I'm more conscious. I look
around and try to make sure.
I'm not very good at
it. . . . I distrust myself,
these days. I feel I made
the wrong decision, about
which direction to turn. I
had a choice of going down
one street or another, and I
felt that, in this instance,
I should have taken the
other street. I *know* there
was no way I could have known
what was going to happen, but
both were quiet streets; it
was really a matter of chance.
I'm not exactly ashamed, but
just . . . I felt I took the
wrong turn. I usually feel
that there is a reason for
doing things, and probably
the reason was, in some
sense, I *had* to go through
this incident. It's *not*
preordained, but it's "on
tape"—my "Karma," if you
want to call it that: I

I'm afraid when . . . someone follows me or when I'm in an unknown environment where I feel my mobility is limited; when I think about the consequences of defending myself whether successfully or not; when I'm in deserted areas at night; when I see a gang of kids or adults loitering in my way; when I'm immobilized in a crowd or on a subway; late at night on the subway; when I see people playing with knives or other weapons; when I think about being vulnerable; when I think that action can have disasterous consequences, and inaction—hesitation—is equally deadly; when I consider the dramatic increase in violent, anonymous crime; when I think about the backlash that will come in response to crime as it is now.[23]

Self-blaming attributions take many forms. Victims often point to something they did before the crime that made it possible for the criminal to succeed: The unlocked window invited the burglar; the wallet in an outside pocket encouraged the pickpocket; the short skirt incited the rapist. The victim seems almost eager to take the responsibility. . . . Blaming oneself is bound to be pervasive in a society that values individual effort and personal reward. Most Americans are encouraged to take personal credit for their achievements. We also tend to feel responsible for our shortcomings, fail-

had to go through it.
Because once a thing has
happened, that's true, it
is. And the interesting
thing is that after the
incident [my friends] said to
me that they had had a
feeling that I was going to
go through a bad thing. They
didn't know what, and when
they got the call from me
they decided that this was
it. That was what they were
sort of feeling—that I was
going to go through a bad
time. . . . I'd like to
spank the [perpetrators],
because they are children.
They're bad children and I
also think one of the worst
things that you can do to
these kids is to pull their
pants down publicly and spank
them, like babies. We should
go back to the stock—it's
not a bad idea, public dis-
play. I don't want to shoot
them, I don't want to kill
them, I'd like to . . .
humiliate them, and to get
them *to feel* something. . . .
[There] was a show on TV last
week, called *Victims*, where
a group of raped women get

*ures, and personal suffering. In such a
society, it is not at all surprising that
many people explain their victimization
in egocentric terms. The self-blaming
attribution is self-punishing, but at least
it restores a sense of order to the world.
Victims may see their experience as a
kind of expensive education. They may
resolve to correct their behavior so that
they can avoid being victims in the future.
Believing that they know the cause and
that the cause is in themselves, these
victims can plan for their experience to
be a lesson that will not be repeated.
Such planning can be useful in reorder-
ing the fragmented self because it allows
the victim to feel that he or she has
regained control.*[24]

**If the perpetrator of the crime came
into this room right now I . . . would
cripple him and turn him over to the
police. I feel like that's not quite fitting
the punishment to the crime, so maybe
I'd only cripple him a little before I
turned him over to the police. On the
other hand, even now—a year later—I
have a desire to cripple him a lot. Then
I have the thought that I'd have to kill
him to feel secure that he wouldn't try**

togther because they know who assaulted them. It was terrifying! Did you see the end of it? She puts *him* through what happened to *her*, and he cowers and concedes the terror. I would want to do that to these kids! I don't know if I *could* put a gun to their heads to make them feel how it felt, but I would like to be able to. That was one of the dream scenes I'd play. To be . . . able to hold a gun to their necks and make them believe that I was going to shoot, so that they could experience what I did. . . . After the first session of the Crime Victims' group, I began to realize what you were doing. I came back for reinforcement on the "permission" to feel *bad*. It was *okay*! That came through to me in the group. Just by listening to everyone's stories. Some of them were worse than mine. Some of them were horrifying. Some of them were, well, they who had survived—yes, like me. Some had much more worse traumas than I did,

to come after me later—painful line of thought. I feel a kind of pleasure in being in control—ultimately—of him in this way. Then there's a sadness in seeing him dead—unmoving in my imagination and I feel like I don't truly—in my heart—want that. I do want him stopped—absolutely; and I would like to do to him what I was afraid he was going to do to me, to exorcise my pain with his.[25]

The best things that I have gotten out of these sessions are several things. The first and most important thing, I believe, is the sharing of the traumatic experiences with our fellow crime victims. To know that others have suffered greatly at the hands of perpetrators and that I am not alone in this suffering is a very consoling feeling. Just talking about the experience has helped me greatly as I know it has

and they were walking around
and coming to the meeting,
and that was one of the first
things that hit me. I
[understood] that I was
not alone, and that,
relatively speaking, I had
gotten off "easy," because
there was no physical damage.
After all the sessions were
over, I felt that I was glad
it was there, and I was glad
that I had found it early
enough in the whole thing.
I have since spoken to
people who have been through
this kind of thing, even had
tried to forget it, from a
year or so back. I still
tell them they should go.
It makes a difference, it
made a difference in me. It
just made me relax and not bet
against myself. It's enough
trouble dealing with the problem
of what these kids are
doing, but at least I don't
have to be angry or afraid of
myself. It helped me deal
with my own feelings in such
a manner that I felt freer
to have them, explore them,
and kind of get back to who
I am. I think it was quicker

helped everyone in this group who has been a crime victim. Another very important thing is the learning about what to do to prevent, as much as possible, future crime against us.[26]

Every person lives in a kind of steady, moving state, adjusting to changes within the self and in the outside world all the time. The balance is continually shifting. Most people live from one stress to the next; their equilibrium is always being upset in little ways—a family quarrel, a bad report card, a bout with the flu, an unexpected bill. People who live fulfilling lives have learned to roll with the punches, adjusting to these everyday shifts in the order of things. They are able to change in the needed ways so that they regain their equilibrium at more or less comfortable intervals.[27]

than if I didn't have it, too.
It would have taken a lot
more time. What was most
useful was the group sharing,
the talking together in the
CVCS groups. Mostly, hearing
the experiences of others.
Listening to how they had
survived. And the fact that
they were terified, also.
It was all right to be
terrified. For them it was
all right, so why not for me?
Before I came to the group,
it wasn't so good to feel
terrified, but indeed I was
terrified—it was somehow
inappropriate for me to be
feeling it. We're all
raised not to be, and I've
been in the habit of enjoying
the city and going about my
business, so it was hard for
me to let myself really feel
that. After the group, it
was *okay* to feel it; there was
nothing wrong with me. We're
not all John Wayne! The
counselor articulated the
permission to *feel* what I
was feeling. The others
gave me the permission by
the fact that they *had* the
same feelings. The counselor

I'm afraid when . . . I see someone whom I don't know suddenly appear in front or behind me. I find myself becoming uptight and tense. I will try to stay in the middle and not pushed up to a wall or an alley. If I am of the opinion that this is a mugging situation, I would try to use a set of keys with each key between my fingers, so that I could jab him. This also makes me afraid, for fear of seriously hurting him, and then being blamed for maiming him. I find myself also being afraid of little sounds. I become startled easily, and have to fight myself to overcome this. I'm afraid of letting my feelings take over the functioning of my life.[28]

"I hope that my story can help others survive an attack of violence, that seeing how I've dealt with it will give courage to others." Sharon's candor in describing her reactions to violence, her matter-of-

actually, specifically, said the words. That took the pressure away—it helped me reduce my anxiety a lot. It reinforced some old nonsense of my own, about not being worthless. Some stuff that I have been trying to get past for many years. So it merely brought that up— "I can't do it for myself." It got triggered off all over again, but the counselor helped me deal with that a lot better—made me more comfortable, yes. [She] helped me get it off my chest and there was no one around to talk to. The specific incidents I don't remember offhand, but I had the journal in use a lot (but I haven't continued it). But there were incidents that would pop up, and then I would write the whole scene out, and then it was all right. [The journals] helped me master it, and relieve some of the anxiety. Sometimes just writing it out, or talking it out, makes the difference, and it's worth doing. It seems nonsense, but it works.

fact recital of her adjustment, leave an indelible impression on everyone she meets. And everywhere she speaks, those who hear her come away, as I did, with a deeper understanding of the meaning of inner strength, determination and courage.[29]

A great deal depends on the kind of help the victim receives. The victim of a personal crime has been violated by another person. If the victim's recovery is supported by other people, their help provides a kind of counterbalance to the violation, reassuring the victim of the essential trustworthiness of most people. The victim who receives appropriate help from family and friends, for example, will come out of the crisis with a heightened appreciation for them and a greater ability to seek their help again. Weathering a crisis can be a strengthening experience for victims and those who love them.[30]

After a lively discussion last night of crime and my own robbery—during which I sometimes grew very emotional—I went home and slept soundly. However, I sweated quite a bit. Sometimes I have to change pajama jackets twice in a night because of these night sweats. . . . And at times like last night when I'm all "het up" over reliving

I think I did it for a week more. I continued it for another week. I was carrying the book around, then I found that I was carrying the book for nothing. I should mention that I found that, in being under stress situations in the past, writing things out was helpful, and this just started me doing it again. I hadn't thought of it. As an artist, [I used my] art to get the feelings out, too. Oh, yes! That's one of my things that *I* had that other people don't have. I went to the studio, within my first week, and I did a painting. It just poured out of me. It came out—one of these rare things—that comes out in a half hour or an hour. The whole painting was done. And I just slashed it on in a style that I haven't used in many years—with a palette knife, which is the most powerful medium. I used to go through canvas with those, and the painting is there. I have it out and it's very insolent, it's not

the robbery, I find myself sweating on the chest area more than usual. Can there be a connection? I'm almost sure that the sweating has been worse since the robbery. . . . Wrote up the story of my robbery. It might be well to type it later. Had some thoughts of making the story more interesting(?) by injecting humor, playing it as a bad joke on a stupid fellow. Anyone who opens the door to muggers must be a little stupid. However I can't make up my mind to run myself down so. Anyone might open the door to a criminal unknowingly—and no doubt too trustingly. Anyway I doubt if one would do it twice. . . . [30]

something that anybody would buy, but it was my catharsis. . . . It's the overall program, rather than one part of it, that did the most for me. I gradually dealt with the problem within myself. I know it's not over or ever will be. Some changes will be permanent, but under control. I will never be as trusting. I will never be able to walk down a city street in quite the same freedom. It has already eased off, but I still look around and I don't plan to change it. I have a fear that these things are going to become more and more frequent. Maybe I should have learned it years ago. I had no need. It's the first time I had ever run into anything like that, since I was a kid. As a child, everybody chased everybody, and you got beaten up, and you had your problems. But as an adult, I hadn't experienced anything like it. I also should mention that I had my apartment burglarized three times over a period of five

Victims never entirely forget the crime. Their suffering lessens, but other effects of the experience remain as part of the self. Their view of themselves and of the world will be permanently altered in some way, depending on the severity of the crime and the degree of its impact. The violation of self can hardly be called a positive experience, but it does present an opportunity for change. One of two things will happen: Either victims become reordered, reborn, put back together so that they are stronger than before, or their experiences during the crisis will promote further disorder with long-term negative consequences.[32]

I'm afraid when . . . I have to go in or out of my building, afraid that if the incident were to happen again I would be vulnerable again as I was the first time. I'm afraid because if it were to happen again I would be just as helpless as I was the first time, not being able to defend myself or rather, protect myself against them. Even though I am aware of what's going on around me and I am cautious whenever I leave or enter my building, and also walking on my street, the thought keeps popping up in my mind, "What would I do different from the first time if it were to happen again?" What frightens me is that I don't have an answer to that question that satisfies me or makes me feel secure.[33]

years, but that didn't affect
me the way having a gun
pointed at me did. After
each time, I felt a little
less secure about the place
I live in, and I moved
from that place, so that I
changed that atmosphere. But
I didn't get personally hurt.
I felt violated, but it wasn't
the same as having a gun in my
neck, or having another human
being do something to *me*,
directly. There's a
difference. I always knew
there would be a difference,
but I didn't know *what* it
would be, and I don't think
anyone can surmise that
without having the experience.
The other victims in the
group, who did have a similar
experience, were therefore
important to me, because I
knew *they* knew how I felt,
and I knew how *they* felt. I
felt worse for them, because
most of them actually had
been physically harmed. I
felt that they were fortunate
to have come past that, and I
thought they did extremely
well. I figured, if they can
deal, I should be able to.

Crimes that involve personal confrontation threaten autonomy much more directly. In any face-to-face encounter with a criminal the victim is painfully aware that his or her survival is on the line. Whether the threat is stated or implied, the loss of autonomy is absolute—the victim surrenders control on pain of death.[34]

The most important thing to me about the sessions was the realization that I am not alone with my fears and anxieties about crime. Just talking with others who had similar encounters helped relieve some of these fears, not to mention learning of the different strategies and safety measures for survival. E.g., some of the tactics of the criminal, knowing what to look for and what to do or how to size the situation up.[35]

So their example of dealing
with it was useful to me,
too. Especially some women.
They get beaten up very badly.
They take a lot of punishment. . . . Now it's about
nine weeks or so after. I'm
glad it's in the past and
I'm not spending my time
dwelling on it. I just don't
want to be bothered with it.
I'm going on with my life
and living one day at a time.
It crops up only when I walk
the street. But, the other
day, someone rang the bell
and I wasn't expecting anyone, so I wouldn't open the
door. I looked through the
peephole and somebody was
trying to sell me religion,
and I wondered what the hell
he was doing in my house.
How did he get in? I almost
decided to call the police
and ask them to get him out
of the house. I don't know
who he is. And I never
behaved that way. I was not
going to open the door. I
don't care what church he
was talking about. "Just
stay out of my building." . . .
I'd certainly recommend the

I get angry when . . . men make lewd remarks as I pass them on the street. Men joke about rape (or make light of it). My freedom to run alone in the park is curtailed because of high crime rate. Anyone expresses the opinion that it was somehow a woman's fault when she is sexually assaulted.[36]

"I've never operated on fear in my life, and I refuse to do so because of this incident. This was an isolated, freakish occurrence, and the fact that there are a few insane people out there who would harm an innocent person doesn't mean that all people are bad. I believe that human beings are basically good. I've always operated on that philosophy, and I will not become a negative person now and stop enjoying my life. How can I survive and live a healthy life if I worry every time I'm alone? That's why I go to restaurants, attend social functions, refuse to stay home and hide. Basically I'm still the same person, and this bizarre incident isn't going to make me recluse. Not ever!"[37]

CVCS groups to other crime victims. I think it would make life easier for them, quicker. Help them deal with it faster. I don't say that it's absolutely essential, but it's *easier*. It made it easier for *me*, that's for sure. The only thing I would like to see is more people get into it. I would have appreciated it even more if there were *more* people. They were small groups, so they made it easier to deal with. More people should be availing themselves of the CVCS service. It would be more helpful, to the individuals and to the group as a whole. The more you hear from other folks. . . . When you get to feel empathy for the next guy, that helps you with your own problem. . . . I'll be glad when [this interview] is over, because it's bringing up some of the stuff, but if it will help the group function, or to grow, or do it some good, I think it's worth it. It's a situation that we have to

This idea of counseling for victims is a wonderful idea. I'd like to see it enlarged by more victims taking part. I've seen quite a number of victims before I was mugged, and many of them seemed very distraught, full of painful thoughts and emotions. Yet most of these victims will just try to forget about it. I doubt if you can forget a violent episode. The fears and doubt and guilt are simply repressed and may show up later. How can the public be educated to know that some counseling is necessary and highly useful? Probably a lot of people are afraid of counseling from a professional therapist. It seems to show that they're weak-minded or crazy.(?!) It seems to be more common for rape victims to get counseling. Women are learning to accept this. But why not counseling for *most* crime victims?[38]

deal with in our culture
today. I'm afraid that, with
the way things are going,
it's going to get worse.
Is there anything *I* want to
say? Just . . . thanks.

NOTES

1. Pileggi, p. 20.
2. *The New York Times*, November 12, 1980.
3. Pileggi, p. 26.
4. Martin Symonds, "Victims of Violence: Psychological Effects and After Effects," p. 4. Paper delivered April 24, 1974.
5. *The New York Daily News*, November 1, 1981.
6. CVCS group exercise.
7. Arthur H. White, "Coping With the Cost and Fear of Violence," *Public Relations Review*, (Vol. VIII, No. 1, Spring 1982), pp. 40–41.
8. Heinz, July 20, 1982.
9. Pileggi, p. 23.
10. *The New York Times*, November 17, 1981.
11. Bard and Sangrey, pp. 34–35.
12. Pileggi, p. 21.
13. Friedman, p. 24.
14. Symonds, "Victims of Violence," p. 8.
15. "What You Should Know About Rape," p. 3.
16. CVCS group exercise.
17. Spates, p. 14.
18. CVCS group exercise.
19. CVCS group exercise.
20. Bard and Sangrey, p. 43.
21. Symonds, "Victims of Violence," p. 5.
22. CVCS group exercise.
23. CVCS group exercise.
24. Bard and Sangrey, pp. 55–57.
25. CVCS group exercise.
26. CVCS group evaluation.
27. Bard and Sangrey, p. 17.
28. CVCS group exercise.
29. Wayne W. Dyer, "Against All Odds: An Inspiring Story of Survival," *Family Circle*, September 1, 1981, p. 138.
30. Bard and Sangrey, p. 16.
31. CVCS victim's journal excerpt.
32. Bard and Sangrey, p. 47.
33. CVCS group exercise.
34. Bard and Sangrey, p. 15.
35. CVCS group evaluation.
36. CVCS group exercise.
37. Dyer, p. 122.
38. CVCS group evaluation.

HOW TO READ THIS BOOK

Writings appearing in this left column, widely spaced in the typeface you are reading, are always and only edited transcripts of audiotaped interviews with crime victims who availed themselves of the group sessions offered by Crime Victims' Counseling Services.

Writings appearing in this right column, in the typeface you are reading, are always and only from books, newspapers, magazines, journals, reports, brochures, and similar sources.

Writings appearing in this right column, in the typeface you are reading, are always and only the author's responses.

Writings appearing in this right column, in the typeface you are reading, are always and only from group exercises and evaluations by members of Crime Victims' Counseling Services group sessions.

Five: JENNY

There were actually two crimes. The first one was not that bad—I wasn't harmed or anything. The second one I wasn't harmed seriously, physically. But emotionally, both times. This second time, I was going home after visiting a friend, and I was walking along the pavement and two guys came running up, you know, in jogging suits. Came jogging behind me, and they just ran past me. One actually ran on my right while the other one ran on my left, cutting me off because I made an attempt to step down off the curb into the street. One grabbed my handbag and kept running while the other one held on to me and was choking, actually choking me. His hands were around my neck and one hand was holding my other arm right up behind my back, and really pulling it up.

Monday, December 21, 1981, is the shortest day of the year. It is also the first day of winter. It is the day when Johnny Cash, the famous country singer, was attacked in his home in Jamaica. He and his family were threatened and robbed and terrorized for four hours. He called it the most terrifying event of his life. For me, too, this was one of the most terrifying days of my life.[1]

You should fear the criminal, take the security measures widely advised. But if you are caught nevertheless, don't panic or you will freeze when you should be actively alert. Dr. Symonds urges that you go along with the criminal's every demand and be actively cooperative to minimize the danger to your life. If you panic and freeze and can't give him what he wants, or do as he demands, he may make you do it forcibly and you can get

157

Well, I started screaming, and I think when he realized that the first guy was far away, he left. He dumped me on the ground. I mean, not just let me go. Really, he dumped me, he threw me to the ground, and he ran off, and by then I was in the street. I was panicky, I was crying. It was about nine-thirty or ten, I'm not too sure of the time, at night. . . . The assailants were anywhere between nineteen and twenty-one, and it happened in another neighborhood, not in mine. I got up and I noticed there was a little boy, around eight, coming from the same direction. I wasn't sure whether he was one of their accomplices, because these people come in all ages, so I turned towards him and was backing away. But I was crying and he said, ''Miss, what happened, what happened?'' but I couldn't answer him because I wasn't sure who he was. He looked sincere, in the dark. I could see

seriously hurt. You can protect yourself also by understanding that criminals are predators who prey on the weak and the stragglers from the herd. They will attack the person who's standing outside the crowd. So make it a point to stay with others. If you are all together, you will be less vulnerable.[2]

Crime and new District Attorney Liz Holtzman brought out a large crowd of people last week. The occasion was a Town Hall meeting on February 4 called by Assemblyman Roger Green (57 A.D.) for the residents of Fort Greene/Clinton Hill, held in the area's 100 year old Emmanuel Baptist Church. . . . Green called the issue of crime "one of the things folks are most concerned about." He said fighting it was one of the most troubling problems, and that there were no clear cut answers. "We've begun to coin an expression," he said. "Freedom from fear of crime is a human right."[3]

Last year [1980] was the worst year of crime in New York City history, the Police Department reported yesterday. There were more reported murders, robberies, burglaries and thefts of automobiles and other items than in any previous year since the department began compiling such statistics 49 years ago. In only two of seven categories that make up the crime index—rape and assault—were there declines. The total number of reported crimes last year, 710,153, represented a 14.3 percent increase over the 1979 figure of 621,110, and a 7.9 percent increase over the previous record of

his face, so I said, "I was just mugged," and he said, "Okay, just a minute. I'll just run and go get help," and he ran to get help. But in the meantime I didn't want to stand there alone, so I walked out to the main street (where I was going in the first place, to catch my bus home) and there was a carpet place right on the corner so I went in there and they called the police, who came about twenty minutes later. They took a statement, and they took me home. . . . The girlfriend who I was going to visit (who was ill) told me that in the same neighborhood, close by, just about a week before, she noticed two guys. Well, they fit the description that I spoke about, that I told her about. They were shadowing her, so she saw a policeman and she told them and they took her home. So when she said that to me, I called up the station, the precinct, and I told them and they said it could be anybody. So

658,147, set in 1976. As is the department's custom, the statistics were released without explanation of interpretation. They came as no surprise to department officials and others. For many months, officials have said that 1980 would establish records in many categories of crime. Officials feel that the actual number of crimes is much higher, possibly twice as high, because many victims do not report crimes. The city's increase exceeded the nationwide crime increase, according to the most recent compilation by the Federal Bureau of Investigation. Over the first six months of 1980, the city's crime index increased at a rate 50 percent greater than that for the nation as a whole. Among the nation's 25 largest cities, New York City ranked ninth in the relative crime index. . . . Last year there were 100,550 robberies, a 16.6 percent increase over the previous record, set in 1976. Criminologists generally consider robbery the most accurate yardstick for measuring the extent of predatory street crime in a community. New York City last year ranked first in the number of reported robberies.[4]

I'm afraid when . . . somebody's steps are heard behind me on the street. Of course, many New Yorkers who have not been robbed are a little anxious when on the street. But I had never been particularly concerned during daylight hours. Now I get anxious when I hear steps. I stop to see who it is and let them go by.[5]

It should be noted that victims recounted their experience to more people than they listed as supporters. Although "talk" was considered an important form of emotional support, an effort was made to distinguish between talk victims found therapeutic and other conversations. Vic-

they really didn't look
into the matter. They never
really called me back. I
got the impression that they
just didn't care. They were
annoyed that I should even
call, because the policewoman
once said, "If there is anything, *we* are going to call
you, you don't have to call
us." [That made me feel],
angry, because I felt that
they should be trying. I
mean, on any little bit of
information, they should try.
They should look into it,
but they didn't. I never
heard from the police after
that. Never. They never
called me, because I actually
called them about two or
three times before I really
got to speak with someone.
And then she acted in an "I-
don't-care" manner, so I
figured it wouldn't be worth
my while to call them back.
There was nothing that I
really could do about it.
I'm depending on them to find
this person, to find my handbag, to find my identification,
but they didn't seem to be
particularly interested.

tims reported they had mentioned the incident to neighbors, co-workers and friends, but distinguished between those to whom they felt talking was helpful and others. In some instances the victims believed they were doing others a service by telling them about the crime and thereby warning them to be more careful.[6]

In 1975, Robert Grayson was a 10-year veteran newspaper reporter—an old hand at the police and government beats. Then a single event put him squarely in the middle of the legal and bureaucratic systems he had until then observed only from a distance, and changed his life. One night, Grayson was mugged. The attack left him blinded in his right eye and psychologically battered. It was only then he got a first-hand view of the system and how it deals with—or rather, ignores—the human element in the crime: the victim. Today, Grayson is a crime victim advocate in the first government-funded department in the country. It was established in October 1978 in Paterson, N.J., when Mayor Laurence Kramer appointed Grayson to head the Office of the Crime Victim Advocate, a function Grayson had been performing on a volunteer basis after his own ordeal. Even now, with crime becoming a fact of urban life rather than an event that happens to someone else, Grayson is one of only about 300 victim advocates in the nation. But this is about 100 more than a year ago, as interest in setting up such offices spreads. The advocate attempts to ease the aftershock of a crime for the victim, and acts as a liaison between the victim and the various social, medical and legal agencies in obtaining aid and restitution.

Another thing she said was,
"Hundreds of people are
mugged every day, and a lot
of these guys fit the same
description. You know, they
always wear dark clothes
with hoods or caps pulled
down, so it could be one of
hundreds of people," but I
felt that two people from
basically around the same
area, with two descriptions
actually matching, I think
that was something to look
into it . . . I felt
frustrated and angry about
it all. . . . I didn't
come in contact with any
other part of the criminal justice
system. I was looking
at television one day, I
think it was Channel Thirteen.
I was looking at, and they
actually had a program on
crime victims, and after the
program they said, "This is
where you can call," and
they gave the Crime Victims'
Counseling Services number.
I was actually glad that
there was somewhere I could
turn, so the very next day
I called up. . . . But
right after this second

But perhaps more importantly for the prosecutors who are thwarted in their efforts when victims fail to follow through as witnesses, the advocates help the victims make their way through the obstacles placed in front of them by a cumbersome and insensitive legal system. In his own experience, Grayson found that all too often, instead of finding aid and comfort, the victim is blamed for being a victim.[7]

Psychological services also become important in order to help the victim overcome the trauma, and even the sense of guilt at being somehow responsible for the crime taking place. . . . [Grayson] notes that a forerunner of crime victim advocacy started in the late 1960s. "Some states started developing compensation programs, but never advocacy. But money is only part of the problem."[8]

When Charles walked into the bare fluorescent-lighted room at St. Francis College, 180 Remsen Street, he saw four other people who had had similar experiences after being mugged, robbed, burglarized, or raped. "I no longer felt emotionally isolated," Charles said. The woman guiding the discussion was Shelley Neiderbach, a psychotherapist who co-founded the service a year ago four years after muggers leapt into her car to steal it and tried to split her head open

crime, I went to my friend's house, after I got home, because she was very concerned. She felt responsible, simply because I was on a mission to help her, for her benefit, since she was ill and I was coming to her assistance. . . . But, funny, just last week I was speaking to someone, and I remembered it reminded me of some of the things we spoke about during the sessions. He was trying to impress upon me that somehow it was my fault, "blaming the victim," blaming me. "Do you think it was your fault? I mean, don't you know that you're not supposed to be in places like that? You should not walk alone at night." But I had to tell him I cannot always be everywhere with someone, and I do have to travel. There are things I have to do. It's supposed to be okay for a citizen to walk on the streets. I got that kind of response from about half of [the people I told]. One of the first things they said was that I

with a pistol butt. She was mugged a second time after she began her service. "We started the service because we were frustrated that there was no long-term program or groups to deal specifically with the psychological and emotional trauma that accompanies a crime," Neiderbach said. "Nothing other than short-term crisis-intervention hotlines and brief psychotherapy on a one-to-one basis was available." . . . Neiderbach said her agency has helped over 150 people in its year of existence. Those people, she said, ranged in age from 14 to 67 and came from as far away as Yonkers. She said that, surprisingly, nearly 60% of her participants are male. . . . "We also have a phone network similar to Alcoholics Anonymous or Gamblers Anonymous," Neiderbach said. "Whenever one of the group's participants feels a wave of anxiety, they have the numbers of other members who they can talk to." For further information, telephone [718] 875-5862.[9]

"Society finds it hard to accept violence. So rather than accept the fact of violence, people feel the victim must have contributed in some way. Even families inadvertently blame the victim—especially in rape cases," Grayson observes.[10]

"I don't look at it as protection for me," Mr. Barouh said. "I could have an armed chauffeur and an armed guard outside my house. But what does the average guy do who has to take the subway? It's wrong for me to have extra protection, it's wrong for the Mayor to have it. Everybody should be entitled to the same protection. Every single human being on this earth, if they are decent people, deserve all the benefits enjoyed by the middle and upper class."[11]

should not be alone. "Every woman should have an escort service!" And the only response I could give to them then is that I cannot have somebody with me every time I go out, and I don't think this justifies the crime. I think something could be really done. I think what happened is that the penal system is probably not tough enough, and it's making it easier for these people. They find it's easy, it's easy—they can get away with it. So it really doesn't bother them when they're going to go after you. I feel angry. I really think that something should be done. [I'm not sure what;] it would be easy to say jail terms, but maybe youth groups could help. I don't know. Maybe some other form of counseling for young people. Groups that young people can get into. I also think that the home, the home plays a very important part in it, and a lot of people would say that, well,

"Crime is the hidden social issue of the 1980s—not abortion or busing," said Representative Charles E. Schumer, Democrat of Brooklyn. "Ten years ago, crime was a Brooklyn issue. Five years ago it was a metropolitan New York issue. Now it's a national issue." This concern has caused a change in the political climate. A decade ago, most liberals saw "law and order" as a cover phrase for racism and a threat to civil liberties. They shunned the issue. But now, Senator Edward M. Kennedy's office distributes a pamphlet entitled, "Violent Crime: It's Time to Act."[12]

Time can be a powerful ally of crime. When suspects remain loose on the streets for long periods because the courts are overcrowded and the case backlog forces plea bargaining—often to ridiculously low charges—time becomes the enemy of public safety. In 1980, for example, only 2,100 of the 20,000 persons indicted for serious crimes in New York actually went to trial—most of the other untried cases were disposed of through plea bargaining. Next Monday, a group of concerned Bronx residents will begin an unprecedented project that may lead to speeding up trials in the criminal courts—and, at the same time, add another weapon to the arsenal in the battle against crime. Every day for three

it's a cycle. Okay. Well,
then, if it's a cycle, have
adult groups for parents,
on how to educate their
children to be good citizens.
A part of the cause of crime
is some kind of family
breakdown. [Also],
sentences are not long
enough, and justice is not
swift enough. The word
"swift" shouldn't even come
into play. Although I am
angry at the muggers, I am
even more so at the system for
not caring about me, for
not trying to help me. I
still feel that way. I don't
feel any different, now. . . .
[My family was] concerned,
but actually I don't have
very many family here, and
they are far from me anyway,
so after the mugging I didn't
have any close contact with
them—they are back home in
Trinidad, where I come from,
more than a phone call away.
I'm alone, here. There was
not much family support for
me during this crisis. None,
really. . . . [People at
work, the next day] were
really concerned. I mean,

*weeks, teams of volunteers from the
Bronx Citizens Court Monitoring
Project, Inc.—after training by experts
from the Fund for Modern Courts—will
go to Bronx Supreme Court and sit in on
the start of trials. With one eye on the
clock and the other on the jury box, they
will record the time it takes to select a
jury.[13]*

*[He] noted that juvenile crime was a
big problem because "There are not
enough diversions for youth," particularly during the evening hours. "A good
strategy when I was growing up," he
said, "was that there were a number of
night centers open. They allowed you to
come in off the street and engage in
productive activity." To that end, Green
said some funds were being made available from the [New York State] Special
Delinquency Prevention Program. He
called it "a drop in the bucket" but "a
beginning also." Encouraging adults to
provide "ideas, purpose, and direction," Green said area youth were prepared to "change their lifestyle" if given
the chance.[14]*

*Maceo Singleton and Richard Jenkins,
the defendants, are in jail on Riker's
Island, unable to make $50,000 bail.
April 5 will mark the 13th time they have
appeared in NY State Supreme Court
since their arraignment last June when
they were both charged with first and
second degree assault and robbery. Tom
Noel, the 70-year-old victim, waits in his
Clinton Hill apartment, slowly recover-
ing from injuries sustained in the crime
police say Singleton and Jenkins committed. He will never see out of his left eye
again. Noel's daughter and his neighbors
wait with growing impatience to see if on
April 5 the judge will set a trial date for
a crime committed 10 months ago. They
have been in the courtroom on each of the
13 appearances so far in this case, and
this chain of experiences has given them*

they were supportive, but
there was not very much
they could do because they
also feel, "Well, what can
we do? There's nothing that
can be done, and this is
how it is." They felt powerless, like me. Like during
the crime—at the time I was
scared. I was afraid of what
they could do to me, and there
was nobody within earshot.
Afterwards, I felt angry,
angry enough that if someone
would look at me on the train,
or anywhere, I would put up
a defense. In fact, even
now, I'm ready to hurt
someone who would make the
slightest attempt or gesture
towards me, you know. If
somebody is walking close
to me, I feel afraid. I'm
very alert, now, and ready
to swing back. Always. I
don't even know if those
people had a weapon—I've
got to be honest: I didn't
see any. It was just the
strength and force of two
people that was sufficient
to frighten me. They "just"
choked me and put my arm
behind me, but then, the

a unique, if frustrating, view of how the legal system proceeds to mete out justice once an arrest is made in a case. What they have seen is not a reassuring picture.[15]

Types of help provided by supporters varied according to the supporter's relationship to the victim. . . . Emotional support and long-term assistance were given more often by relatives or friends than by neighbors or landlords, by members of the victim's social networks than by non-members, by people who knew the victim more than one year and by people who saw the victim at least once a week. Long-term assistance included practical forms of assistance, such as driving victims for subsequent visits to the doctor, but in most cases consisted of emotional support. For example, victims reported that family and friends called to check on them or dropped by to see them more frequently than before the crime. In one instance a burglary victim's friends took her out to dinner on five consecutive nights following the incident.[16]

I'm afraid when . . . I see a group of rowdy fellas yelling all kinds of profanity and with hostility written all over their movements, and when I am on Remsen Street walking twoard the Jay Street subway station in the dark at 10:30, with no one in the streets and a group of blacks turn the corner, and when someone is arrogant around me. I am scared when I feel I may have to defend myself. I may get hurt as well. I don't like the idea of getting hurt, either with fists or with words.[17]

I'm afraid when . . . I awake during the night—sometimes when I hear the digital clock move or the bed creaking. I am afraid on first opening the door to

realization of what *could*
have happened. . . . For night
after night, I couldn't
sleep. I think I even
dreamt about this. I would
wake up, and the fear! Even
now, I find it hard to
really fall asleep, into a
deep slumber. I'm always
"there," in one way,
expecting something to
happen. It was that way for
five or six months. When I
called and made the CVCS
registration appointment,
I was glad. I looked forward
to getting help. I didn't
know what kind of help,
actually. I didn't know
what form it was going to
take, but at least I'd
really be able to talk about
this with someone. The
thought that maybe they
could help me by telling me,
or showing me, how to deal
with my fears made me feel
better. Even before I
actually went. . . . Most
of the time I stayed home,
especially if there was
nobody to go out with me.
If I had to go I would go,
but I was always afraid. I

my apartment, when getting into my
car at night, thinking someone may be
hiding inside. When answering the
phone—probably because the phone
was ringing so often prior to the incident without anyone saying anything
or asking for someone else.[18]

Ms. Shelley Neiderbach
Crime Victims' Counseling
  Services, Inc.
GPO Box 3003
Brooklyn, New York   11202

Dear Shelley:

*Let me take this opportunity to thank you
for taking time out of your schedule to
make the presentation on crime prevention to our clients August 30. . . . Your
presentation focusing on safety precautions in securing their apartments and the
need to be awake and alert to their
environment as they move around the city
on buses, subways or walking the streets
of their neighborhood was informative
and direct. The clients themselves were
most appropriate in their questioning
which further indicates their concern and
desire to know more adequately how to
deal with this issue. I was impressed with*

was afraid just coming across here, just tonight, walking on my way here. I was so afraid, becasue it is a bit lonely coming here, and I had my umbrella snug across my shoulder, and at one point I took it off. People walking behind me, or looking funny in any way, would start my heart pumping. I would become a little afraid. I *still* have some anxiety; I think for a while it abated, but it seemed to be coming back again, especially during the winter months, when it's dark early. . . . Powerless-ness? It's just that—not being able to do *anything* about it. You know, being a victim of a crime and the perpetrators were never caught. Just another crime that happened to another person, that was about it. There's nothing that I can do about it. I had no recourse, nowhere to turn to. I'm truly a victim. . . . Now, I distrust people, in general. Just people, I would say. Well, if you really think about it deeply,

your delivery; your understanding of their concerns was evident and you handled the material without causing them undue alarm.

Again my sincere thanks.

Yours truly,

*Carol Collins, Exec. Dir.,
    Association for the Rehabilitation of
    the Mentally Ill*[19]

I'm afraid when I hear a sudden noise behind me on the street; when my dog jumps up on me from the back I go into sudden, instant shock/fear; when I hear a noise from below going up the stairs to my apartment; or someone in intense anger/rage; or men on the street who I think could hurt me; when walking down a city block at night and absolutely no one else is on the block; taking the subway to areas I'm not familiar with as well as just taking the subway; I am afraid when going into my apartment building and turn around and go in backwards; walking the dog at night; I am afraid when I go into Central Park; afraid to walk along the East River between Sixty-Third and Seventy-Second streets during bright daylight, with the dog; I think I am just somewhat fearful in going out at all.[20]

I feel powerless when . . . I am power-less—when someone else (i.e., a robber/ mugger/whatever) has control of a sit-uation and I don't trust that person. Actually, I get angry when I feel pow-erless, so most of what I wrote last week about anger applies here, too—especially regarding fighting "The Sys-tem."[21]

yes, it would also be mistrust of the criminal
justice system. They didn't
do anything to help me. You
know, this is something that
they should have looked into.
I don't trust people who look
like them, but also almost
everyone, male or female.
And not as much female as
male, but also male or
female. I get vigilant
especially if they are close
behind me. I would stop and
let them pass me. . . . At
first I dreamt about things
happening to me at night,
but that didn't go on for
long. But the sleep! Even
now, I'm always afraid.
Because I live alone, I
think that someone is
always going to come and
that I'm not safe, even
though I try to secure my
doors and windows. I do
not feel safe and I sleep
very lightly. It has come
to the extent where some-
times I'm not asleep by
one, two, and even when I
do fall asleep I wake up
several times. The first
time I was mugged, I was

I'm afraid when . . . I leave my apartment—when the elevator's open I always check to see if it's empty. If it is,
I'm afraid of who may get in next. I
can never get my mail alone, and it
even makes me nervous when I'm with
someone. I get frightened whenever I
know someone is behind me. I'm always aware now of the people around
me. I almost run from the subway at
night, and I don't feel secure until I
reach the security people who walk me
to my apartment each night. I have not
felt comfortable being alone since the
robbery, whereas before I loved walking around by myself. This crime has
made me a prisoner in my own home.
And, unfortunately, I don't feel secure
there, either.[22]

afraid. I was afraid,
yes, but the second time
enhanced it, enhanced my
fears. What happened the
first time was I was
living with my relatives
at the time, so I guess
having them around helped.
But this time I was alone,
so that made the difference.
I think about what happened
and what could have happened,
and where I might have been.
That will, I think, drive
feelings into you again,
and fear, generally. I mean,
fear of everybody, almost
everybody. And I've
received no help from any
agency, actually, apart from
calling Crime Victims'
Counseling Services. From
you. After I made the
appointment, and went to the
first session, I felt, I
think, relieved. A
little . . . a little elated,
a little bit of the tension
loosened. I guess being able
to talk about it with others,
realizing it is really a
problem that we all share,
and knowing that there are
ways in which to deal with

I want to thank you, in fact, for putting this together, for providing this service—(and for free!). Not so much from anything said or done in particular, but perhaps just from the positive action of doing this has made a great deal of difference to my way dealing with the event. I give myself more credit now for handling it as well as I did, for surviving, and even winning. Thanks![23]

it, I did feel a little
relieved. . . . I can't
say that all my fears went
[after the sessions were
over], but I did feel better
just knowing that there is
a group there. There are
people that I can turn to,
because we can actually call
each other if we have
problems and talk to each
other, and again I would say
finding ways in which to
deal with my fears, and wish
to deal with the perpetrator,
and how to defend myself, for
example. The self-defense
part was useful. I mean,
never that I had to use it,
but at least I now have an
idea of what I can do when
something like that happens
again. Some of the "do's"
and some of the "don't's,"
some of the things that I
wasn't aware of. At the
time when I was mugged I
didn't know what to do. I
didn't know how to defend
myself, but finding out
that there are do's and don't's is
being able to be able
to defend yourself.
I may have just tried

If the perpetrator of the crime came
into this room right now I . . . would
like to smash him, punch him, slash
him with a knife and watch his blood
flow—I wouldn't feel any remorse, I'm
afraid—I probably would scream at
him how horrible he is and demand to
have my things all returned. I can't
feel sorry for him. He deserves the pain
he inflicted on me. My rage would be
best directed at him, but since he's not
here I'm afraid sometimes I directed it
at myself, blaming myself. It's frightening.[24]

defending myself. I was
just trying to do one of
the don't's, at the time,
and could have gotten myself
into more hot water. . . .
I just felt that sharing,
being able to talk with
someone, people who have
actually experienced, who've
actually been crime
victims. . . . You know, you
hear about crime. I mean,
you hear it on the air, on
the television, but most
people haven't actually
experienced talking with
others who have gone through
the trauma. I think to know
that you're not alone is so
very, very important. It
gives me a sense of comfort,
and takes away some of that
sense of fear and being out
of control, as well. . . .
I remember I was talking
about some of the fear, some
of the things we felt, and
you actually interpreting it
in such a way that it made
sense to us, that we actually
knew. Knowing how to deal
with the different
experiences, I mean emotional,
our emotional feelings . . .

Again and again, crime victims expressed relief and support from knowing that others—i.e., other crime victims—understood what they had experienced and were trying to overcome. As with other peer counseling groups (such as Alcoholics Anonymous), the issue of true empathy was paramount.[25]

In a high crime area or at a time of an acute disaster, I think there is a need to develop a specialized program for victims in order to have the capacity of being responsive to both their acute and long-term needs. But I also feel that victimization occurs throughout society, and that it is quite important to train and sensitize a broad range of health, mental health, and social service professionals to the

it did help, for clarity. Actually, because it's easy to talk about tangible things. But one's *feelings* are a little bit hard, and another thing, too, is you having the information ready for us. How to defend ourselves, also. Not just physically, but emotionally. *That's* the important part, and knowing that the counselor was a crime victim, too. It helped to know that here was someone who has actually experienced it—she's not talking about something that she heard or read. She actually *felt* the fear, the trauma. She actually felt the muggers' hands on her, as I did. The empathy was important to me. It's the winter months and I do have these fears again. I hoped it will go away when the spring comes and it gets light again, and there are more people around. I hope in the meanwhile, though, that something is going to be done. What possibly can be done? I'm talking about the penal system, to help

issue of victimization. Anyone showing psychological distress may have a history of victimization, and it is quite important to be able to deal with it. Generally, I favor a broad approach to victims' services, but in highly specified situations I think that there is a need for specialized services.[26]

I'm afraid when . . . I see a black-haired foreigner, especially Turkish, Arabic, etc. When I am alone. I look at people's eyes. I look at myself. Really afraid that this crime, and my holding in all the pain, will twist and contort my mind and body. I am afraid when someone is phony to me. I am afraid of everything. I am afraid to feel horny. I am afraid to feel pain and be alone. I am afraid of nothing. What's there to be afraid of?[27]

these young men. I don't know whether some of them really want to be helped and I think the most harmful part of fear is maybe society, how society deals with it, how the justice system deals with it. It's easy for these people to go out there and mug. I mean, in one day they can bring in a few hundred dollars, the "career criminals." [It's a way] of making a living, and the only reason why they would do it to the extent that they do it is because it is easy to do. Easy in that there aren't enough cops, there aren't enough arrests, and they can get away with it. They know that. They know that they are going to get away with it. I think something should be done about it! [There should be more police, more patrol cars, more arrests]—that would help, but it would not help if they arrest the muggers, or the criminals out there, and then they go into the courts and it takes a year before their case is at

District Attorney Elizabeth Holtzman is less circumspect; she blames much of the reasons for delays on defense lawyers. "Unnecessary delay is the plague of the criminal justice system," Holtzman said last year in a statement criticizing defense lawyers for "delaying tactics." . . . Defendants are denied the right to a speedy trial, the deterrent value of swift and certain punishment is lost and as a result public confidence in the system is destroyed." Holtzman ordered her 300 assistant district attorneys to seek strict enforcement of the rule requiring defense lawyers to file pre-trial motions within 45 days of arraignment. "New guidelines require all assistant district attorneys to have their cases ready for trial within 45 days of arraignment. For certain crimes, prosecutors must be ready to go to trial immediately," Holtzman's statement reads.[28]

trial, and they're still
out there. [I want them]
in jail, fast, or somewhere
being helped. [I] see
rehabilitation as part of a
criminal justice program.
I'm not saying that it's
going to happen in all
cases, but there are cases
where it can help. Take,
for instance, that little
guy, how old is he? Nine
or ten: "The Littlest Bank
Robber." But now, again, he
took, what was it? A
bicycle. He's now, himself
and his two sisters or
brother, they're now back
in the courts again. I
mean, he's only *nine*! He's
starting his career! He
should get help *now*! . . .
[Doing this research] shows
that you care what happens
to the victim as time goes
by. You know how they are
coping. You should [also]
get more people in [to the]
CVCS groups, because it
helped, it helped me,
knowing that you are there
and being able to come to
counseling, talk my problems
out, get help from others,

*Noel passed over a set of black and
white photos taken of him in the hospital,
as he continued his story. The images
show a seemingly lifeless man laying in
bed with his head swathed in bandages,
his fingers badly swollen, and numerous
cuts and bruises. It was himself in
Brooklyn Hospital. Noel's injuries were
extensive: a fractured wrist, a fractured
left eye socket, bone fragments lodged in
the eye socket, and a blood clot formed in
the front lobe of his brain, which caused
internal bleeding and necessitated surgery. It was six and a half weeks before
he left the hospital, and only then with
assistance. As he left the hospital for
home, the doctors had recommended
Noel's family look for a nursing home.
Today, however, the only visible signs of
the injuries are the scars above Noel's
bright blue eyes. What you can't see on
the surface, is the continuing pain. He
has a severe numbness and deadness in
the balls and toes of his feet, a recurring
bladder infection, and no sight in his left
eye. Miraculously, he is living back in his
own home, independently. "It's changed
my life," Noel says quietly of the attack
on that May morning. "These guys broke
my health, I was in excellent health, and
now I go to a doctor almost every
day."[29]*

*Along with my New Year's greeting to all
Cadman residents and my best wishes for
a healthy and happy year, I want to share
with you my growing malaise about the
increasing crime in our city. On January
1, my day began with a New York Times
article informing me that subway crime
rose during November and December.
Since I am a regular straphanger (as are
many of you) this was hardly startling
news. However, as I read the article, I*

you and other members. They help. Yes, I would recommend. I would. Totally. Actually, I have been telling people around, but they haven't been mugged or anything. But I keep telling them, if ever you know anybody, there is a counseling service that could help you.

experienced a growing concern for those people, old and young, who are the victims of a mugging, robbery, assault or rape. Their continued anger, fear, shame and/or helplessness is perhaps the most overlooked aspect of the crime. It is often weeks or months before the victim of a crime can resume a normal life without the difficult feelings that often linger in the aftermath of the crime. Later that day, I learned of a new organization created to help crime victims cope with the emotional and psychological after-effects of the crime. Crime Victims' Counseling Service, founded by two psychotherapists in 1981, offers ongoing free counselling assistance for those who are the victims of any criminal action. The counselling groups are free of charge and are held Mondays (7–9 p.m.), Wednesday (10 a.m.–noon) and Saturday (10 a.m.–noon). New groups start each month. All groups meet at St. Francis College, 180 Remsen Street, Brooklyn. At a time when we are trying hard to reduce crime and prosecute the offenders in a timely manner, the experiences of the victim are often quietly forgotten. The Crime Victims' Counseling Service is establishing outreach programs through civic and political groups, churches and synagogues. But, more important is the immediate assistance they offer through their 24 hour hotline: (212) 875-5862. Or, write to them at GPO Box 3003, Brooklyn, N.Y. 11202.[30]

NOTES

1. CVCS victim's journal excerpt.
2. Freese, p. 89.
3. *The Phoenix*, February 13, 1982.
4. *The New York Times*, February 25, 1981.
5. CVCS group exercise.
6. Friedman, p. 140.
7. "Victim Advocate: A New Style of Crimefighter," *Ms. Magazine* (September 1982), p. 78.
8. *Ibid.*
9. *The New York Sunday News*, January 31, 1982.
10. "Victim Advocate," p. 78.

11. *The New York Times*, March 8, 1982.
12. *The New York Times*, March 16, 1982.
13. *The New York Daily News*, May 23, 1981.
14. *The Phoenix*, February 13, 1982.
15. *The Phoenix*, March 31, 1983.
16. Friedman, p. 147.
17. CVCS group exercise.
18. CVCS group exercise.
19. Letter to Crime Victims' Counseling Services, September 2, 1982.
20. CVCS group exercise.
21. CVCS group exercise.
22. CVCS group exercise.
23. CVCS group evaluation.
24. CVCS group exercise.
25. Author's note.
26. Sharfstein, quoted in Salasin, "Caring for Victims," p. 19.
27. CVCS group exercise.
28. *The Phoenix*, March 31, 1983.
29. *Ibid.*
30. *The Cadman Complex*, January 1981.

HOW TO READ THIS BOOK

Writings appearing in this left column, widely spaced in the typeface you are reading, are always and only edited transcripts of audiotaped interviews with crime victims who availed themselves of the group sessions offered by Crime Victims' Counseling Services.

Writings appearing in this right column, in the typeface you are reading, are always and only from books, newspapers, magazines, journals, reports, brochures, and similar sources.

Writings appearing in this right column, in the typeface you are reading, are always and only the author's responses.

Writings appearing in this right column, in the typeface you are reading, are always and only from group exercises and evaluations by members of Crime Victims' Counseling Services group sessions.

Six: RITA

My apartment was burglarized. I have a son who is now seventeen; at the time he was sixteen, when this happened last June. He's a hard-of-hearing boy—he has about an eighty percent hearing loss and he wears a hearing aid, which does help him to have pretty close to normal hearing. However, he's been handicapped since birth. He has a language problem because of this, but he goes to regular school so he's not a retarded child or anything like that, but he's been characterized by medical people who worked with him as immature because of his language problem. There is a boy who lives in my building who is the same age as my son; I've had previous problems with this kid coming in and stealing things. The first time it happened he was ten years old; I had two hundred dollars missing

1. *PROTECT YOURSELF AND YOUR HOME*

   - *Request a confidential police Home Security Check—it's free! Call (212) 793-2727.*
   - *Join Operation ID. Mark your valuables so they can be recovered and be used as evidence, if necessary. Call your local precinct today.*
   - *Report all crimes and suspicious persons immediately. Cooperate fully with the police.*
   - *Be on guard at all times. Stay alert. Plan ahead. Do not resist if you are the victim of a hold-up or mugging.*

2. *ALWAYS CARRY A WHISTLE WITH YOU*

   - *Attach a high-pitch whistlestop whistle to your key ring. (You can order one by mail for $1.50 from Edgewater Community Council, 1112 West Bryn Mawr, Chicago, IL 60660.)*
   - *Use your whistle in emergencies, whenever anyone needs help . . . including yourself . . . and keep blowing until help arrives.*
   - *In a life-threatening situation, CALL 911.*

3. *STUDY UP ON WHAT IS WRONG WITH THE COURTS*

   - *You can order a copy of the paperback book* Blow the Whistle on Crime *by sending $1.50 to: Citizens Action on Crime, Box 273, Church Street Station, New York, N.Y. 10046.*

from my apartment and I just couldn't imagine what happened to it, because it would never occur to me— that the kind or relation- ship I have with my son and with my family in general— was just, you'd never dream that anyone in your family. . . . I couldn't imagine what was going on, and a couple of days after this happened, [Paul's] mother came with the man she was dating. The man came in and said, "Can I talk to you?" and he gave me forty dollars. He said he seen the boy with the money, a lot of money, and he knew that [Paul] didn't get it from his family, and he talked to the kid and asked him where he got it. The kid was buying all kinds of crazy things and he had spent most of it. Ever since then, I'd come home and I'd find things missing—a piece of jewelry: you know, you wear it and put it on the dresser. Or a couple of dollars for grocery money would be in

4. *JOIN US IN OUR FIGHT AGAINST CRIME*

- *Send a contribution to Citizens Action on Crime, Room 711, 36 West Forty-fourth Street, New York, N.Y. 10036.*

BLOW THE WHISTLE ON CRIME.[1]

Recent efforts to maintain standards of decency in prisons result in an anomaly: A convict is thereby eligible for many state-paid benefits—psychological help, education, vocational training and medical care. But not his victim. The victim, who may desperately need some of the

the drawer. . . . This has been going on since, well, about seven years. Anyway, I try to be more and more cautious. After about two or three of these incidents happened, I absolutely forbid my son to play with him. [Paul] is the kind of kid that took great sport in making fun of my son because he's handicapped, and he just hung around [with boys] from another neighborhood. And on quite a few occasions these boys had beat up my son. It would be a case where he would be coming home from school (see, I always work) and I would come home a couple of hours after my son—I'm a single mother. So, anyway, this one particular day (it was last June) my son graduated junior high and he was off for a couple of days. [These boys] went over to my son and told him, "Let's go over to your house and do weightlifting." They like keep insisting, they won't take no for an answer—and, like I said previously, he had been

same services as a direct result of the crime, usually must fend for himself. That's why some localities have set up programs to offer crime victims counseling and help in applying for state assistance. The programs also give victims advice about testifying in court and take responsibility for notifying them, as well as other witnesses and the police, when trials are to begin, saving time and sparing frustration. Though judges, prosecutors and police officers praise these programs, they are threatened by Federal cutbacks. Assemblyman Richard Gottfried wants New York state to put up enough money to make sure the victim programs continue. Well it should. Help for the victim is no expendable afterthought; in moral and practical terms, it is an essential part of the criminal justice process. Recent hearings have offered dramatic examples of how much the victim service agencies help. A woman who saw her former lover murder her new boyfriend told how the defendant's friends tried to intimidate her after she agreed to cooperate with prosecutors. They made death threats against her and her baby. A gasoline bomb exploded in her hallway. But a victim services agency helped her find a new apartment and move, with police protection. She went on to testify and help convict the defendant of murder. In part because of the victim services agencies, the number of people willing to testify at trials has risen sharply in New York City. One agency estimates it saves the city $4 million a year by reducing the time the police wait to be called to court. About 20 such programs are operating in New York state, most of them still on a "demonstration" basis, with pieced-together funding. To rescue programs severely threatened by Federal cutbacks, the Legislature last spring provided $1.5 million of interim aid. Assemblyman Gottfried would increase the amount in next year's budget to $5 million, to guar-

beaten up by these kids one
time, and he felt he
couldn't refuse them. They
were forcing him. You know,
like pushy. So they went in
the house and I guess they
were lifting weights for
a while, 'cause he said they
told him again (that pushy,
insisting way) that when
you're lifting weights, it's
very good for your muscles,
to develop muscles, to go
into the bathroom and take a
hot bath, and they insisted
he go into the bathroom.
Now, again he said, "Ma,
I didn't want to take a
bath," and he said he
didn't take a bath, but they
insisted he go into the
bathroom and he stood in
the bathroom and they went
looking around my apartment.
They went into my bedroom and
they were looking through the
drawers and under the one rug.
I have a closet in my bedroom,
and in the closet there is, I
had kept hidden (hidden in
the sense that I had it
wrapped up, put away in bags)
photography equipment. I had
two expensive cameras and

antee the agencies' future. They have earned the right to permanence. Humanity, efficiency and public respect for the law offer powerful justification for a larger investment. Official neglect compounds the trauma of crime.[2]

On Wednesday afternoon, 11-year-old Lubomyr Waroch was mugged moments after he boarded a bus across the street from Intermediate School 88 in Brooklyn.

With the dexterity of accomplished felons, one boy clapped a hand around the sixth-grader's mouth and forced him back while a second went through his pockets. A passenger alerted the driver, who parked the bus and chased the muggers to the rear. Meanwhile, another youngster helped himself to the driver's transfer tickets.

Throughout the ordeal, the victim's expression remained impassive, as if such indignities were familiar. "It's happened before," he said later with a shrug. "On the second day of school they stole my bus pass."

When Angela Owings, 11, refused to surrender a friend's earrings to five boys at the bus stop near I.S. 391 in Brooklyn last month, the boys followed her onto the bus and chased her to the back. One punched her in the stomach and went through her pockets. She got off at the next stop, but the boys pursued her. A teacher driving by helped her home, and now she has nightmares.

"It's had a pretty bad psychological effect on her," said her mother, Scottie Owings, a District 17 board member. "We have had to go in the night and wake her up and deal with that."

The beginning and end of the school day are frightening times for some New York City public- and private-school children. While aboard either public buses or specially designated Transit Authority school buses, the pupils are easy prey for older children seeking their cash, bus and lunch passes and even their clothing.

three lenses. I had a
strobe—all this stuff that
was wrapped up and put in
plastic bags, put in camera
bags. They were buried.
On top of them were old
clothes, papers, boxes of
shoes, what have you.
Because I had these previous
experiences of these kids
coming in my apartment and
taking things. And they
were looking through all
this stuff and my son came
out of the bathroom and he
said, "What are you doing
in the closet?" and they
said nothing. Also, I had
this box (and I had
remembered I had put away
the things dear to my life,
my most precious stuff—I
was afraid to wear it. Not
that it was so valuable,
but of sentimental value).
I had my wedding ring, a
pair of gold earrings I
had bought for my niece
that I was going to give
her for Christmas, something
special. I had a watch that
my mother gave me, a gold
watch, from graduating
junior high school. . . .

The Transit Authority, school officials and the police say they do not have statistics on the number of such attacks. Edward Silberfarb, a spokesman for the Transit Authority police, said that he had no figures broken down by borough but that the situation in Brooklyn was the worst.[3]

Juvenile offenders in Moore County plow fields and chop wood to pay back thousands of dollars to their victims, but few of the recipients ever learn the source of the money.

In its first year, the program has helped 34 youths raise money to repay victims, said Gary Crutchfield, the county youth coordinator and director of the project.

The Z. Smith Reynolds Foundation has donated $30,000 to the program, Mr. Crutchfield said. He said he also hoped to expand the project, which involves boys whose ages range from 10 to 15, to include offenders up to the age of 21.

Nearly all the young men might otherwise have been sent to training schools at a yearly state cost of $15,000 each, he added.

"Once a child is sent to training school, there's no way for a victim to receive restitution," Mr. Crutchfield said.

Most victims who have received restitution have no idea that the money came from juveniles who committed the crimes, Mr. Crutchfield said. The juvenile simply turns in the money to the court clerk, who writes the checks for restitution.

A year ago, Moore County's courts sent 17 youthful offenders to training schools, 16 of them because they had not paid back their court-ordered restitution. "Ninety-five percent of the time it's because they don't have a job," Mr. Crutchfield said. "They don't have the means to pay."

Under the restitution program, juvenile offenders spend Saturdays and school holidays working, either cutting

The photography equipment—
I've been interested in
photography since 1973—
the cameras were stuff that I
acquired by trading up,
by saving, by having things
made for me. On my dresser
I also had a little box that
I would throw things in—I
had spare keys that would go
in there. You know, it's
just like for convenience.
You don't think people will
come into your house and
take things. I mean, you
don't until you experience
it. I came home and [my
son] didn't say anything
to me, never said a word.
I had no idea that anybody
was in the house; I didn't
see anything missing. A few
days later, I'm at work and
I get a call—guess it was
about three o'clock in the
afternoon, and it was my son,
and he said, "Oh Ma, something terrible happened!"
So I asked what and he said,
"When I came home I knew
right away something was
wrong, because the door was
opened." I asked, "Wide

*wood in the fall and winter or farming all
spring and summer. The average offender owes about $200, primarily for
larceny or breaking and entering offenses.*

*The young people are paid $3.35 an
hour for the work. But $2.85 of each
hourly wage is set aside for the victims.
The remaining 50 cents per hour is saved
in a contingency fund that also goes to
the victim if the offender does not meet
his obligation. If he pays off the entire
amount, the youth gets the contingency
fund.*

*Judge Michael Beal of Moore County
District Court said he had sent most
juvenile offenders in his court through the
program. "I think one of our biggest
problems in criminal law is restitution for
the victims," Judge Beal said. "This
gives us an alternative when there are no
jobs available."*

*The program's woodcutting operation
raised $7,000 in its first year. It has
collected $2,000 more in just the last
seven weeks, and telephone calls are still
coming in from buyers wanting wood.*

*In its first summer, the farming oper-
ation grew seven acres of corn, tomatoes,
cabbage, cucumbers, watermelon, canta-
loupe, lima beans and okra on land
donated by Police Chief Sam Prim of
Whispering Pines. But the farming operation has yet to be profitable.*

*All but one of the 34 youths have paid
back what they owed. The one exception
moved out of Moore County and could
not complete the program.*[4]

*Once you are inside your apartment,
police still urge caution. Far too many
New Yorkers are not careful enough
about whom they let into their apartments, police say. No one—especially
unexpected workers or deliverymen—
should be admitted without proper identification and a call to double-check.*

open?'' and he said, ''No, it was like, when you see the door, you saw it was closed tightly and I thought oh, the door's not locked,'' so he opened the door and he went in. The living room was messed up. He had baseball cards. There were baseball cards *glued* on the wall. The living room wasn't ransacked, but it was like kids fooling around in there. They were hanging out. There was a bottle of soda on the floor. I had club soda in the refrigerator and there was a bottle of soda on the floor. But in the bedroom it was ransacked. They had pulled everything out of the closet and everything was thrown all over. I was missing the jewelry I had that was up in the shoe box. The shoe box was there but it was empty. The stuff was taken out of it—the cameras, all of my photography equipment. The bags were there but they were empty. They took all of my equipment. It came to about two thousand dollars, with

Push-in robbers and holdup men will use any ruse to get into an apartment they suspect may hold valuables or cash. Such bandits have been arrested in painters' clothes, toting brushes and pails, and in utility-company uniforms complete with tool-laden belts and fake identification cards. Always direct that ID cards be slipped under the door, not passed through the crack in a door held by a chain. Most chain mountings are so flimsy that they can't withstand a real shove.

Laminated identification cards should be scrutinized carefully. Such cards, especially those with photographs, are very easy to fake. "It's a snap," says one anti-crime detective. "The hood puts his own snapshot on top of the picture already on the ID and then has the whole card re-laminated, identifying himself as the owner of the card. It's scary how well it works. Unless you look carefully at the picture and compare it with the physical characteristics usually listed on the card you're going to be had."

Important as it is to keep strangers out of your apartment, it's also vital to make sure that an intruder isn't already in your flat when you come home. There were nearly 174,500 burglaries reported in the city in the first ten months last year, and on too many of those occasions hapless residents were further victimized when they stumbled in on the burglar.

According to police, the average burglar spends about three minutes in an apartment. He usually wants to get in and out as quickly as possible. One trick suggested by veteran detectives to avoid interrupting a burglar in action is to leave a $20 or $50 bill within sight of the entry hall. Thus, if the money is gone when you open your door, you know that someone has been inside your apartment and may still be there. In that case, don't go in. Quietly close the door and run to a neighbor's apartment and call the police. Tell the 911 operator that there is a

jewelry and the photography
equipment. It was about two
thousand dollars worth of
stuff and it also happened
to be everything that I had
that was of value. . . . I
didn't call [the police] from
work. I came home immediately
and figured, let me see what's
going on. My boss said to
me, "I heard your phone
call—go home," and I left
right away. I got home at
four o'clock and I walked
into the house and saw what
was there. My son was white.
He was very, very upset. I
mean he was white. He
couldn't talk. I looked
around and went into the
bedroom and my heart sank.
By the time the cops came I
knew what had happened.
[My son] told me about the
key, and that he saw [Paul]
take it, and what have you.
I told this to the cops.
When they came in they looked
around. The baseball cards
were pasted on the wall. I
had like a photo-mount that
you spray. They had done
this and stuck the baseball
cards on the wall in my

burglary "in progress," so that a radio car will be dispatched as soon as possible. Completed burglaries rarely get an immediate response from the police.

If you are asleep in your apartment when you hear a burglar, do not give any sign of being awake. Let the burglar take what he wants, and as soon as you're certain he is gone, call the police. If you are far enough from the burglar to call for assistance, remember that a dial phone makes so much noise it may alert the intruder. It is best to have a silent, Touch-Tone phone near your bed.[5]

In pocket picking and purse snatching, the target of the criminal is some extension of the victim's self—the money, the credit cards, the wallet. The victim loses these symbols of self and experiences the violation of trust and autonomy that is at the center of every personal crime. A person expects to be able to walk down the street without having his or her property stolen. When a wallet or purse is taken, the victim suffers a rude reminder of vulnerability. Usually these crimes involve only momentary contact, but they are still personal affronts.[6]

. . . the psychological response to sudden and unexpected loss is easily recognizable as the same phases seen in depression. This concept is of clinical value in the psychological treatment of victims. What has the victim of violence lost? It is more than just the loss of money and the loss of physical functioning. They have lost the feeling of individual invulnerability. They have lost their trust in society, which they have depended on to protect them from harm. Many have lost their self-respect when they view their compliant behavior with shame and they have gained the unenviable status of being a victim.[7]

New Yorkers are hiring their own troops in the war on crime. They are paying

living room, but to me it's telling me these are not burglars, professionals. It was kids, with the soda on the floor. So I told the cops what had happened and they said, "Did they glue the pictures on the wall?" and I said yes. They took one down to see it. They found fingerprints. They made a report and they looked. They looked at the closet, they checked for fingerprints on the card, and then they said they didn't have any fingerprints, and they wrote CASE CLOSED on the paper. I saw him write down, "Case closed." I thought that was a hell of a note. I'm standing and telling him where my stuff is and he's writing "case closed" on the paper. I knew right there, where I stood. I told him what happened and I said, "This guy came and took my key. He lives next door." I said, "Please, if I could get my cameras back, would you please just go over there?" "No, we can't go over without a warrant.

sizable sums to private security firms for guards to patrol their blocks during the high-crime hours. Private guards, long commonplace in Manhattan's richest neighborhoods, are now watching over a growing number of communities throughout the city. And a host of security outfits—ranging from giants like Pinkerton's, Inc., to mom-and-pop operations—are scrambling for their business.

Hiring private security, however, is more complicated than simply putting up the money and calling in the help. The very job of raising that money—usually delegated to block or neighborhood associations—can be a daunting experience. Then, too, neighborhoods have to be prepared to provide their own systems to ensure their paid guards are doing the job.

In the end, though, private security is often worth the effort. Many of the neighborhoods using private guards say that crime has been cut back on their blocks and that residents tend to feel more at ease.[8]

During questioning, the victim may be asked things that seem irrelevant or unnecessarily personal. The victim should feel free to ask police officers about anything he or she does not understand, including matters of procedure and the meaning of unfamiliar terms. Sometimes an officer will seem reluctant to answer questions or seem annoyed by them. The police can forget that what is routine for them can be puzzling or upsetting for a crime victim. Occasionally a victim's questions are experienced as second-guessing by the officer. These attitudes may be understandable, but they should not dissuade the victim from seeking clarification.[9]

Did anyone see him?'' they
said. That's all I got out
of them and I said no, my
son saw him take the key.
"Did anybody see him take
the cameras? Did anyone
see him with the cameras?''
and I said no. "But see, to
me, I can't make the leap.
Everyone else seems to, but
I can't make the leap that
this kid did come in and
take the key,'' the cop said.
They also asked my son,
"Does your mother have any
money or gold jewelry around?''
No. To me if a person comes
into your house, steals the
key to your apartment, and
asks if there's any money or
jewelry around, to me it's
telling me that they're
looking to steal something.
But the law cannot make that
leap. They say that one
incident has nothing to do
with the other. . . . Exactly
a year before, for a good
time they were going to hurt
him, break my son's arm. I
wanted the police to protect
us and I went and told them
what happened, and I wanted
this kid arrested for

Sometimes a victim will remember something about the crime several days or even weeks after the police have asked their first questions. For example, burglary victims commonly discover, over a period of days after the crime, additional items that have been stolen. It is important to let the police know about these additional facts in the case, even if the information seems trivial. Part of the police investigation involves constructing what is called an MO (from modus operandi, "a method of procedure"), a description of the way particular criminals operate. By accumulating details and arranging them in a pattern, the investigators can sometimes develop a unique individual portrait of the criminal.[10]

*97th Congress
2D Session
S.2420
IN THE HOUSE OF
REPRESENTATIVES
September 16, 1982
Referred to the Committee
on the Judiciary
AN ACT
To protect victims of crime.*

Be it enacted by the Senate and House of Representatives of the United States of America in Congress assembled, That this Act may be cited as the "Omnibus Victims Protection Act of 1982."

assault: You did this act,
you pay the consequences,
you must understand that
society won't accept this.
You can't go around kicking
somebody's face because you
feel good. When I went to
the police, there is a
woman there, a switchboard
operator. She's sitting at
a kind of telephone console
and you cannot get past
this woman. She talks to
you like you can't believe,
like you're an idiot. I
kept insisting, "Lady, a
bunch of kids are having a
fight." "The police can't
be bothered with this," and
this is all I got. I was
there for a couple of hours
talking, insisting with
these people. The hardest
one to get past was this
woman. She's screaming at
you and the cops come over
and start telling you, "Don't
yell at her," and that's how
they come over. Right away
you're telling them my son
was beat up and the cops
say, "Hey, lady, you stop
yelling at her." My point
was, I wanted this kid

FINDINGS AND PURPOSE

Sec.2. (a) The Congress finds and declares that:

(1) *Without the cooperation of victims and witnesses, the criminal justice system would cease to function; yet with few exceptions these individuals are either ignored by the criminal justice system or simply used as tools to identify and punish offenders.*

(2) *All too often the victim of a serious crime is forced to suffer physical, psychological, or financial hardship first as a result of the criminal act and then as a result of contact with a criminal justice system unresponsive to the real needs of such victims.*

(3) *Although the majority of serious crimes falls under the jurisdiction of State and local law enforcement agencies, the Federal Government, and in particular the Attorney General, have an important leadership role to assume in ensuring that victims of crime, whether at the Federal, State, or local level, are given proper treatment by agencies administering the criminal justice system.*

(4) *Under the current law, law enforcement agencies must have cooperation from victims of crime and yet neither the agencies nor the legal system can offer protection or assistance when such victim as a result of such cooperation, is threatened or intimidated.*

arrested. He assaulted my son. After the cops finally saw they weren't getting anywhere, they told me to go in the back. There were some cops to talk to in the back. There were two cops, oldtimers, and you couldn't get past these guys. They were telling you and treating you as if you were a hysterical woman. After a lot of insistence, they said I needed to talk to the detectives. This is another run. See, I know this police station. The next runaround. The detectives are upstairs and there's no one there. The detectives are out, there's a bomb threat at LaGuardia, there's a double homicide in Forest Hills, they can't see you, come back tomorrow. Got a runaround. You have to keep insisting that you're not leaving. Finally, the detectives saw that they weren't getting anywhere with me, so one came over and he sat down and talked, and they said to me—"Well, you see, we can't arrest

(5) *While the defendant is provided with counsel who can explain to him both the criminal justice process and his rights, the victim or witness has no counterpart and is usually not even notified when the defendant is released on bail, the case is dismissed, a plea to a lesser charge is accepted, or a court date is changed.[11]*

(b) *The Congress declares that the purposes of this Act are—*

(1) *to enhance and protect the necessary role of crime victims and witnesses in the criminal justice process;*

(2) *to ensure that the Federal Government does all that is possible within the limits of available resources to assist victims and witnesses of crime without infringing on the constitutional rights of the defendant; and*

(3) *to provide a victim/witness model for State and local law enforcement officials.[12]*

Brooklyn's new District Attorney Elizabeth Holtzman is making a bold beginning. She is reorganizing her office to upgrade the investigation of crime cases in the crucial hours following an arrest when assistant DAs determine whether and on what charge a suspect can be prosecuted.

Holtzman's action goes to the nub of a damaging row which has been raging for several years between New York City's cops and assistant DAs throughout the five boroughs over the treatment of crime suspects.

The ADAs contend that the police do not bring in enough evidence to make many of the arrests stand up and that's why felony charges must often be reduced

him because you son doesn't have any marks on him,'' and they all insisted that this was the reason. Later, I was told by the Assistant District Attorney as well that the police were *right*! They can't arrest someone if there aren't any marks on the person. Now, I don't know whether this pertains to adolescents, because I think they have rights like anyone else. I think, imagine anyone trying to break MY arm! But according to the police, if you don't have any marks on you, you haven't been hurt. But what I'm saying is that I have my opinions of the police. . . . *This* time, I asked them [to go next door], and I explained to them what had happened last year. They told me they couldn't go because there was no eyewitness to this boy taking this stuff, so they had no cause to get a warrant. . . . I mean, I can't accept it like that, you know, ''Case closed,'' and they leave, goodbye. I couldn't accept that.

to misdemeanors. The cops, on the other hand, argue that the ADAs prefer to build a record of convictions and tend to set aside the more complex cases.

Of the 98,923 felony arrests in New York City in 1980, the five District Attorney's offices secured only 20,041 indictments. In Brooklyn last year, there were 29,000 arrests but only 6,000 indictments.

In sum, almost 80 percent of felony arrests in the criminal justice system appear to be deteriorating into misdemeanors or violations, or are being dismissed without being brought to court.

The Brooklyn DA's office will now have a Deputy Bureau Chief with the sole task of supervising the examination of cases as they are brought in. Between 5 p.m. and midnight, peak crime period in Brooklyn, additional ADAs will help handle the load.

A computer system is being introduced to reduce the time police, victims and witnesses have to spend in the DA's office providing evidence. Right now this takes 1 1/2 to 5 hours.

A computer will also tell prosecutors immediately whether a defendant has a record or is awaiting trial on another case in Brooklyn.

Finally, Holtzman is ending the system of referring cases back to the police for further investigation. This has usually resulted in such cases being written off completely. Instead, police will be told specifically what aspects of the case need strengthening and the DA's office will then check back after two weeks.

Many of these improvements were outlined by Holtzman during her campaign for DA last year. If they increase the number of indictments, it will be compelling reason to introduce them throughout the city.[13]

Another common, and sometimes overwhelming, feeling after the crime is an intense anger toward the criminal. Feel-

First, I called [my councilman's] office, because I
knew he was a person that
tried to help citizens. I
explained and the man that
answered the phone said to
me, "You know, we have free
legal advice on Tuesday
evenings, so come down."
There was a young lawyer
there. I explained to him
the situation. Oh, before
I did this—excuse me,
it's a long story—I got to
talk to this detective. It
bothered me that they just
walked off, and that was
the end of the case. I
went to the police precinct
[that night] with my son
to tell him what happened,
and I talked to a detective
to see what happens, because
I know the next level after
the patrolman is detective.
To me, like I say, when you
hear this story I don't know
how you can say I don't have
a case, so I said to myself,
"Well, that was *those* cops.
Let me go down and talk to a
detective." I did, and let
me tell you something—to go
from my house to the police

ings of rage can be especially difficult
because victims usually have no realistic
means to vent their anger on the criminal. Most victims never see the criminal
again. Even if the offender is apprehended and successfully prosecuted, the
legal proceedings will take months. The
absence of the criminal creates an emotional vacuum; the victim has no way to
confront the person who has made him or
her so angry. One way to release these
feelings is through fantasy. Fantasies and
dreams about revenge are not uncom-
mon, especially among victims who have
suffered physical violence. The imagined
retribution may be quite graphic and
violent; in some cases it will seem shocking to the victim.[14]

*TITLE   V—FEDERAL   GUIDELINES
FOR FAIR TREATMENT OF CRIME
VICTIMS AND WITNESSES IN THE
CRIMINAL JUSTICE SYSTEM*

*Sec.501.(a) Within six months after the
date of enactment of this title, the Attorney General shall develop and implement
guidelines for the Department of Justice
consistent with the purposes of this Act.
The Attorney General shall assign re-
sponsibilities for the implementation of
each of the guidelines. In preparing the
guidelines the Attorney General shall
consider the following objectives:*

*(1)   SERVICES   TO   VICTIMS
OF CRIME.—Law enforce-
ment personnel should en-
sure that victims routinely
receive emergency social
and medical services as
soon as possible and are
given information on the following—*

*(A)   availability of crime
victim   compensation
(where applicable);*

(B)   community-based vic-

station is two-and-a-half
hours on the train, because
I live in Jackson Heights
and this is in Astoria. You
got to take the train, a bus,
and a train. There's no
local precinct; they are
building one now. But anyway I went, but I'm not
doing this because I don't
have nothing better to do
with my time, right? We
went over to the precinct
over there and I told my
little story. Again, getting
past the same woman, the
receptionist, is the hard
part. She's telling me I
don't want the police. I
want to go down and file
for harassment, and she's
telling me this *is* harassment. I'm telling *her* what
happened with my boy (see,
you have to explain the
story before you get past
her to a cop), so I'm telling
her what happened and she
said to me, "Lady, that's
not burglary, that's
harassment." So we waltz
around with that, and a cop
came over and told me to
shut up and stop yelling at

tim treatment pro-
grams;

(C) their role in the criminal justice process, in-
cluding what they can
expect from them;

(D) key points in the criminal justice process at
which they might want
to request information
as to the status of their
particular case and
suggestions on how
best to request this in-
formation; and

(E) ability of law enforcement officers to protect
victims and witnesses
from intimidation.[15]

The provision of transportation, housing,
subsistence, or other assistance to a person under section 3521 may be condi-
tioned by the Attorney General upon
reimbursement of expenses in whole or in
part to the United States by a State or
local government.[16]

A violent crime occurs every 24 seconds in our nation. Every 6 minutes a
woman is raped. Every 58 seconds someone is robbed. Every 23 minutes a life is
lost to murder. And these statistics reflect
only those crimes reported to the authorities. How can we urge others to come
forward when we know the reception
awaiting them by those officials charged
with enforcing the laws that have been
broken? How can we ask victims and
witnesses to pore over mug shots, sit
through lineups, offer testimony, relive
the experience, when their trauma is
entirely overlooked? In my opinion, we
cannot. What we can do, however, is
reform a system far out of balance.[17]

her, but this is their routine. This is how you're treated. Like you're the criminal, like a real nothing. The criminal they treat real nicely. You are treated like a total idiot. . . . I went upstairs to the detectives and naturally they're gone—come back tomorrow. So I said, "Look, I can't come back tomorrow. If I come back tomorrow I have to start all over again, and nobody is going to know me tomorrow. Could you give me some piece of paper of the times?" They would not. I knew the next day I would go through this all over again, which I did. I got up at six o'clock in the morning. I called my boss and said I would be in late, and then went back the first thing in the morning. Finally, we saw a detective. There was a detective there and he said, "We'll call you." He listened to my story. We talked, and they kept all along insisting (from day one they have insisted) that I have no

I get angry when . . . I was robbed last year, some of my personal belongings were gone. Although I reported to the police station, what's the good of it? I get angry when I was almost raped in the elevator. I felt so angry towards the landlady because of her negligence in not fixing the door. I was almost raped. I could have been killed, raped or anything, although I considered myself so lucky. But I can't help but feel so angry, so blue. I wish I could strangle, or kill something, yet I could not. I want to scream at someone, but whom could I scream at? I had to control myself.[18]

A crime victim's assistance program, funded by state money and implemented through coordination of eight Nassau departments and the courts system, is in place and functioning, County Executive Francis T. Purcell announced recently.

Called the Community Justice Program, the system aims to assist the victims of crimes and witnesses in criminal cases. It also offers dispute mediation through the American Arbitration Association at no charge.

"This program is designed to assist needy victims of crime quickly and effectively," Purcell said. "It is not a compensation for losses of property, since that is addressed elsewhere in the state law. It is a helping hand for the victim to proceed through the criminal justice system, to get counseling where it is needed, to get carfare for court appearances, and to get compensation for wages lost in court visits.

"Too often the poor victim of a crime

eyewitness, so I don't have a case of burglary. But you see, the whole thing that I'm trying to say is that, from day one—from the minute this burglary is committed (and I think that I'm typical) the criminal's rights—everybody's worried about his rights, everybody's worried about him. Not a thought is given to you. I mean, as a human being who something has happened to them. Not even what would you call sympathy. . . . There was this detective, I'll call him detective D. He calls me and I explained the story on the phone. I said, "Would you please just come and talk to my son?" I asked the detective to come to my house, please, and listen to my son and listen to our story, and he did. We talked and my son described the whole thing to him, and he said he couldn't [make an] arrest because I didn't have an eyewitness. He said, "You're probably right, it

is reluctant to assist authorities because of the expense of court appearances or the loss of modest wages. Then too, a victim sometimes suffers trauma and needs professional assistance and support."[19]

Thirty percent of the nation's households were touched by a crime in 1981, the same percentage as the year before, a Justice Department report said today.

The report, from the Bureau of Justice Statistics, said nearly 25 million households experienced a crime of violence or theft last year, 2 percentage points less than recorded in 1975, when 32 percent of households were affected.

The statistics, based on a twice-yearly survey of 132,000 people in 60,000 households, also showed that in 1981 10 percent of all households were touched by a burglary or a violent crime by a stranger: rape, robbery or assault.

"The kinds of households that were the most vulnerable to crime in 1975— black households, higher-income households and households in central cities— remained so in 1981," the report said.

CRIME RATE DROPS 2 POINTS

The Federal Bureau of Investigation said last month that the number of serious crimes reported to law-enforcement agencies in 1981 remained virtually unchanged from 1980 and the country's crime rate dropped 2 points.

The crime statistics were made public at a time when the Reagan Administration is pushing tougher anticrime measures in Congress. Last week, President Reagan proposed a legislative package for Federal courts that would limit the insanity defense, revise the rule of excluding illegally obtained evidence at criminal trials and limit a defendant's ability to obtain Federal court review of convictions returned in state courts.

The Justice Department report said American families were more likely to

probably did happen,'' and he
was sympathetic. Talked
nice but couldn't do
anything. . . . After that
I had this feeling that I
couldn't accept this, so I
wanted to talk to somebody
who knew about these things,
[at the councilman's place].
The lawyer there told me,
first of all, ''You have a
witness, your *son* is a
witness.'' See, the police
never told me, never
mentioned it. All they kept
telling me is that I *don't*
have a witness and the lawyer
said, ''Your son is a witness.
He saw him take the key,''
and he said right there he
should be arrested for that.
So I had to call the
detective back and tell him
that, and he said, ''Yeah,
I know your son's a witness.''
I mean, he didn't tell me
that until *I* told *him*, and
then he said, ''Yeah, okay,
[Paul] will be brought in
for questioning.'' But the
next time I called the
detective and asked him
what happened, he said, ''He
didn't do it.'' Well, really,

have a member attacked in a serious violent crime, meaning rape, robbery or aggravated assault, than to suffer a residential fire or have a family member injured in a car accident.

More than 20 percent of American households were subjected to a larceny, and in 7 percent of the cases someone broke in or tried to burglarize the home, the report said.

Almost half of the households touched by violent crime in 1981 experienced only simple assault. About 3 percent of all American households had members who were victims of rape, robbery or aggravated assault.

Last year, a higher proportion of black than white households was touched by crime: nearly 35 percent for blacks and 29 percent for whites.[20]

I get angry when . . . I experience or hear of the so-called justice system permitting most criminals to either obtain reduced sentences or to be freed outright. I also feel angry when I know that the drug (heroin, cocaine, etc.) business functions outright in this country; that corrupt politicians and the police, who after getting paid off in graft, either purposely impede justice or disrupt the legal system for their own benefit and the aims of the drug distributor. I also get angry when I sense the situation of lawyers paying off judges in order to get a favorable decision. I get angry when I realize that crime will never diminish in this country. I also get angry believing that this government wasted 56,000 soldiers in the Vietnam War due to the fact that they all died defending a society where most criminals, especially those involved in the drug trade were, and are, still able to profit from the lives of their captives.[21]

I felt like, I don't know
how to explain it, but a
feeling like, "It doesn't
work for you." I'm telling
these people this, I'm really
not being facetious, but I
felt through this whole
thing like Alice in Wonderland talking to the mad
rabbit. They come out with
these stupid things. . . .
So I called the Assistant
District Attorney. I went
back to the lawyer and told
him what happened and the
lawyer said, "Look, if you
want him arrested, insist
he be arrested, because
your son is a witness and
they should arrest [Paul]."
So that's when I called the
Assistant District Attorney.
There were a couple of calls
to the Assistant District
Attorney, then it was a
couple of calls to the
detective, and finally the
detective said he was going
to arrest [Paul] and time
kept going by. I mean, a
month would go by, because
I didn't want to bug these
people. I mean, I would say
a month went by and the kid

I get angry when . . . I feel threatened
and abused, taken advantage of and
defenseless. I feel anger when I feel
that I'm not getting what I need from
another or when I feel something is
being taken away from me that I need.
I get angry when I feel unappreciated,
diminished, or belittled. I get angry
when I have worked hard for something I feel I deserve and that reward is
denied me or taken away. I feel angry
when I am at loss in knowing how to
handle a difficult situation and wish it
had never arisen. I often ask, why does
life have to be so hard?[22]

ain't arrested and I see him
walking around . . . and in
the meantime, you can be
sure all of my equipment is
gone by then. Every time I
would call the detective and
ask him what happened he'd
tell me, "Gee, you know, I've
been to his house a couple of
times and he's never home."
So this went on *a couple of
months*, and again I called
the Assistant District
Attorney. This is why I
called him a few times and
finally they must have got
on his tail. I mean, I
kept persisting, and finally
he was arrested on a mis-
demeanor, for stealing *a
key*. So I went to the
complaint room, because I
felt that they should know
the story. I just wanted to
be sure that the Assistant
District Attorney knew the
story, because on paper a
kid stealing a key could be
nothing; this Assistant
District Atorney said that
the key was worth maybe
seventy-five cents, it's a
very minor charge. He was
really angry because I kept

*The testimony of one of the victims still
rings in my ears. "Don't confuse cold
with professional," she said. "We need
to examine our own feelings about crime.
Because of our discomfort with the issue
of crime, society tends to treat its victims
as anathema. Ask them to emphasize
respect."*

*It is distressing to think we must
statutorily define the justice system's sensitivity toward people. But the needed
changes are obvious—and overdue. The
challenge is for Congress to act before
too many others are victimized, both by
those who choose to break the law and by
those who are charged with enforcing
it.[23]*

*TITLE   I—VICTIM'S   IMPACT
STATEMENT*

*Sec.101. Subsection (c)(2) of rule 32 of
the Federal Rules of Criminal Procedure
is amended by striking "", and such other
information as may be required by the
court" and inserting in lieu thereof:
"The report shall also contain verified
information stated in a nonargumentative
style assessing the financial, social, psychological, and medical impact upon and
cost to any person who was the victim of
the offense committed by the defendant.
The report shall also include a statement
of any need of the victim for restitution
and any such other information as may be
required by the court."[24]*

insisting that this guy
stole my stuff, and he kept
insisting that you don't have any
eyewitnesses, you
don't know if he did it.
He said to me, "Do you want
to see a boy go to jail for
a seventy-five-cent key?"
Those were his words. Like
I came out of the woodwork
and bothered this boy,
persecuted this innocent boy,
because I'm a crazy lady or
something. . . . At the
arraignment [that night] we
sat there from six-thirty and we
got out of court that night
at eleven-thirty. It's a desk
appearance ticket—[Paul]
was supposed to be in court,
and the complainant is
supposed to be there. Well,
the fella [in the complaint
room] that we told the story
to charged [Paul] with two
counts of burglary, because
both times he entered my
house was against—you
know,
he never had my permission
to come into my house on
both occasions—grand
larceny, for stealing
two thousand dollars worth

Hundreds of public school administrators and key law enforcement officials gathered yesterday for the first time to discuss ways of coordinating their handling of the growing problem of juvenile crime in New York City and its schools.

"Crimes for which juveniles are arrested today are more ruthless and remorseless and criminally sophisticated," Deputy Police Commissioner Kenneth Conboy told 300 people at Manhattan's Park West High School.

The impetus for the meeting, said Deputy Mayor Robert F. Wagner Jr., was that "some numbers from the year before were quite alarming."

Among these, Mr. Conboy said, are statistics showing that the arrest rate for children 15 years and younger in New York City was four times the national average, that one-eighth of all arrests for juvenile crime in the United States are made in this city and that from 1970 to 1978, the arrest rate for serious and violent juvenile crimes in New York increased 81 percent.

Hampering past efforts to reduce the crime rate, officials acknowledged, was the frequently poor coordination among principals and superintendents, school safety officers, the police and the courts. The gathering's practical purpose was to introduce representatives from each of these areas to one another.[25]

of equipment, and a mis-
demeanor for stealing the
key. [Paul] was there with
his mother, and I heard the
Legal Aid lawyer (he was
appointed a Legal Aid because
his mother has too many
dependents or something) ask
him did he work, and he said
no. I heard this lawyer
talking and she asked him if
he went to school and he said
no, and to me it tells me
something: He was a kid (at
that time he was sixteen).
If the kid stops going to
school when he's fourteen
years old, and he doesn't
work, it tells me that
something is wrong there,
because how is this kid
going to make a living in
his life? I mean, people
might feel that you can't
legislate, a person has the
freedom, you can't force a
person to work, or after a
certain age go to school, but
all I'm saying is that, isn't
that telling you something
about a person??? Because
he's out of work, and not in
school, so he has no source
of income. . . . So, anyway,

Terry Selzer, a former Brooklyn Legal Aid lawyer now in private practice, said that what is happening in Tom Noel's case is not unusual, under the circumstances. "When you don't feel you have a strong defense you wait . . . and the practice has been when the case has been around for a long time, the charges will come down."

But, there may be other possible reasons too for delays on the part of the defense legal aid attorney. One of them is the exhaustion factor. "I did back-to-back trials for two years straight," he said. "It gets exhausting. If you finish a trial and start another the next day, you might do anything to get a breather."

Solman said, from his viewpoint, that the single biggest problem bogging down the courts is volume. "Every lawyer's got a lot of cases, a crowded calendar, it just multiplies." He said he normally works on 20 to 40 felony cases and 20 to 40 misdemeanor cases at any one time.[26]

he was arraigned. They were
very shocked because of these
charges. Then we went to
court. The next one was
like a hearing. I testified
and my son testified, and I
remembered when I came out
(see, this is another thing
very strange to me), when I
came out of the room and
when I testified, my son
wasn't there. They told him
to leave the room. He
testified and they told me
to leave, and when I finished
testifying they told us *both*
to wait outside, so we
didn't hear the deliberating.
But I remember the Assistant
District Attorney coming out
and saying, "You won everything because he's going to
be tried on felony charges."
Now, the *next* time I went
to court, they told me that
the felony charges were
dropped. He's only going to
be tried for the misdemeanor,
for stealing the key. The
felony charges were dropped
because I didn't have an eyewitness. . . . The case
isn't closed yet. Again I
sat for three days, and I'm

*Students and professionals in the crimi-
nal justice system have become increasingly aware that a victim of a criminal
becomes—more often than not—also the
victim of the criminal justice system.
Once the victim reports his victimization
to the police—the gateway to the criminal
justice system—he or she is routinely
faced by postponements, delays, resched-
ulings, and other abuses. All this means
loss of earnings, waste of time, frustration, and the painful realization that the
system does not live up to its ideals and
does not serve its constituency, but instead serves itself and its underlings. As a
consequence, many innovative proposals
have been advanced, such as the creation
of central citizens complaint and service
bureaus; witness coordinators at police
stations, courthouses, district attorneys'
offices, and defenders' offices; participation of the victim in plea bargaining by
prosecutors; reports, at some point, by
police to victims on whether they are
making progress in investigating and
solving their cases; the provision of the
services of an ombudsman who would
assist the victims of crime by intervening
in the crisis, acting as a community
facilitator, and referring the victims to
the community's and other resources; the
establishment of Rape Crisis Centers,
and other victim assistance organizations.*[27]

*Programs to aid victims of crime have
been emerging across the country in recent years as criminal-justice authorities
and social scientists have increasingly
advocated their establishment with public
funds. The problems that crime victims
face can be immediate or long-term,
practical or psychological—or all of
these.*
*They may involve the need for emer-
gency funds for a poor family whose
breadwinner has been slain by robbers.
Another murder victim's family may need
help coping with the psychological im-*

telling you, you're there
at nine-thirty. We had left
the court at five o'clock
all three days, sat there
all day one day, on standby.
Now, another point I'm
bringing out is that this
boy was appointed a Legal
Aid lawyer—it won't cost
this family a penny. Our
case has been postponed
because she's been called
somewhere else and she has
to leave, and he's entitled
to have her for a lawyer.
If she can't be there the
case is postponed. It don't
matter if *I* have to sit there,
if *I* have to take off from
work another day, or my son
has to take off from *school*,
that doesn't matter. [Paul's]
precious right to have the
same lawyer comes first. . . .
Victim's rights in this case?
Even though you have been
ripped off, and you know that
your boss may dock you, nobody asks *you* that. Ever.
But I have to say that every
Assistant District Attorney
that I have talked to since
then, there's been maybe
four or five, have all been

pact of the crime. A poor victim of a burglary may not be able to pay for a smashed-in apartment door.

And whatever the crime, there are the often confusing, inconvenient, even intimidating court proceedings, for victims and witnesses, that follow arrests. With their multiple hearings, adjournments and other delays, these proceedings can add to the anxieties and burdens of victims and witnesses, and have discouraged many from participating in prosecutions.[28]

The median length of time that it takes for a felony case to go from indictment to disposition—either guilty or innocent—in New York City is 151 days, according to the 1982 Felony Processing Report soon to be released by the State Division of Criminal Justice. And in Brooklyn, between January and October 1982, the median was 190 days or more than six months. Judge Joseph D. Williams, an Administrative Judge for Criminal Courts in New York City in charge of the Felony Backlog Program, says it is hard to identify single factors as the cause for delays. He cites requests by attorneys, the availability of witnesses and courtrooms, timely motions, and missing materials all as variables that could affect the length of time between arrest and disposition of a case. "The court has set a standard for itself in trying to dispose of felony cases within six terms of the court, almost six months," Williams said. "But it depends . . . "[29]

The Victim Services Agency grew out of a pilot project run in cooperation with the Brooklyn District Attorney. Mayor Koch made the effort citywide by establishing the agency in 1978. Its current budget of $4.5 million a year comes largely from

very nice, very under-
standing, very reasonable.
This last bunch I was with
in court tell me they really
felt bad about the felony
charges being dropped. They
told me that they really would
like to see this kid get it.
He strikes them as a real
punk and they really think
that something should be
done, like to see this kid
get it. He strikes them as
a real punk and they really
think that something should
be done, rather than letting
this kid go on with his
behavior. . . . I have to
say, this detective—I mean,
point of fact, he's right.
He knows this case was
going nowhere. He didn't
care about my feelings, but
in fact the man wasn't wrong.
It's going exactly the way
he said it was going, no-
where. And he knew it. . . .
Victim Services Agency were
very nice. I talked to a
woman and she came and she
asked if I had any problems,
if I didn't understand what
was going on in court. I
went to them because the

*Federal community development funds
and city grants. . . .*

*The agency explains court proceed-
ings to victims and witnesses, notifies
them when they are needed in court and
provides places for them to wait until
their cases are called. In Brooklyn Criminal Court and Bronx Family Court, it
also has day-care facilities for the children of those involved in the courts'
cases. . . .*

*"Without the support services that the
Victim Services Agency offers, the pros-
ecution of cases would be even less,"
Mr. Keating said.*

*"They are serving a real need that
exists," District Attorney John J.
Santucci of Queens commented.*

*But Mr. Merola, while stressing that
he favors such efforts, added: "I'd like to
see more of the money go to victims and
less to the bureaucracy. . . .*

*While bureaucracy and jurisdiction
are discussed at the higher levels, people
like Elaine Smith, the agency's supervi-
sor in Brooklyn Criminal Court, focus on
more immediate matters.*

*She helped the elderly burglary victim
from Flatbush sign papers needed to
prosecute a suspect arrested in the case,
and had an aide arrange for a taxi to take
the woman home at the agency's
expense. . . .*

*Nearby, Wanda Soto, an agency
counselor, was helping a young Bedford-
Stuyvesant woman prepare for a criminal
proceeding against her former husband,
whom she had accused of assaulting and
harassing her.*

*"When they come into court," Miss
Soto said, "they want to know, 'What's
going to happen in my case?' They also
need emotional support."[30]*

*It became clear to McGuire in New York
that if felony arrests were to become
felony convictions, witnesses and victims
could not be treated thoughtlessly. Detectives assigned to . . . cases would need*

first encounter with an Assistant District Attorney was very upsetting to me. He was yelling at me, asking did I want a boy sent to jail, and I thought, *"This man is representing ME? My God, I'd be lucky if I don't get sentenced."* So I was very upset. There was a sign in the complaint room about Victim Services, so I figured, let me talk to someone there, because I really felt like Alice in Wonderland. And they referred me to Crime Victims' Counseling Services. These nitpicking details are what being a victim *is about.* It wears you into the ground. See, I've lived this. I feel strongly and maybe it's too vague a thing to say, but I think our approach to the system is wrong. I'm not a learned lawyer or judge or what have you. You knew this before, but it just kind of confirms things, and you watch and you know very well that people are let go and let go. What I'm saying is so

patience to pursue reluctant victims. They would also have to be given what the street cop seldom has, the time and money to make the case.[31]

The agency is generally lauded by criminal-justice authorities in the city as providing services that are vital and long overdue. . . .

    "The large bulk of cases that fail do so because of witness problems," said Robert G.M. Keating, New York City's criminal-justice coordinator. "And the victim is the key witness in almost every case."

    Until recently, victim-aid advocates say, such concerns have taken a back seat as the rights of defendants have received the lion's share of attention from civil libertarians and the courts. But now, they say, there is not only increasing recognition of the aid often needed by victims and witnesses, but also realization that failure to provide such aid can slow down or thwart the criminal-justice process.[32]

. . . and for others whose lives have been touched by crime, the pain never ends. All too often, Mayor Koch said, much of that pain stems from the criminal justice system. Yesterday at a City Hall rally, Koch proclaimed this week Victims Rights Week.

    "In the past, it was all too common for victims of crime to be victimized twice: the first time by the criminal, the second time by the system itself," he said.

    In 1978, Koch created the Victims Services Agency to provide victims and their families with financial aid, counseling and help in cutting red tape. Since then, the agency has served 150,000 people.

    Alvin Pierce, whose 17-year-old son was gunned down last May at the South Bronx grocery store where he worked, spoke at the rally on behalf of the families

obvious: They are so
worried about these people's
rights that they let them
get away and they know they
are getting away with it. I
see this kid [Paul] all the
time. That day I came home
from court he sticks out, I
mean deliberate like, this
kind of look [gesture] but
he could care less. I really
feel the whole approach, the
crime, is one about worrying
about the criminals' rights,
about protecting the criminal.
Any intelligent person—I
mean, look, we certainly
don't want a police state,
but it's very obvious to
anybody that sees the
judicial system, the court
system, the police, that
nothing works. I don't
blame the police, believe
me. I don't think we have
enough of them. As I say,
this detective was right,
he wasn't wrong. He was
saving himself, he was
saving the government a lot
of money, he was saving himself a lot of time. I do
think the man was very busy.
I don't think they have

of murder victims. He said that they seek the right to protest plea bargains, to argue for a speedy trial, to be informed of the progress of the proceedings, to obtain a free trial transcript and to describe to the sentencing judge the impact of the crime on their lives.[33]

I feel powerless when . . . I don't know my rights—I am being sloughed off (i.e., victimized)—out-talked—timid—afraid they won't like me—etc. etc. etc. I know I am powerless when I lose my temper—anger makes me a victim. Again, knowledge of rights—prior knowledge so I won't be surprised if I *am* powerless. There are things I *cannot* control—realization of these and let it go—know the things I can do something about—*that* is power![34]

The effectiveness of victimology should reach the level of the requirements of the cosmic environment and of its energies, of the nature of man, of the technological level of contemporary civilization and of its social trends with respect to the factors which create victims.

In order to reach this goal, nothing must be ignored, not even the results obtained through routine work, though these must, of course, be considered carefully and without blind conformity. On the contrary, victimology must concentrate, with initiative and sustained effort, on the essential needs of society. Finally, it must select methods which meet the realities of the situation, so as to find the solutions of various scientific and practical problems and open new roads.

The essential needs of society lead victimology first of all to become involved with the search for methods of preventing, to the full extent possible, individuals from becoming victims: from the physical or psychological point of view (death, injury, shock, etc.), as well as from the point of view of his possessions

enough police and detectives, but *where does that leave the victim*? I think a very strong case to me that points this up, the whole approach, is the recent incident where the woman, the pregnant woman, was raped. The man stabbed her baby and they determined—a lot of intelligent people with books—determined that this wasn't murder. What right do they have to tell a woman that her baby wasn't murdered? They're so worried about the criminals' rights. "The fetus doesn't breathe on its own until it's six months old." What kind of bull crap is that? This is a mother, and you killed her child, and it's murder. What about her rights? She was raped, she was stabbed, and her child was killed, and you're telling her that this man can't be charged with murder, blab, blab, blab. . . . The approach is wrong. I mean, in my case—not to harp on it, but I speak about it because it's something I'm

(damage, loss, etc.), of his honor (slander, etc.), and of the rights of man (annulment or limitation).

If and when an individual has become a victim, victimology shall search for methods of diminishing the harmfulness of the situation and of lessening the extent and the severity of the results, and for methods of preventing individuals from relapsing, that is becoming victims again.

It is important to emphasize that research must not be limited to anything less than the vital interests of society, and that it must reach the full potential made possible by progress in science, technology, education, legislation and administration.[35]

As all of you know, crime today is an American epidemic. It takes the lives of over 20,000 Americans a year, it touches nearly a third of American homes and results in about $8.8 billion a year in financial losses.

These statistics suggest that our criminal justice system has broken down, that it just isn't working. And many Americans are losing faith in it. Nine out of ten Americans believe that the courts in their home areas are not tough enough on criminals.

And the cold statistics do demonstrate the failure of our criminal justice system to adequately pursue, prosecute and punish criminals. In New York City, for example, less than 1 percent of reported felonies end in a prison term for the offender.

The perception is growing that the crime problem stems from the emergence of a new privileged class in America: A class of repeat offenders and career criminals who think they have a right to victimize their fellow citizens with virtual impunity. They are openly contemptuous of our way of justice; they do not believe they will be caught, and if they are caught, they are confident that once their

close to and I understand—
I say, if you know me, just
a neighbor, here's a woman
who for years goes to work,
comes home, doesn't bother
anybody, comes in, goes
out, works. And here's a
kid who hangs out, goes in
and out of apartments
stealing things, hangs out
with a gang that goes around
stealing things, and you're
telling me I don't have a
witness. If you knew me and
you knew him, you know I'm
not making up a story. I'm
implying there's something
wrong with the system.
Nobody knows. I think years
ago, when they had police
on the beat, policemen knew
the neighborhood. They know
Mrs. So-and-So, she goes to
work, she don't bother
nobody. They know the punks
who hang around the corner,
they know what's going on.
I got two-and-a-half hours to
get to my precinct. All
right, they're building
another one now, but I'm
saying, who knows you from a
hole in the wall??? I'm
talking to people, they can't

*cases enter our legal system the charges
will be dropped, postponed, plea-bar-
gained away or lost in a maze of legal
technicalities that make a mockery of our
legitimate and honorable concern with
civil liberties.*[36]

LET THE CRIME BILL DIE

*An anti-crime package left for President
Reagan by the last Congress will die
unless he signs it before Friday. It contains some good provisions—heavily out-
weighed by bad ones. The bill deserves a
peaceful death.*

*One laudable feature would provide
$127 million in sorely needed assistance
to local law enforcement agencies. It's a
modest amount, but at least it revives the
undervalued approach of the Law Enforcement Assistance Administration,
which encouraged innovation. Another
positive feature would strengthen drug
laws and make it easier for the Justice
Department to claim the assets of major
drug dealers.*

*Neither provision, however, justifies
acceptance of the bill's "career criminal" proposal. This misguided idea
would—with the concurrence of local
prosecutors and United States attorneys—let Federal courts try twice-
convicted felons charged with street*

even relate to you as a
human being. Where's the
touch? Where's the human
touch? Where is the humanity?
. . . Naturally, the people
that I'm close to, what I
have of a family, my brother
and sister-in-law were very
sweet. She has a large
family and that's about all
I have of a family. I have
another brother, but he's
a bachelor and he's floating
around. He called up and
said, "Gee, that's a shame
that someone had burglarized
you." He had caught some
burglars breaking into his
landlord's apartment and
chased them, but they got
away with it, so he was
commiserated in one phone
call. Couple of times we
talked about it, my sister-
in-law, and she's asked did
they catch the guy, but the
thing is, it came to a point
where I don't talk about it
because I feel like, "How
many times can you go
through it?" . . . [My boss]
just said, "You know, you
better go home." But you
see, the people that I work

crimes. Federal jurisdiction would sup-
posedly permit speedier trials and access
to Federal prison space. The bill also sets
a mandatory 15-year sentence as the
minimum for the repeating offenders.

All that may be desirable, but not
desirable enough to distort the Federal
role in the war on crime. Defining Federal jurisdiction and penalties by individual criminal rather than the type of crime
would violate accepted principle, create
an intolerable burden on Federal law
enforcement and grant excessive power
to local prosecutors. Washington best
fights street crime by limiting handguns,
pursuing its war on the drug trade and
leasing Federal prison space to states.

Also poorly conceived is the proposal
to create a Cabinet-level "drug czar."
The fragmented agencies that oversee
drug enforcement could indeed use more
coordination. But this bill would give one
Cabinet official authority over various
activities of Justice, Treasury and State.
Would he then bypass the chiefs of those
departments? Any attempt to exercise
such power would in fact increase conflict, not reduce it.

In any case, President Reagan has
already taken steps to coordinate anti-
drug activities. Vice President Bush over-
saw the Miami Task Force that claims
some success in a drug crackdown, and
the President's Cabinet Council on Legal
Affairs helped the Justice Department
with a plan for task forces in 12 cities.

What's more, the White House already has an adviser on drug policy, Dr.
Carleton Turner, who now concentrates
on education and prevention. Why not
simply expand his role? Effective coordination doesn't require a new law so much
as attention from the President.

The failure of the 97th Congress to
come up with a better crime bill creates a
challenge for the 98th. Assistance for
local crime efforts and strengthened drug
laws are a good place to begin.[37]

with don't relate. They
don't live in apartments.
They live in these houses in
New Jersey and Westchester,
and I don't think they
relate to having your
apartment broken into like
we New Yorkers do. They
think it's a shame. They
know that the criminals are
let go. I got some support
from them, but not much.
Everybody's got their
problems, some are worse
than yours, and I feel
there's no sense in harping,
so I stopped talking about
it, after a while. . . .
I want to say it's a funny
thing to have your material
possessions taken from you.
As bad as these things
were for me, I know there
are far worse crimes. God
forbid you have someone
murdered, or a woman is
raped. All of these terrible
things that we pick up the
papers and hear and see
what's happening every day.
I don't want you to feel
like it's the most terrible
thing that can happen, but
at the time when it did

N.B.: No commentary at all regarding provisions for victim issues.[38]

This study reinforced findings from previous network research about the tendency of individuals to turn to persons with whom they have well-established ties in times of crisis. Eighty-one percent of supporters were individuals that victims saw at least once a week, 64% of supporters were persons that victims had known for five years or more, and 61% of supporters were persons that victims had named as members of their social networks. Forty-two percent of supporters were blood relatives of victims and 57% of supporters lived in the same neighborhood as the victim.[39]

Personal crimes, crimes that violate the victim, span a broad continuum from pocket picking and burglary at one extreme to rape and murder at the other. Although the injury to the self intensifies as the crime becomes more serious, the degree of violation experienced by an individual victim finally depends on the meaning of the crime in that person's life. What seems a minor incident to one victim may be a personal catastrophe for another. But crimes against people can be differentiated according to the degree of violation inherent in the crime. Rape, for example, is universally experienced as a more serious violation than burglary.[40]

happen, the first thing you
feel is that your apartment
is very dirty. I can imagine
what a physical violation
must be, but for a long,
long time I felt the apartment was dirty. If I could
move, I'd just leave it.
The closet—I just threw
everything back and I
didn't use that closet all
summer. I shut the door, I
couldn't go to that closet,
because every time I tried to
touch that stuff, pick it
up, it felt like it was
dirty. The bedroom itself—
I mean, it was my bedroom,
my bed was in there. I
would wake up in the morning
and look at the closet. I
felt powerless in the sense
of that somebody can do this
to you, know they can do it,
know that they can get away
with it. And what's wrong
with me? Why do I let them
get away with it? I really
strongly feel now that I
can't count on our "judicial
system," or whatever you
want to call it, because
that has no meaning. It has
no meaning, it makes no

I feel powerless when . . . someone is
abusive toward me for no justifiable
reason and I need to ignore or "force"
myself to walk away from a possible
hostile situation with this person. I also
feel powerless when I think of how
there are so many destructive things
going on around me at different times,
whether it is easily seen or not, and I
am in no real position to do anything
about it.[41]

sense. . . . I wanted to
come to the Crime Victims'
Counseling Services groups
because of the frustration.
I remember—I think I spoke
about it in the group—that
you really can't talk to
people. As I say, you talk
to relatives or your friends,
and maybe once you tell the
story and you might allude to
it once or twice again, but
after that you really feel
you would be making too much
of it. If a friend of mine
was involved in a court case
I think I would just be
interested in what's going
on, but when I tried to talk
to people I would say, "Gee,
you know, I went to court
yesterday, I was in court
all day." "Oh, yeah?" they
say. I felt that being in
a group with victims would
be good, because we're
interested in each other. . . .
The helplessness is a kind
of frustration, because you
feel people should say,
"Yeah, you're right, nobody
should come in your house
and take your things," but
you don't hear that. You

I feel powerless when . . . confronted by law enforcement authorities. That is, the people who are supposed to protect you from criminals or criminal activities against you. As a victim, it always seems as if I'm in an Alice in Wonderland cartoon trying to reason with the White Rabbit. Instead of the person in authority (read "responsible for justice and law enforcement") at least listening to you describe your problem and then giving "wise council," the scene is reduced to its lowest possible denominator. Either these people are very stupid or they treat you as if you are. This instills in me a tremendous rage for the so called "Establishment." I don't know how else to put it, but I cannot blame people for feeling they have to take matters into their own hands and to hell with the system. [42]

hear this, that, and the
other thing, so you feel
helpless because you say,
"I am the only one thinking
like this. I must be nuts
or something." It's worse
than the fear. . . .
I was afraid for my son.
I said, "Who are you so
afraid of?" and he said,
"I'm afraid of everything."
Anyway, I mean the fear when
he goes out and comes home,
he's seventeen, they go out
and come home ten, eleven
o'clock. These thoughts
particularly, right after
it happened, these thoughts
have come into my mind.
Suppose they do something
to him because there's him,
and there's a gang? [My
son] called me up at work
and he said, "Ma, [Paul] has
been standing outside the
door across the hall, staring
at the door for a half hour."
Sometimes I can't explain the
feeling, as a parent, that my
kid is lying dead somewhere.
Those streets would be empty
and you'd go outside and say,
"Where is this kid?" Then you
look up and down those

I get angry when. . . people (or someone) hurt(s) me. When I'm not treated
fairly or when someone else is not
treated fairly. When my or someone
else's feelings are not taken into consideration. When I am or someone else
is inconsequential. I get angry when
frustrations build up and I don't let
them out. I get angry at myself for not
acting in my own best interest. I get
angry when I see other people being
abused or when I'm abused. I need to
work at recognizing my own anger.
When do I get angry? And how do I
express anger?[43]

*Current law also does not address the
most common form of intimidation—verbal harassment. Testimony given to the
ABA suggested that sometimes innocent
acts, such as telephoning a victim to say
hello, coming to his home, or even driving a motorcycle by, may be extremely
effective in preventing a victim or witness
from testifying. This type of activity is not*

streets and there's nothing
out there and you say, "My
God, my kid's lying some-
where." But I can't explain
the real terror. . . . I
think the shame—I don't know
whether I'm distinguishing
it from that helpless
feeling—that people can
just *do* this. Why are you
in such a position that
people can do this to you?
Did it happen to other
people? You know it's you
they do this to. So it was
a feeling like some kind of
inferiority. You feel like,
"It's being done *to me!*
Why???" I feel like somehow I failed, somehow I'm
a letdown. I feel that I
should be in a place where
this doesn't happen, but
mainly because I can't afford
anything else. It's a
rent-controlled apartment.
I feel that I'm a failure,
that I can't provide better.
I mean, I look at my kid
sometimes—he's sleeping in
bed and I look at him and
say, "This is all that I can
do for you. I'm sorry, I
should have more than this

covered by section 1503 which requires corruption, threats or force for an offense. Section 1510 includes intimidation as a method of obstructing criminal investigations in addition to force, threats, bribery and misrepresentation; however, nowhere is intimidation defined. The Committee believes a clear and straightforward prohibition of such activity will increase prosecutions of such cases, where warranted.[44]

If the perpetrator of the crime came into this room right now I . . . would feel very uptight. I'd get nervous and get a flurry of thoughts in my head at once. I'd check where I could run out if I have to get out fast. I'd see what I could use to block him physically—a chair, table, etc. My fantasy in my mind would be to want to knock him out, punch him and take his unconscious body to the police department. But I feel bad about myself because I'd really not want to hurt anyone. It repels me to see violence. It hurts me. I feel sorry for other people. I feel sorry for myself, though, if I *don't* do something about it. I guess I have a conflict. But here I am thinking this now while I'm writing. I wouldn't have a chance to think in a real situation. I'd have to make the choice of attack, retreat, and exit—get him or get out of this place.[45]

for you." I wouldn't feel bad if these things didn't happen *here*. This, as I say, has been going on for a while. The kid is a victim of this particular person. First time I talk to people and tell them, the first thing they say is, "Why don't you move?" Well, if I could, I *would*. And they don't seem to understand. . . . I still have the feeling—I had it very, very greatly then, but every time I had to go out and leave that apartment empty it made me sick. They would be standing there. It was not just leaving the apartment, but it was knowing that one of them *saw* you leaving it. They know my movements. They know I come home from work at six o'clock, they know I leave at eight-thirty in the morning, they know I work Monday through Friday. If we go out Saturday or Sunday and they see me going out, they know that there is nobody else in that apartment, they see me go out, they see [my son]

I'm no attorney, I don't know anything about the law, but I've been watching a little more carefully since this happened, and I see no real justice. For the victims. I don't know. I think that everyone should have a fair trial, a good, honest, fair trial, and a chance to question that, to appeal it. After that I think that it's stupid to keep on with this appeal, appeal, appeal. What the hell are they doing? . . .

I'm still irritated that the situation in this country is such that you can't feel comfortable to come and go in freedom. We should be able to do whatever we want, go wherever we want. Be perfectly safe and comfortable. And until that day happens, we're damn fools for tolerating things the way they are.[46]

The problem of victim and witness intimidation which this Title addresses was brought out clearly in two days of public hearings held in 1979 by the American Bar Association Criminal Justice Section's Victims Committee. Testimony by some 80 witnesses showed intimidation to be a widespread and pervasive problem which inherently thwarts the administration of criminal justice. These findings have since been confirmed by the prestigious Victim Services Agency (VSA) in New York City which reports that intimidation occurs in at least 10 percent of criminal cases. According to the VSA study, intimidation usually takes the form of direct verbal confrontation but can also occur as vandalism, threats with a weapon or actual physical attack.[47]

go out. To me it's like
they know that the window
in the back leads into your
apartment. It makes you
feel very vulnerable. . . .
After the first session of
the CVCS groups, I felt
relieved, that finally you
were people that understood.
As they say, you talk to
your friends and relatives,
and you got, "Oh, gee,
that's a shame, why don't
you move? Why don't you do
this? Why don't you do
that?" but you didn't feel
they were really under-
standing what you were
saying. I don't think until
people really experience
something that they are
really listening. I'm sure
I do, I'm sure we all do it,
but it's tough to really
relate to what someone is
saying. They say, "Gee,
it was a terrible thing that
happened," and "That's a
shame," because you're not
really relating. . . .
After all the sessions were
over, I realized that it
was the talking that just
did it. I felt there was

*. . . there appears to be extensive dissat-
isfaction with the quality and quantity of
information available about victims
needs and victims services. Yet, despite
this uncertain knowledge base, when
asked what kind of service is appropriate
for victims, all 45 respondents included
some form of in-house counseling in their
recommendations. Because many victimologists discourage the view that victims
of personal violence are merely a special
class of psychiatric patient, the apparent
emphasis on a relatively conventional
approach to the development of services
for victims may indicate that current
knowledge and awareness is too forma-
tive to make "victims services" as yet a
fully distinct concept. In order to bring
the field to a higher state of readiness for
specific programs, a systematic victims
research and development effort may be
necessary.*[48]

*. . . nonvictims often feel that they and
the crime victim are different in some
crucial way. How else can nonvictims
assure themselves that they will not be
victimized? If victims can be seen as less
competent, less strong, less smart, essentially less human than other people, a
person who has not been victimized can
feel immune to victimization. Seeing the
victim as basically different, the other
person can say, "It won't happen to me.
I'm safe."*

No one is invulnerable to personal

understanding on your part, because you had been a victim yourself. You had described your experiences and you kind of related. You realized what the people going through this were going through, and it helped me when I had to do battle with the Assistant District Attorney and the detective, because I think if there hadn't been anyone to talk to, I might have said, "Well, gee, I must be crazy, I must be the only one." But having talked, it gave me the feeling of a relationship—that other people have been through this and it's almost as if you're not alone, there are other people and they *do* understand, and they *do* hear what you're saying. Otherwise, the other diet you got, of everybody seeming to be going against the grain, you know—maybe I should just drop it, maybe I'm crazy. I felt really supported. You know that after certain disastrous experiences you go through hell, but having

crime, of course. Given the right set of circumstances, any person can become a crime victim. But most people need to deny that possibility. One form of denial is the feeling that somehow the victim just isn't like other people, including yourself.[49]

Judges, prosecutors, the legal profession and the police still are somewhat removed from the personal plight of victims. I recently spoke to a judge about victims and he said: "You know, I never really thought about it. My concern was always the application of the law. I thought of the criminal act and what to do about the criminal, but not the victim." This diffident attitude towards victims is derived from the legal model which is based on the adversary principle. It is not the truth but the better argument pro and con which wins the case. The victim's plight is exploited or attacked when the adversary principle of law is applied. It would require another paper, and a long one at that, to discuss fully the psychological trauma which victims receive from all aspects of the administration of criminal justice.[50]

All too often, crime victims become emotionally unhinged as a result of the crime. Such a psychological crisis is obviously a searing experience for a period just after it strikes. It can also produce long-term, deleterious results for the victim, and for the police and prosecutors as well. How-

people *talk* about them, and
then the other members of the
group speaking of *their* fears
and *their* anger and what
have you, you realize that
this is what *human beings* do
when something happens to
them. You kind of put it
into place and say, "Okay,
I'm through this anger and
I'm going through this fear."
There was a couple of bad
nights, as I say, when my
son would be out and I don't
know where he was, and I was
going crazy with fear. I
didn't know who there was to
call. You know, you want to
call somebody at ten or
eleven at night and say, "I
don't know where my kid is."
You don't know what to do,
so you tell yourself, "Well,
this fear is part of it."
You kind of almost explain
it to yourself, you know that
this fear happens, that it
was appropriate. I've had
feelings of anger and you
tell yourself you understand
what's happening and you
know that it's not just you,
that this is what happens.
It's helpful to understand

*ever, specialists in "crisis intervention"
can usually help the victim avoid the
worst repercussions of the experience,
both in the immediate aftermath and in
months that follow. When successful, the
service frequently redounds to the benefit
of law enforcement. . . .*

*What makes crisis intervention so in-
telligible, so lacking in mysterious technology, is that it basically aims to restore
to a victim his or her ordinary coping
skills—skills that virtually all of us use
and observe in others throughout our
lives, but which can be knocked out of
commission if only temporarily, by a
severe shock.*

*None of this is meant to indicate that
effective crisis intervention lacks form or
subtlety. The fact that some individuals
come by these skills more or less naturally does not in any way debase the
extraordinary value of the service.*

*Nor should one conclude that, be-
cause crisis intervention derives from
ordinary human experience, it is an
"easy" service to provide. It is, in fact,
hard, often trying work. Unfortunately,
the more skillful a crisis intervenor becomes through experience, the greater
the risk that he or she will suffer too much
emotional wear and tear. This occupa-
tional hazard is magnified by the tendency to assign the most experienced staff
member or volunteer to the most tragic
cases, such as dealing with youngsters
whose parents have just been killed.*[51]

**I'm afraid when . . . I'm in doubt
about what to do about anything and
then I'm sure to make the wrong decision. There are times when I feel a
strong urge to do something, no matter
what, and I've learned from experience not to do it because that feeling
stems from anxiety and then I wait till
I'm more comfortable and do it because I want to do it. I'm also afraid
when I don't recognize my own emotions and where they are coming from**

these things. I don't think
you're really going to get
that understanding from
people, be they your friends,
relatives, no matter how
good friends they are. I
mean, I'm talking about
good, good friends for
years, and you tell them
and they really don't want
to hear about it. There's
no question that CVCS has
been beneficial to me. The
only thing I can say is that
it should be more well known.
I don't think that people
really know about this, and
there's plenty of victims,
I'm sure. I know *I'd* say,
"Yes, it helped me and it's
a good thing." I really
don't know what victims do
if they don't really have
someone to help them understand what's happening to
them. It just makes things
all that tougher, if there's
no one who understands.
Keeping a journal was great
for me. One time [the
perpetrator] was walking
down the street with some
other kids, and they were
kicking over garbage bags.

**and I get panic stricken. My personal-
ity is such that I MUST KNOW everything and why.[52]**

*Victim services also have proven so far to
be not much different from general mental health programs in that they lack
integration. Each agency has different
priorities, and frequently victims receive
a succession of referrals instead of defin-
itive intervention and help. What is missing is special victim advocacy and bro-
kerage, similar to the concept of case
management in community support
projects, by which clients are more effi-
ciently directed to the kinds of assistance
they individually need. A related problem
here is the lack of organized outreach to
find victims who have not availed themselves of existing services, either because
they don't know about them, are fearful
of re-victimization, are simply apathetic,
or because they have little confidence
that the programs will really deliver the
services they purport to offer.[53]*

**Where was my alertness? This man
without tools had calmly announced
that I needed a new pipe and went out
to see about it. I knew very well that it
was a tremendous job to get my landlord to fix leaks, much less put in
pipes, unless he had to. And yet I took
the word of this confident young
stranger that he was going ahead with
the job. He soon came back and**

It bothered me very much. They were the plastic bags that the super works his back to bring out the garbage, so you shouldn't have garbage all over, and they were kicking them open so the garbage all went over the street. I felt, "This scum. You know, *that's* making your life bad. They're scum," and writing that out helped, in the sense of almost making a note, like. Some day I'm going to tell somebody, you know, and I want to remember it so I would write it, but I did feel that once I wrote it I'd read it over, those feelings, and I would under- stand it and say, "Okay, I'm not crazy," and then it would go, be gone, I'd get it out of [my] system. . . . The self-defense stuff you taught—that, too, I think, is very good, and I keep telling myself I really should get more into it. The more you hear about things and all you think— I mean, I've really been very lucky. I'm a single

knocked again. I let him in again and this time the missing partner came in with him, also with no tools. The part- ner now got down on his knees to check the pipe and then went into the bath- room, saying he'd have to shut off the water. I got him a screwdriver and the partner I'd talked to went and got my wrench from below the sink. Surpris- ing how he'd noticed those tools. I glanced in the bathroom and saw one fellow on his knees unscrewing the handle on the hot water shut-off valve. Even in this technical work, I noticed that his unscrewing the handle was meaningless. Yet I didn't feel the least suspicious. If I had, could I have beaten them to the door and gotten away?[54]

person, I like to go out and I have many interests, and very often I'm going home (not that late alone, but ten or eleven o'clock, you know) you walk in and you say, "What would *you* do?" and it's then on my mind. The self-defense stuff encouraged me. . . . Right now, some of the feelings are still with me. The basic idea behind it, is still there—but those very passionate feelings have dissipated. The next time I have to go to court is March second, and they tell me that will be the final time. The Assistant District Attorney did get up and say, "Look, Your Honor, this woman has been sitting here for three times. She's come here, she has to take off from work, her son has to take off from school." I am well prepared that *nothing* is going to happen—I say "prepared" in that this is what I expect will be the outcome. I really think it is a very bad thing. I'll see it through, but I think

In each offense category, and with every victim, the impact of a crime will vary. Some victims are, of course, cushioned by highly supportive family situations, insurance, and the ability to purchase private medical care and counseling. But those most often and most easily victimized are rarely so lucky. Victims are predominantly residents of the inner city. They are predominantly the young and old. They are likely to be poor and undereducated. The victim of crime is the very person least able to cope with the problems of crime, to locate and utilize existing services.[55]

Courts, prosecutors, and defending attorneys are, of necessity, offender-oriented. The victim is only one of many possible trial witnesses. Courts could, however, inform victim-witnesses what to expect. Coordination could be improved so a victim need not tell his story repeatedly—to police, to several prosecutors, then to the court. Victims also should be better informed of court scheduling. In most courts, all witnesses in any case, expected to be heard on a given day are subpoenaed to appear at the same early hour in the morning. Yet, the case might not be heard that day at all, due to over-scheduling or continuances. Efficient use of court resources requires victim-witnesses to be available when a case is actually called, but many victims could be alerted by telephone. Considering the victim from the start would ensure

it's a very bad thing on
this kid's part to know
that he is going to get away
with this. I think it's
a very bad thing on his
mother's part to feel that
her poor son has been
persecuted for nothing. I
think it's going to be a
very bad thing, but I
really suspect that's what's
going to happen. I'll have
to accept that fact and then
live with these people
afterward. I pass them
every day—it isn't fear so
much as the person who did
this is looking you right
in the face and saying, "Hey,
I did it and got away with
it." Before I'd just *think*
that the system doesn't
work. I think if you *think*
it's going to work for you,
you're making a big mistake
and you're in for a real big
disappointment. I think that
the people who think that the
system works have never really
been through it, and this is
what you have to face. I'm
living in this society, and
it doesn't work. You sit in
court, the questions they

*his cooperation if legitimate delays in
prosecution and trial arose. Considering
a victim's view in sentencing is another
new and important possibility for court
involvement is being tried in some juris-
dictions. Courts and prosecutors' offices
are increasingly sponsoring information
and assistance programs to begin to address these needs of victims and witnesses.*[56]

*The concept of commensurate punish-
ment is so vital that no punishment is
almost preferable to an insufficient one.
That some people "get away with murder" is simply part of the generic principle that "life isn't fair"—and we all
know that. But when the opportunity for
fairness is presented and when the insti-
tutions that carry the label of justice and
are presumed to serve it seem to deny that
purpose, the sense of outrage becomes
unbearable.*[57]

*In our system of justice, a trial by jury
represents the most comprehensive and
formal means available for judging a
matter in dispute. In addition to the
already elaborate rules of evidence and
procedure common in court trials, jury
trials involve the complexity of selecting
an impartial jury, providing jurors with
instructions regarding the law, and con-
ducting jury deliberations. Jurors are
asked to judge the past actions of a
defendant in light of relevant legal standards and to arrive at a verdict of guilt or
innocence. This decision is typically the
result of many separate judgments on the
part of jurors. Jurors may need to ask
themselves first whether the defendant*

ask! I mean, a couple of
times I've been there. One
man was held up in a men's
room at knife point, and
they went on and on about
where were you standing, and
the man said, "This man came
up to me with a knife and
said, 'Give me your wallet.'
Now, it was him, that man.' "
So they ask him, "Where was
he standing? Where was the
door? Where was the window?
How big was the knife?
Where were you when he said
this?" and meanwhile, P.S.,
the guy gets off. What is
all *that* about? It's all
for his protection. God
forbid they should bother
the person who did it.
And nothing for the victim.

actually committed the alleged offense
and second whether the defendant intended the offense to occur. In short,
jurors must conclude that the defendant
was legally responsible for the offense.[58]

Coda: Rita telephoned crime Victims'
Counseling Services after the last hearing. She said, during a long and tearful
conversation, that the judge had thrown
the case out of court; [the perpetrator]
was let go without any penalty; Rita and
[her son] were admonished by the court
to refrain from bringing such nuisance
cases before it, and to make peace with
their neighbors. Case closed.[59]

NOTES

1. Citizens Action on Crime, "Pocket Facts About Crime in New York," brochure.
2. Editorial, *The New York Times*, March 11, 1982.
3. *The New York Times*, November 15, 1981.
4. *The New York Times*, December 18, 1981.
5. Pileggi, p. 23.
6. Bard and Sangrey, p. 17.
7. Symonds, "Victims of Violence," p. 7.
8. Randy Young, "Putting a Guard on the Block," *New York Magazine* (February 8, 1982), p. 36.
9. Bard and Sangrey, p. 112–113.
10. *Ibid.*
11. United States House of Representatives, Bill S.2420, pp. September 16, 1982 pp. 1–2
12. *Ibid.*, p. 3.
13. *The Phoenix*, January 25, 1982.
14. Bard and Sangrey, p. 44.

15. United States House of Representatives, Bill S.2420, pp. 24 –25.

16. *Ibid.*, p. 16.

17. Heinz, July 20, 1982.

18. CVCS group exercise.

19. *Newsday*, August 5, 1982.

20. *The New York Times*, September 20, 1982.

21. CVCS group exercise.

22. CVCS group exercise.

23. Heinz, July 20, 1982.

24. United States House of Representatives Bill S.2420, pp. 3– 4.

25. *The New York Times*, February 7, 1982.

26. *The Phoenix*, March 31, 1983.

27. Emilio C. Viano, "Victimology: The Study of the Victim," *Victimology: An International Journal* (Spring 1976), pp. 3– 4.

28. *The New York Times*, February 2, 1981.

29. *The Phoenix*, March 31, 1983.

30. *The New York Times*, February 2, 1981.

31. *The New York Times Sunday Magazine*, January 24, 1982.

32. *The New York Times*, February 2, 1981.

33. *The New York Daily News*, April 20, 1982.

34. CVCS group exercise.

35. Beniamin Mendelsohn, "Victimology and Contemporary Society's Trends," *Victimology* (Spring 1976), pp. 8–9.

36. Ronald Reagan, speech, October 14, 1982.

37. Editorial, *The New York Times*, January 10, 1983.

38. Author's observation.

39. Friedman, p. 143.

40. Bard and Sangrey, p. 17.

41. CVCS group exercise.

42. CVCS group exercise.

43. CVCS group exercise.

44. Report of the Committee on the Judiciary, United States Senate, to Accompany S.2420 To Protect Victims of Crime, August 19, 1982. (No. 97–532), p. 15.

45. CVCS group exercise.

46. Byron Haisbitt, quoted in Gary Kinder, *Victim* (New York: Delacorte, 1982), pp. 304 –305.

47. United States Senate Report, p. 15.

48. Sander Lund, "How Ready Is the Mental Health System To Adopt or Expand Services for Victims?" *Evaluation and Change* (Special Issue, 1980), p. 143.

49. Bard and Sangrey, p. 89.

50. Symonds, "Victims of Violence," p. 8.

51. John Hollister Stein, "Better Services for Crime Victims: A Prescriptive Package," *Evaluation and Change* (Special Issue, 1980), pp. 106 –107.

52. CVCS group exercise.

53. Zigfrida T. Stelmachers, "Evaluations of Victim Services: Is Enough Being Done?" *Evaluation and Change* (Special Issue, 1980), p. 127.

54. CVCS victim's journal excerpt.

55. Mary E. Galuss, "Services for Victims of Crimes: A Developing Opportunity," *Evaluation and Change* (Special Issue, 1980), p. 96.

56. *Ibid.*, p. 97.

57. Willard Gaylin, *The Killing of Bonnie Garland*, New York: Simon and Schuster, 1982), p. 12.

58. Daniel McGillis, "Biases and Jury Decision Making," *New Approaches to Social Problems*. Irene Hanson Frieze, Daniel Bar-Tal, and John S. Carroll, eds. (San Francisco: Jossey-Bass, 1979), p. 265.

59. "Pity runneth soon in the gentle heart." (Chaucer)

HOW TO READ THIS BOOK

Writings appearing in this left column, widely spaced in the typeface you are reading, are always and only edited transcripts of audiotaped interviews with crime victims who availed themselves of the group sessions offered by Crime Victims' Counseling Services.

Writings appearing in this right column, in the typeface you are reading, are always and only from books, newspapers, magazines, journals, reports, brochures, and similar sources.

Writings appearing in this right column, in the typeface you are reading, are always and only the author's responses.

Writings appearing in this right column, in the typeface you are reading, are always and only from group exercises and evaluations by members of Crime Victims' Counseling Services group sessions.

Seven: BARNEY

It was the early afternoon, about the middle of August of last year. I was going to my apartment and walking along the corridor towards the entrance to my apartment, when all of a sudden someone put a bag over my head. It was a large bag and they pulled it all the way down towards my waist and pinned my arms together. Someone fished through my pockets and took my wallet out. It was very close to the stairway leading down to the exit, and they ran down the stairway before I could do anything. When I pulled the bag off they were gone. I found out later that there were two assailants, but I couldn't see anything because of this black bag. I couldn't see a thing. I called the police, of course, after it happened, and they took the information down. Later on, a detective called

"And I'd go outside, see the fellows, get high. And all of a sudden one of us would say, 'Let's go get some money.' And we'd decide we wanted to do a store or we going to rob some, and I'd go home and get my pistol."

Mr. Wilder, who is black, said he robbed both blacks and whites: "It didn't

me and told me that, let's
see, what did he tell
me . . . ? They were very
helpful and of course they
wanted to know if I had
seen them. I hadn't seen
either of them, so there
was nothing they could do
because I couldn't identify
anyone. It might have been
a few days afterwards, I don't
recall exactly when, I had a
phone call from a detective
and he told me they had caught
someone who attempted a mugging in my neighborhood.
One person attempted to mug
someone who had just come
out of the bank and had some
money on them. [The police]
thought it might have been
the same one. The person who
was mugged saw who had
mugged him, and told the
police. He described the person
and they picked him up. Then
they found in his possession two
of my credit cards.
Then they called me, and
told me about this; they
came over later on and had
me sign a form. I had not
given these credit cards to
this person, and the detective

*make no difference—money was money.''
But, he added, "I was the brains. I wait
till I see somebody with a attache case.''
. . .*

*He never tried to get a job. "I just
always knew I couldn't make the kind of
money I could make robbing, working,''
he said. "I always wanted to have
money—to do whatever popped in my
head.''*

*Robberies were fairly easy, he said:
"You get a nice block that ain't too
crowded and just snatch the first person
you see," he commented. . . .*

*He began to be concerned about
prison sentences when he was 16, he
said, "because one judge tell me, 'I see
you in here again, I send you upstate,
and you won't come home till there's
another tree in that parking lot.' I got
worried then.''*

*He also heard about "these times
these fellows was getting.'' "I said," he
recalled, "'Oh, man! Seven to 13. Four
to 12.' I said. 'Man, not ever. That's too
long to be off the streets.' I decided I'd
just have to be more careful.''[2]*

*Victims want to know whether an assail-
ant has been caught. If they fear a repeat
attack or reprisal for prosecuting, they
want to know if the assailant is out on
bond. They want to know why their possessions are being held as evidence, and
when they will be returned. They want
follow-up information—for example, police often pick up a suspect linked to
several incidents who is later prosecuted
only for those offenses supported by the
strongest evidence. A victim may hear
that "his case," though never directly
prosecuted, is considered closed. Or a
victim may be called to identify a suspect
and never be called to court due to plea
bargaining or some other procedure that
changes the nature of the prosecution.
The victim's response is to lose whatever
confidence he might have had in police,
prosecutor, and courts.[3]*

told me that they had
questioned this young man
about these credit cards
and during the questioning
the detective found out that
there were *two* people that
evidently mugged me, and
that one of them lived in the
apartment house where I
lived. He got a name of
this other person but
eventually it was the wrong
name, and they couldn't find
out who the other person was.
They never found out who it
was, to this day. He
probably gave them the
wrong name or something, but
they didn't find out who the
other person was. I got a
letter from the Assistant
District Attorney, asking
me if I would testify in
a case involving this person
who had attempted this
mugging, who had my two
credit cards. I said, "Sure,
I would testify," and that
was about two months ago and
I haven't heard from him
since. . . . I don't have a
family here in New York and
my closest relative is my
sister up in Malden,

*Often times we draw distinctions between
violent crime and sophisticated crime or
between crimes like drug-pushing and
crimes like bribery. But the truth is crime
does not come in categories, it is part of
a pattern. If one sector prospers in the
community of crime, so ultimately do the
others.[4]*

*Interviews with two dozen victims, some
of whom asked that their names be with-
held to protect them against possible
retribution, showed a pervasive feeling of
despair over their personal experiences
as well as a profound skepticism about
the criminal justice system. No matter
how much they had anticipated an attack,
many said, they remained unprepared
for it.*

*"You just react from the gut," said
Maragret Weintraub, a 32-year-old ad-
ministrator for the College Entrance Examination Board who was assaulted in
late September on 93rd Street, off
Lexington Avenue. "You forget things
you planned to do. You suddenly feel
someone has done something to you and
you're going to get him." . . .*

*Many victims of robberies and bur-
glaries . . . say they have been seriously
scarred emotionally, if not physically,
and have altered their habits and ways of
moving about the city and their views on
political and social issues that relate to
crime.*

*Victims who once considered them-
selves "liberals," and some who still do,
say they have little sympathy for their
assailants or for political leaders and
scholars who emphasize poverty or other
environmental factors as causes of crime.*

*Although many of the victims have
found the police to be more caring than
effective—and have little faith in the
readiness of the courts to impose stiff*

Massachusetts, but I never spoke to her about it. I don't speak to anyone. She's the only closest person to me. I'm sixty-three years old and I live alone. I wasn't hurt in this, you know, but just scared and frightened. Very frightened. I told my neighbors who live on the floor that I live on, and I told the guard and the superintendent. I gave them, the guard and the superintendent, the name of this person that the detective had told me. They tried to find him but they couldn't find him. They didn't know anyone by that name. They couldn't find anyone with the name that I gave them. . . . My neighbors were supportive. They sympathized with me and they gave me all sorts of advice, and told me if they could do anything they would be glad to help and all that. I was so scared. It was a complete surprise to me. I hadn't seen a thing, up to that point. It was sudden.

sentences or in the reforming capacity of prisons—they seem generally prepared to cooperate with the authorities. Moreover, a number of the victims, some of whom recalled being assaulted or being victims of burglaries in other cities and suburbs, said they "don't blame New York."[5]

Omnipresent joke in criminal justice circles:
Question: "What's the definition of a neoconservative?"
Answer: "A liberal who's been mugged."[6]

Age, race, sex, and income are among the most consistent correlates of all measures of fear of crime, reflecting (we argue) the underlying dimensions of physical and social vulnerability to crime. In rough order of the strength of those correlations, females are more fearful than males, older persons are more fearful than young people, Blacks are more fearful than whites,and poor people are more fearful than the relatively well-to-do. Further, these effects are generally linear and additive; fear "accumulates" among successively more vulnerable groups, but without significant interaction effects.[7]

I'm afraid when . . . I get this creepy low feeling inside of me. I'm afraid of losing control of my feeling. Somehow I need to think I am in control and when I think I may not be, I feel a sense of panic throughout my body. . . . I'm afraid when many good things happen and I'm not feeling worthy of the good things. Since last week after our meeting, I have been afraid of dealing with many of the feelings I seem to have and do not want to face. I was surprised at how much pain I still had and during the week, the pain was very obvious to me. I'm afraid of letting this incident be more than it was.[8]

I just got very frightened.
I got so frightened that I
said, ''Take my money and I
don't care. Just don't
bother me.'' I was very
frightened. I didn't scream.
I just didn't do anything.
I just spoke to them. They
didn't say a word. I didn't
hear anything. They didn't
say a word. I just knew
what was happening and said,
''Here, take my wallet.''
Then I went into my apartment
and called the police and
told them what happened.
Then I went out and found
one of the guards who works
in the building, and I told
him about it. Then I met
one of my neighbors and
another neighbor, later on—
I still felt frightened.
I was still frightened for
maybe about several weeks
after it happened. It took
quite a while for me to get
over it. I became more
worried and afraid it might
happen again. I was a little
more watchful after that,
and whenever I came into my
apartment house I would look
around. I'd walk slowly

The Figgie Report, Part I *revealed that fear of crime has penetrated the foundations of our lifestyles. About one-quarter of the respondents replied that they no longer participate in community activities because of fear of crime—a startling finding with serious implications for the social health of our communities. More than six out of 10 respondents dress plainly to avoid drawing attention to themselves; telephone back to a friend or relative to say they've arrived safely at home; and report keeping car doors locked, even when the car is stationary. About half of the survey respondents say that they plan their routes to avoid potential dangerous places all of the time. About 50 percent of the population also have extra locks on their doors.*

These umbrella findings about the pervasiveness of fear in modern American daily living may not surprise some people, but they themselves are matters of concern. If we are disturbed about the future, specific findings about the distribution of fear of different segments of the population offer even more cause for alarm. It was expected—and confirmed— that fear of crime is prevalent among the most victimized groups in our population: residents of large urban areas, women, and blacks. What was not expected, because previous studies had not confirmed it, was that young people in their twenties are quite fearful.[9]

I'm afraid when . . . I feel helpless, stuck, unable to make a decision, flooded with emotions, out-of-control. I think of all the consequences of my behavior and the unknowns. I think of the worst consequence and maybe the best. I jump from one idea to another. I'm obsessed and become paranoid about acting on my decision. Sometimes I wait to the last moment to act (when the pressure builds) and I can't act. I become afraid as I do what I have decided to do. I become afraid when I

towards my apartment and I'd keep looking around, look behind me to make sure that there was no one around, or to see if there *was* anybody around. And if I went into the elevator and if anybody came in with me, I just made sure I knew them and if I didn't know anyone I wouldn't get on. I was a little more careful about my movement in the building. Whenever I saw [the guards] they kept asking me about it, and at one time one of them volunteered to walk up with me 'cause I was scared to go up alone. The area that I live in is a high crime area. In my building alone there are other crimes that I've heard of that people have told me about. On the floor that I live on there were two other muggings in the past year. It's a private apartment house, subsidized by the federal government, I would say it's a medium income—I believe it is a Mitchell-Lama funding arrangement. . . . It must have been a short time afterwards,

become dependent. I lose a sense of autonomy, my freedom is in jeopardy. I have to ask for help and I'm seen as weak and to be pitied. I'm afraid when I feel vulnerable, drained emotionally and physically. I'm afraid when my defenses are down and I'd like to believe that the world is not such an awful place. I'm afraid when I don't know if I've made a clear decision or am unsure about how to proceed or have the courage to proceed. I know that I need not be brave all the time and my fears are warranted. I know that sometimes my fears/anxieties far outweigh reality and I can handle the situation.[10]

Even more, perhaps, than residents who have not encountered violence, the victims have circumscribed their lives by staying at home more than they wished, particularly after dark; riding taxis that some of them can ill afford instead of using mass transit; watching suspiciously over their shoulders when they walk, even in daylight; investing in expensive door and window locks and alarms, and figuring out elaborate strategies for pacifying the next mugger.[11]

I think possibly within a
week, that I called Crime
Victims' Counseling Services.
I heard this broadcast and
after I heard it I called,
right about that time,
because after it happened I
felt that I needed to talk
to somebody about it. I
didn't have any family and
I spoke to my neighbors, but
that didn't seem to be enough.
I felt that I wanted to talk
to somebody about it and
it might be helpful. I
live alone and I don't have
much contact with people, so
I thought it might be helpful
if I tried to make more
contact with people. I just
felt I needed contact with
somebody to talk about it,
have somebody to talk to.
I was a little worried
because it was in Brooklyn
and quite a distance from
where I lived, and I'd
have to go there at night.
That's what bothered me
most about it. But I did
go to all of the sessions
despite that, and I
traveled alone, even though
that was arduous for me.

*Special types of services required that
have been raised by the efforts of crime
victim groups in seeking treatment for
this disabling condition that are of rele-
vance to the mental health services development agenda include:*

   *1. Development of a responsive out-
      reach capacity.*
   *2. Refinement of short-term, crisis-
      oriented services.*
   *3. Development of support systems
      for family members, particularly
      those who may be "at risk" for
      related difficulties.*
   *4. Development of treatment ap-
      proaches that tend to mediate or
      reverse the long-term effects of
      victimization.*
   *5. Establishment of useful goals in
      the treatment of victims that en-
      courage further self-development.*
   *6. Development of standards for
      evaluating the success of each of
      these initiatives.*[12]

*. . . the research findings have begun to
tell us regarding the consequences of
criminal victimization. What is known
. . . is that above and beyond the immediate problems posed by physical injury,
loss of valued property, and demeaning
interactions with governmental systems,*

You're the first one I spoke
to at length about it, and
what you told me was
supportive and made me feel
a little better. I was so
upset about it, of
course. . . . The main thing
was that I was more careful
in my movements and more
watchful about what was going
on in the building, and it
made me want to contact
other people more so that
I could have someone to talk
to, about my fears and everything else. I didn't do anything else. I have two locks on
my door—a bolt lock and
an apartment lock. I think
that's enough. Then I have
a sign on my door that states
that items of value in my
apartment have been marked
and are on record with the
police department, Operation
Identification. . . . I was
thinking about it, and it was
on my mind most of the time.
I just kept going over and
over what happened, and what
I might have done, or what
else I might have done, and
I was thinking about how I
felt at the moment it

*the victim is at risk for delayed psycho-
logical reactions with unexplained "flash-
backs" of the event, continuing fear and
a sense of loss, with depression and
physical disabilities not necessarily related to injuries that occurred at the time
of victimization, together with a much
greater probability of premature aging
and death.[13]*

OPERATION I.D.

*The Police Department's Operation Iden-
tification program was designed to benefit New Yorkers by discouraging theft of
valuables, decreasing the resale value of
the stolen items to the thief, and assisting
in the recovery of stolen property. The
program costs no more than a few hours
of your time, which is spent marking your
property with a special etching tool
(loaned free to citizens for a three-day
period), recording all marked property
and registering your name with your
local precinct. The program includes free
decals for your doors and windows. The
decals carry the Police Department logo
and warn would-be burglars that valuables are marked for identification by the
department. Contact your local precinct
to become part of Operation I.D.[14]*

happened. This went on for
four or five or six weeks,
maybe, the most. Gradually,
I kept thinking less about
it. Probably it was right
after the CVCS groups were
over that I thought about
it less than I had. . . .
When it happened I just
felt that I should have
tried to *do* something about
it *when* it happened, and I
also felt ashamed the way
I acted when it happened—I
got so scared I said, "Take
my money, don't hurt me."
They didn't say anything to
me. They didn't have any
weapon, and I don't think
they were going to hurt me.
I don't know, but I didn't
try to do anything about it.
I don't know what might have
happened, but I just felt
ashamed the way I reacted to
it. I thought maybe I should
have been a little bit more
aggressive about it, or done
something instead of what I
did. But, as you said in
the group, I did the right
thing because I didn't get
hurt. I know you're right,
but I still feel ashamed.

If the perpetrators of the crime came into this room right now I . . . probably wouldn't recognize them. But if I did . . . it's hard to say. I suppose I would give in to their wishes, let myself be robbed if I had no opportunity to escape. I am quite sure that these are violent men who would actually enjoy beating a person half to death. This time I would try harder to fix something in my memory as to what they looked like, what they are wearing, what is different about them.[15]

Not as much as I did,
though. . . . Right after
it happened I was afraid to
go out, especially at night.
I didn't go out at night,
actually, for about three or
four weeks after it happened.
I rarely went out at night.
Lately, I have been going
out more at night, but I still
feel a little worried. The
only thing I do is try to
walk on the main roads where
it's light and I look at
everybody. I watch every-
body who I pass, and whenever I pass someone who looks
a little dangerous, who might
possibly do something, I just
watch him. It occurs to me,
and I keep thinking about it,
when I pass somebody who
looks dangerous. I don't
trust *anybody*. Now, anybody I don't know might be
someone who might do something. . . . I found the
CVCS prevention session very
useful—I found helpful the
items about how to behave in
an elevator, or what to do
if something should happen.
Now, I understand that I
probably would have done

Ms. Shelley Neiderbach,
  President
Crime Victims' Counseling
  Services
GPO Box 3003
Brooklyn, NY 11202

Dear Ms. Neiderbach:

As Chairman of the Senate Committee on Aging, I would like to thank you for testifying at the recent hearings on "Crime and the Elderly."

Your testimony added a great deal toward giving the committee a greater understanding of the problem, and we hope to see many ideas take legislative form in the near future. The waiting period for some witnesses, as you know, was longer than I had hoped, but I do appreciate everyone's patience.

Once again, many thanks.
Best wishes.

Cordially,

Hugh T. Farley
Senator [16]

THE EVERYBODY-TALKS-ABOUT-CRIME-BUT-NOBODY-DOES-ANYTHING-ABOUT-IT EQ TEST [17]

  I have devised a method to reduce crime in New York City.
  My plan is based on the point system—determined by the expendability of the victims of crime. My criteria for victim-points has been established as a result of years of careful screening of media coverage of crime, political response to victims, and the Police Department's ability to pursue selected perpetrators of crime, based, most often, on who the victim is.
  It has been apparent for some time that the media gives more attention to some victims than others. In fact, some cases are headlines for weeks while oth-

the same thing, I think.
The main thing, I wasn't
hurt. I protected my-
self. . . . I felt scared
after I left the first CVCS
group. I hurried down to
the subway. When I was
riding in the subway train
I felt scared; I wasn't
quite sure at that time
that the ride was worth it.
Actually, when I was in the
group and I heard what the
other people were telling
me, I got upset by what I
heard from the other people.
I felt a little more ease
after that, especially about
that other lady who had the
burglary. I thought that
was a rather upsetting thing
to hear about. The young man
who had also been mugged—
it bothered me. I was
thinking about it on the way
home, but I realized that I
felt a little relieved after
I had talked about it. At
least it was a little helpful. At least there was
somebody there to talk to,
and have some contact with
people to get some help.
It was helpful in that way,

*ers hardly rate a mention. Political re-
sponse is usually in concert with media
coverage. Mayors and other vote-getters
lament particular cases. Mayor Lindsay
once referred to the victimization of a
Columbia professor as the most savage
crime he had ever heard of. The rating of
our victims seems to be an indigenous
part of media and political reality. As a
result, law enforcement agencies know
that some cases have to be solved while
others are a nuisance.*

*So I have established a point system of
victims in order to reduce the crime rate.*

*As you can see, there are far more
victims with minus ratings than with plus
ratings. So under my system, we could
show a steady decrease in crime and
people would feel safer. After all, Mayor
Koch has stated that the public's perception of crime is as important as the
reality. My figures relate to that perception, and the news will only get better.*

Female (white)
between the ages
of 18 and 19, pref-
erably blonde and
attractive, living in
Manhattan be-
tween 59th and
96th Streets on the
East Side: 3 EQ

Police Officers
(white, in uni-
form): 3 EQ

Police Officers
(out of uniform, or
black or Hispanic):
2 EQ

to know the others knew how
I felt. That helped. And
exchanging phone numbers,
too. . . . I thought about
what you had told me. I
thought you were experienced
in this kind of thing. I felt
impressed by what you told me
and what you told the other
people (and what they said).
After I had told you about
what happened and you told
me what you thought, and how
I had reacted and what I did
was the right thing to do,
I felt what you had told me
was useful for me. You knew
what you were talking about,
and therefore it made me
feel better. Sharing in the
group aroused my feelings
more of what happened to me
and what happened to the
other people, and may have
gotten my mind off what
happened to me when I
started thinking about what
happened to the other people.
It naturally made me feel
worse at that time, because
what happened to them was
worse than what happened to
me. Actually, I wasn't hurt.
I just lost a little money

Males (white): 1 Expendability Quotient, unless victim is best-selling author, heir, or famed for attending discos, in which case could reach as high as 2 EQ

Female (all other black/ Hispanic women in the city): −½EQ

Teenagers: White teenagers count as 1 EQ (if a varsity player, 1½ EQ; black and Hispanic teenagers are −2 EQ)

Male Homosexuals: Rating depends on whether or not victim is identified as gay (*New York Times* does not recognize the person or the word so this is iffy). Can vary from 1 EQ to −3 EQ. Variations include color, economic status, and place of victimization.

Female (all other white females in Manhattan and other boroughs): 2 EQ

Elderly Males (a sliding scale based on geography and success when younger). Can go as high as 2 EQ or as low as ½ EQ

and it was an inconvenience and it wasn't really that bad. The other victims were sympathetic to what happened; I felt that they had listened to me and were interested in what I had to say, and they said something that might have been useful and helpful. I was listening to what happened to the other people, what they had written on. When they read, I guess it just made me think what had happened to me wasn't quite as bad. . . . I read that little leaflet you gave me on what to do to protect myself if anything should happen, and I was thinking about it, and it was something that I might do. Things I haven't thought of or didn't know before, I might do if it should happen again. I feel better protected. Now, four months after I was mugged, of course, I don't think about it as much. In fact, I haven't thought about it at all, at times. I've just forgotten about

Infants (no color distinction):   1½ EQ. *NY Post* coverage cannot offset *New York Times* low-key reporting of these victims.

Female (black) if employed in white-dominated profession: 1 EQ

Male (all black and   Hispanic men): −1 EQ

Ex-Convicts: −3 EQ

Lesbians: Do not exist in the minds of the media, politicians or police, so have not shown up on the charts.[17]

Most of the crisis intervention specialists working with crime victims conceive of their service as a relatively short-term one, ranging from about a half-hour's conversation to several hours, sometimes spread over several weeks. When the victim has a need for long-term counseling or other social services, the specialist normally sees to it that this help is furnished by appropriate community agencies. In fact, many such workers have discovered that the role of a social service diagnostician and referral agent is one of the most challenging aspects of their job, one which cannot be adequately performed on the strength of the specialist's good will alone.[18]

it, in other words. Except
that occasionally,
especially when I go out
or when I come back to my
apartment house, I may
think of it, but otherwise
I've gotten over it, more
or less. The most important
thing was just the fact that
I had somebody to talk to
about it with at length,
and had some reactions from
people. I think that was the
most helpful; I would
recommend these groups to
other crime victims. I
would tell them that they
could get some advice and
some information about what
to do about it, and also it
might be helpful if they
didn't have anybody at home
to talk to about it. It
would be helpful to have
someone who is experienced
and knowledgeable about it
to talk to; I think that
would be useful to help
others get over it, like
me. I can't think of
anything else, except thank
you.

[My friend] asked if I'd be willing to give a talk to a women's group about this crime counseling course. I agreed with pleasure. This talk should help to spread the word about the advantage of therapy after being the victim of a violent crime. I wonder whether a lot of people are afraid of therapists. Talking or therapy may indicate that you're a weakling or a mental case. Don't let your friends know that you're having mental or emotional trouble. On the other hand, perhaps it seems to show how normal and mature you are if you can just forget about these little things that bother you. My wife told me, "Just forget about the robbery. You're alright. Thoughts of it will go away more quickly if you don't keep stirring them up by talking and writing about them." I know better of course, but it's impossible to argue such points with people who have their minds made up.[19]

Today I made up several "diamond" poems about the robbery which I'll read at the next poetry meeting. It occurs to me that it might be a good idea to read these poems at the next crime counseling meeting. It's given me a great deal of pleasure to think of all the punishing words I can to describe the men who attacked me. Perhaps it's good therapy, too. Here are some of the "diamond" poems I've made up

> Rogues
> roving wreckers
> ranging homes recklessly
> relentless, rabid
> robbers

> Violent
> villainous varlets
> violating aged victims
> vile, vicious
> vipers.[20]

Imagine that I thought the CVCS routine (whatever it was) might be just another bunch of "not-much-help," and I really didn't want to go through that again, or find out that I was *right* to be leery. So it's really a kick to me to be able to say in this evaluation that you had just what I needed—I only wish I had known about it earlier. The combination of other-victims-who-know, *and* a therapist-who-knows just can't be beat. I'm sure that others felt that, too. I hope none of my friends or family ever gets hurt like I did, but if they do I'd send them right to you. (In fact, I'd drive them over myself, pronto). Thanks for everything—like the movie, this is a "ten."[21]

NOTES

1. New York City Police Department, brochure.
2. *The New York Times*, November 17, 1980.
3. Baluss, p. 97.
4. Ronald Reagan, speech, October 14, 1982.
5. *The New York Times*, April 4, 1982.
6. Author's observation.
7. Wesley G. Skogan and Michael G. Maxfield, *Coping With Crime* (Beverly Hills: Sage, 1981), p. 74.
8. CVCS group exercise.
9. John Crothers Pollock, "The Prospects for a Fortress Society in America," *Public Relations Review* (Vol. VIII, No. 1, Spring 1982), p. 17.
10. CVCS group exercise.
11. *The New York Times*, April 4, 1982.
12. Susan Salasin and Robert Rich, "Mental Health Service Needs for Crime Victims." Position paper presented to the Presidential Task Force on Victims of Crime (September 1982), p. 4.
13. *Ibid.*, p. 2.
14. New York City Police Department, brochure.
15. CVCS group exercise.
16. Letter to Crime Victims' Counseling Services, March 17, 1982.
17. David Rothenberg, "The Everybody-Talks-About-Crime-But-Nobody-Does-Anything-About-It EQ Test," *The Village Voice*, September 28, 1982.
18. Stein, p. 107.
19. CVCS victim's journal excerpt.
20. CVCS victim's journal excerpt.
21. CVCS victim's journal excerpt.

HOW TO READ THIS BOOK

Writings appearing in this left column, widely spaced in the typeface you are reading, are always and only edited transcripts of audiotaped interviews with crime victims who availed themselves of the group sessions offered by Crime Victims' Counseling Services.

Writings appearing in this right column, in the typeface you are reading, are always and only from books, newspapers, magazines, journals, reports, brochures, and similar sources.

Writings appearing in this right column, in the typeface you are reading, are always and only the author's responses.

Writings appearing in this right column, in the typeface you are reading, are always and only from group exercises and evaluations by members of Crime Victims' Counseling Services group sessions.

Eight: WANDA

On August twenty-third, I was in Central Park at nine in the morning with my sheep dog, throwing a ball. We were at Seventy-ninth Street and Fifth Avenue when I decided we should take a rest. She was hot and doing heavy panting. So, after a bit, I noticed that I was the only one [there], and [that] there was no one in front of me. So I looked around to see if there were other people and I saw someone sleeping on the hillside, probably had spent the night there. Then I saw another young man just getting ready to sit down, putting down two clubs and a paddle before he sat down. So I thought, "This is a flake." [They were] wooden clubs, like he found himself some really good tree branches, like the size of a baseball bat, and a paddle like for racquetball. So I

There was a mugging in the business section of Cortelyou Road and Sixteenth Street. Imagine a mugger busy in a business section at 9:00 a.m. of a drizzling Sunday morning! The cops got there quickly and everybody stopped to watch what would happen. I could see nothing a few minutes later but couldn't help wondering—as did others—why a mugging at that time of day? I suppose our mugger hadn't got his quota the night before. Or perhaps he had to have money for a fix. But does crime ever take a holiday? We get used to thinking of certain hours (nights) and perhaps certain days, Saturdays perhaps, as being the proper times to expect the crime visitor. But does the criminal keep certain working hours? Can he be trusted to bother his victims only when he's rested or well fed—or perhaps tired and hungry as a wolf? Does overtime pay for Mr. Con Man? Will the professional mugger, like the lion in the wild, pass up possible victims when he's made his quota? We have heard criminals also called animals, but if they are animals do they follow a regular code of practice? Probably not.[1]

waited a few minutes, and
then I looked at my watch
and I decided that it was
time to go back to work, go
back home, 'cause I had to
go to work. And I got up,
turned around, and faced
him—but did not look at
him. I walked down the path
to the base of the hill that
he was sitting on. As I
approached an underpass, I
had a sense of something
happening behind me, and I
thought, "When did he move
his body?" So I turned and
stepped off the path, just
at the edge of going underneath. Meanwhile, the dog
has already gone underneath.
As I stepped off the path
I turned, and there he
was—armed with the clubs.
I started running as fast
as I could down the hill.
All I did was turn my head,
and he hit me across the
back of the head with one
of the clubs. I started to
go unconscious and I said
[to myself], "You are not
going to go unconscious,"
and as soon as I told
myself that, I saw light

*"There are always exceptions," says
Detective Louis Scarcella, a veteran anti-
crime street cop, "but most street muggers are just out for a quick score.
They're not looking to hassle you. They
just want your money fast, and they don't
want lots of noise and people looking out
windows and cops being called."*
*It is also very important for New Yorkers
to get to know their neighborhoods. Find
out what stores stay open late. Plan your*

again. I started to scream
and then, when I saw the
blood, I started to scream
even more. I got to the
top of the hill (which I
think was the road under
which the underpass was) and
two men were coming in my
direction, but they couldn't
help me. I finally got one
young man (who was sitting
on a bench) to just walk
me to a telephone and put
the dog on the leash. Then,
when we got to the boathouse,
by then the blood is running
down my back, down my
front—it's really a mess. I was
fortunate to run into two
young interns, who kind of
calmed me down. Not [so
much] to calm me down, but
they got some ice cubes
for my head and told me that
I was going to have to have
stitches, that I probably
wouldn't pass out, and that
I would have to have x-rays.
And finally, twenty mintues
later, the police came, and
an ambulance. . . . I don't
know what happened with the
assailant. I turned around
and I saw him directly

*route home well in advance. Think in
terms of including as many open places—
such as late-night restaurants, coffee
shops, bars, police stations, hopsitals—
along your route as possible. It's well
worth going a block or two out of your
way at night in order to take the safest
and "livest" route home. If you suspect
you are being followed along a main
thoroughfare and the man or men are still
following you after one or two zigzag
maneuvers, duck into an open shop or
bar and tell the clerk or bartender that
you're being followed and want to call
the police. If you do this, the pursuer is
likely to give up the hunt.*[2]

*The physical residuals of violent crimes
are the ones with which nonvictims are apt
to be the most familiar, and the most
sympathetic. Injuries suffered by crime
victims are usually dramatic, visible,
and painful. Victims are shot, stabbed,
stomped, bruised, burned, slashed, beat-
en, or run over. They may be blinded so
that they cannot identify the criminal; they
may be tortured until they reveal the hiding places for their valuables or submit to
sexual demands against their will. They
lose arms, legs, toes, fingers; faces are
mutilated; organs are permanently damaged. Even the slightest blow to the head
may cause temporary loss of memory,
judgment, and orientation; a more serious
head wound may cause permanent brain
damage and subsequent physical paralysis or mental retardation.*

*Often these serious physical injuries lead
to a psychological wound that may be as
severe or as permanent. Unlike victims of
diseases or natural disasters—hurri-
canes, tornadoes, or floods—who can
rationalize their sufferings, crime victims*

behind me, but I ran. I
have gone back, trying to
see if I can recall how I
got out of there. I have no
recollection. My memory
comes when I really start
to talk with somebody.
Vaguely, before that, I knew
I was on the road and he
wasn't behind me any more.
The dog was alongside of
me, so he hadn't done anything to hurt Butch. I
might have heard it, if he
had. What surprised me was
that my color vision was
off. When I turned around,
my dog was a black and white
sheep dog—was all white
except the black on top of
her head. And it was
looking at—like coming
out of anesthesia, it was
like that. A wall or haze
between me and the intruder,
and he was also all white.
My vision was like this
until I saw the red
blood. . . . I *do* have a
hearing deficiency, and
"tintinnabulation"—ringing
in the ears—too. Maybe,
if I'd had better hearing,
I might have heard him coming

*know that their injuries were willfully
inflicted by another human being. They
were acts of man, not acts of God. In
many cases, the victim sees his attackers—in effect the crime victim engages in
face-to-face combat (or surrender) in a
time of supposed national peace.[3]*

That article about "The Effects of
Muggings on Children" set me to
thinking about my own childhood. Although I was never mugged then—
such things were not so common in
those days—I saw quite a bit of rough
behavior. I grew up in a medium-sized
city in Iowa in a very poor neighbor-

up behind me sooner than I did. I don't know, because he was running through grass in sneakers. I mean, what I saw when I turned was the sneakers. I saw the feet before I saw anything else. Now, my hearing deficiency is between four thousand and eight thousand cycles. Now, that's really high-pitched, so I probably heard as much as anyone could. . . .

After we passed to the boathouse, the young man who was with me walked up to the boats and behind the concession there, and they called the police. And actually brought a towel. I think one of them said, ''Would you please cover yourself?'' I think he thought I was bleeding in the front, too. There was that much blood. When the police arrived, [the guys] were concerned. Somebody said to the cops, ''It took you an awfully long time,'' but I don't remember [who said it]. I think maybe they said, ''Well, you're on the other side of the

hood. I was too small to do much fighting but many times found myself going home quickly, very scared, because I had to go through strange and slightly dangerous neighborhoods. My older brother was the type who was always making enemies and sooner or later they became my enemies, too. I wasn't tough or big enough, so I dreamed of growing big enough so no one would pick on me. ''Might'' seemed to make ''right,'' so it was necessary to have the might in some way. Meanwhile, I developed my running abilities and was always running to and from school. I'm not the only one who ''runs scared.'' I'm sure President Reagan or the Pope have some fear that's always with them of being shot or bombed.[4]

park and we were taking
care of something else,''
and then the ambulance came
a few minutes after. Well,
no, maybe five minutes after.
It wasn't right away. The
ambulance was able to drive
up right next to the police
car, right next to where we
were standing, so the
fellows in the ambulance did
assist me. I was concerned,
actually, more about the
dog. I think it was a
distraction from myself and
I didn't want him to go to
the pound, so the police
were really nice about it.
She couldn't go in the
ambulance, so they brought
her and tied her up outside
of Emergency. They were
really nice except they did
one thing which I cannot
understand—they wrote the
guy up as black, and he's
white. I told the cops that,
but they wrote it anyway.
The guy who helped me had
seen him earlier. I think
he probably passed him on
the way to the hill. At
that time, the cops didn't
know about the distortion

*There are certain cynics who insist that
many New Yorkers think about only three
things: finding the right apartment, the
right job, and romance. This is not true.
There are many New Yorkers who think
about crime almost constantly.*

*Some of them went to the 24th Precinct
station house on a recent night to be
trained as neighborhood watchers for a
group called the West Side Crime Prevention Program, a group devoted to this
preoccupation with robberies, burglaries, muggings, purse snatchings and
other unnatural disasters.*

*The neighborhood watchers are trained
to be aware of and to report to the police
odd, possibly nefarious behavior around
them, like people selling stereo equipment from the backs of cars or sunbath-
ing on fire escapes with crowbars beside
them, and those in the most recent training group seemed well on their way to
being fully sensitized.*

*This kind of neighborliness is just what
the West Side Crime Prevention Program
hopes to foster. Its officers are mostly
leaders of block associations in the area,
and they are convinced that if people
would just stop minding their own business, and mind that of their entire neigh-*

in my vision. In the beginning, I was a little puzzled about it and I didn't really talk to anybody about that distortion. It has taken me a really long time to understand why. It must have been the blow to the head. Another thing that's also very interesting is that I heard ringing at the time of the blow—it was almost but not quite like two cooking pans being hit together. . . . [While I was in the Emergency Room], the police came in and we talked about it again. That's why I do not know how they could have written it up as a black man. We were so explicit in our descriptions, unless the only thing I could think of was they had an early report on some guy on the West Side, so maybe they weren't listening that closely, or that they decided that the guy on the West Side was the same guy on the East Side. Of the two policemen, one was a man and the other was a woman. The woman was black

borhood, they would see incipient crime and be able to inhibit it.

The organization is only 18 months old, but it already counts among its members 300 neighborhood watchers, armed with special Police Department block watchers numbers for easy identification by 911 operators. There are also members who patrol the streets once or twice a week in a car, using walkie-talkies to call back to their 90th Street office if they see anything they think the police should be called about. On the Upper West Side, where people seem to have opinions on everything from the development of Columbus Avenue to the best blend of coffee at Zabar's, the officers think the chance of raising crime consciousness is excellent. . . .

"Someone watched a man come out of my building with a blue canvas bag in one hand and a television in another," [one woman] said. "It was my bag filled with my things, and my television. If he had been trained as a neighborhood watcher, he would have called 911."

The police have had to accustom themselves in recent years, not always happily, to those people who feel that some kind of self-protection is the only answer. This was what the two officers were trying to turn to their advantage the other night. . . .

"He's been following you for two or three blocks," said the detective. "He saw you buy milk and make change. He knows you have money in there. But you're thinking of what's in the mailbox, what you're going to make for supper. I've heard it a hundred times: 'I put the key in the lock and suddenly a guy had his arm around my neck.' That guy didn't just come out of nowhere. He was paying attention and you weren't."

"Do you think screaming is a deterrent?" the mother of the 11-year-old asked. And Detective Cabo replied that, like much else about crime, it depended on the circumstances. . . .

and the man was white. I
don't know who wrote the
report, but the detective
called me that night and
so I went the next evening,
after work, and he pulls
out the report and he goes,
''I understand you want to
see a black man between thirty
and thirty-five, five feet,
seven-and-a-half inches,''
and I said, ''That's all
correct, except he was white
as I am white. He looked
Italian or Jewish. White
skin, dark black hair. . . . ''
Then, I was asked to look at
mugshots. White mugshots.
I mean, suddenly the report
was not incorrect. It may
have been a clerical error,
or it may have been
deliberate: No one will
ever know the answer to that.
As far as I know, the
assailant was never picked
up, anyway. That's the last
I saw of anybody. . . . I
did call the detective maybe
a week later, a week and a
half, to ask what to do
about pursuing insurance
coverage, and he remembered
me. I was really surprised.

It was dark outside, and the meeting had had a chilling effect. ''Just because you're paranoid doesn't mean someone's not out to get you,'' said one woman to her male companion with a jaunty smile, as they went into the night with their eyes open.[5]

Observe as much as you can about the criminal(s). Notice any details which will aid you to describe them and their mannerisms. When trying to determine age, height, weight and appearance make comparisons between them and yourself or people you know.

- *Memorize peculiarities such as tattoos, scars, and prominent physical features.*
- *Notice type and color of clothing worn, but keep in mind that clothes may be changed so try to concentrate on physical characteristics.*
- *Be able to describe size, type and color of guns or other weapons that are used.*
- *Observe direction in which suspect(s) leave. Observe as much as you can about any vehicles they may use . . . if you get a license number write it down immediately and give it to the police.*
- *Remain calm. Robbers usually are excited and may be provoked easily or might be under the influence of drugs.*
- *CALL 911 as soon as possible, the sooner it is reported the greater the chance is that the criminals will still be in the vicinity and can be apprehended easier.[6]*

HOW TO GIVE A DESCRIPTION

PERSONS

1. Sex
2. Race
3. Complexion
4. Age—If unknown, estimate.

I thought of all the cases that come in and out of that place. He did remember. Except for the report, I was treated okay by the authorities. Those that I told—my father's sister, my aunt, was kind of abrupt, but she's the kind of person who never physically complains, ever—those that I told were sympathetic. My father, who lives in Texas, was very concerned. I think in the beginning he didn't understand what happened, and then, a week later, he suddenly called—very concerned. He had tried to get me in the morning. Sometimes I leave early. And then he was calling my sister, so then he actually said, "Why don't you come down here and recuperate for a few weeks?" He was very supportive. The people in the office were fantastic. My boss could not look at me—for a whole week he could not look at me at all. He didn't know that this had happened. Did not make eye contact.

5. *Height—Estimate in 2 inch blocks, for example, between 5'8" and 5'10".*
6. *Weight—Estimate in blocks of ten pounds, for example, 130 to 140 pounds.*
7. *Build—Large, medium, small, fat, stocky, slender or thin, and any distinguishing features on parts of body (tattoos, eyeglasses, etc.)*
8. *Hair—Color, thick or thin, full or balding, sideburns.*
9. *Mustache or beard, describe, color.*
10. *Clothing—Type, color, style, start at top and work down—hat, coat, shirt, pants, shoes.*
11. *Method of escape.*

Example: *Male, white, ruddy complexion, approximately 45 years old, between 5 foot 6 and 5 foot 8, 150 to 160 pounds, medium build, gray hair thinning on top, long sideburns, brown handlebar mustache. Wearing a blue baseball cap, no coat, white shirt, dark pants and sneakers.*[7]

WHO CAN FILE A CLAIM?

(a) *The victim of a crime who has sustained personal injuries.*
(b) *A surviving spouse or child of a victim of a crime who died as a direct result of such crime; or*
(c) *Any other relative dependent for support upon a victim of a crime who died as a direct result of such crime*

Note: *If YOU are the person responsible for the crime upon which a claim is based or an accomplice of such person or a member of the family of such person, you are not eligible to receive an award. If claimant is a minor, claim may be signed by his parent or guardian.*[8]

Then he did a strange thing. [The doctors] told me, first thing, not to cover my head. Secondly, they took the stitches out and [the wound] was infected, and so they had to pack it every day. So I had to start wearing a kerchief on my head, and then they had to restitch [the wound] the following week. He did a strange thing. He brought his son, his two-and-a-half, three-year-old son, to examine my head—my boss! I think I have had The Treatment—to be used as a scientific specimen, while there was no acknowledgment that anything had happened to me! I was very annoyed, but in another sense, it was obvious he couldn't deal with it at all. And it was almost like, "You fool! What are you doing in Central Park at nine o'clock in the morning with your sheep dog?" But the girls [at work] were fantastic. Some of the other men were fine, as much as they get involved with things that happen. There

Yesterday's news had an article about "The Effects of Muggings on Children." I read the article and put it in my files. I was much interested but not surprised to learn that violence can have a very bad effect on even youngsters, especially if the parents aren't helpful and supportive. The article didn't mention professional therapy but probably that would be desirable in many cases. Some parents, it was pointed out, are so insensitive as to blame their child for not taking sufficient precautions. But in this day and place, it's almost impossible for people to completely avoid violence. Kids are often subject to it at school or going to and from school. There are teenage gangs that make a specialty of ripping off other kids. Then the victims may be faced with the problem whether they should report the attacks. They may be afraid to say anything about it to teachers or parents.[9]

I get angry when . . . people automatically say "You're very lucky, they could have killed you. The hell with the jewelry and other stuff that they took." Some people say, "At least they didn't hurt you," and when I say, "But they did," they usually answer, "I mean *really* hurt you bad." I try to explain to people, "Of course, I thank God that we are alive to talk about it, but it is human nature to, afterwards, cry." This really angers me. I'm really finding that most people don't really want to hear about it after they've heard it once. They probably mean well, but they seem so callous. It really makes me mad.[10]

are other people who still
are asking, "How?" It's
amazing how things travel
around on the grapevine—
by the time it got back
to me, I had been raped!
I mean, the look on
their faces, it was *more*
than something terrible. It
was bad, but the gals let me
talk it out, talk it out
and . . . that's how I deal
with things. My friends were
very upset. I mean, the
realization that a friend
could have died. I mean,
I was thankful, I was thankful I was just alive. He
could have just killed me
with another blow. My
friends were just *there*—
calling, really concerned,
really listening. A friend of
mine spent the night, which I
knew would be very difficult,
but, boy, am I ever glad!
But I called Crime Victims'
Counseling Services because
the fear was beyond belief.
By the end of the first
week, for instance, I was
down in the Village with
two friends—I couldn't deal
with traffic lights. I

. . . we need to obtain better normative data on measures of psychological adjustments from non-victim populations. Normative data on selected samples of non-victims would enable us to determine much more about the length of the adjustment process. . . .

But there is another side to this research, one that is comforting and cause for optimism. It comes from the help that was offered crime victims by friends, relatives, neighbors, and strangers. Many of the victims we spoke to discovered care and comfort from unexpected people. The elderly found neighbors delivering meals to their doorstep and calling regularly to check on them. Young victims who lived alone discovered people at work to talk to and previously unnoticed neighbors. Those who got help where they expected to were also thankful and recognized the caring that surrounded them.[11]

I'm afraid when . . . I walk the streets of New York, especially when there are few people around and the neighborhood is shabby. I'm especially afraid after dark. I'm afraid when someone walks up behind me on a less-traveled street. . . . Of course, I haven't felt

continually had this feeling of, "It doesn't matter how many people I'm with, I can be hit on the back of the head again." The tension was so phenomenal, the traffic lights, the head-lights of automobiles and buses, I couldn't do it. I couldn't do it. So we had to take a bus back home. One of them said, "Wanda, you're drunk" and I said I hadn't had anything to drink. I wouldn't dare drink like this. Aspirin was the strongest thing I had taken. But it was the anxiety and the tension that got to me so that I couldn't even walk straight. It was never like that, prior to the crime. Never. After, I couldn't get on the subway without having an anxiety attack, and I felt that I was panicky, and that because of my extreme fear I was attracting people who were nuisance-makers. . . . I felt helplessness. I mean, I got on the subway and tears were streaming down and this is a real kook—

quite so fearful since my robbers (imagine calling them mine!?) have been jailed awaiting trial. But it's hard to forget how helpless I was when attacked, and how happy my robbers were to torment me.[12]

[My wife] and I intend to celebrate by dining at a good restaurant. But even in making pleasant plans, one feels the need to take precautions. The mugger is never far from one's thoughts even though he doesn't seem quite so threatening now. [My wife] decides to leave her bag behind so no one can grab it. Isn't it funny that in this big town one must be always taking the mugger along in our thoughts. I have no bag to leave behind but it occurs to me it would be better to put part of my money in a pocket away from the billfold. But, of course, these precautions are so common one does them without planning.[13]

and the girls, women—were
pacing just so that they
could keep out of his way,
but with my heavy attack I
had a difficult time and
with the fear I had, I was
almost paralyzed—I got off
at an earlier subway stop
and got out. I couldn't
deal with it. Another thing
that happened was that I
live near the Fifty-ninth
Street Bridge, and it was
two weeks before I could
go under it. I live on
Sixty-fourth and I have
friends that live down on
Fiftieth and Fifty-first,
and I couldn't get myself
to go under. It was like
being in the park, again.
[The whole thing] was
absolutely shocking. The
question: "Why did he hit
me???" It's like, "What
did I do to him?" I mean,
that's the feeling, though
there's the rationale—that
here's somebody who's
irrational—but at that
particular moment, you
know . . . "How come my
turn?" I was running to
get out of there. I have a

The fact sheets came today from: Citizens Action on Crime—they not only sent one copy but half a dozen. One can also get a copy of a book they put out for $1.50. I have sent off the letter. Their fact sheet advises carrying a key chain "high Pitch Whistlestop Whistle." I think I will send for this whistle even though one may not have time to blow it if the mugger has already grabbed you. It could be used to call the police and other help when someone else is being ripped off. The fact sheet also advises getting a free police check on one's home or apartment by calling (212) 793-2727. I belive I'll do this right now.[14]

If the perpetrator of the crime came into this room right now I . . . would beat him like he beat me. I would then take him to the police and make sure he would be punished and not allowed to continue his behavior. I would be sure that he would not be allowed to continue to function without changing his way of life. I know that this will not heal my wounds. I feel such conflict. Rehabilitation is something I believe in BUT I know that some people are hopeless. I feel foolish in that I cannot just feel plain hate. I think I am afraid of feeling my anger. I think I might be the quiet person that could kill.[15]

feeling that I went through
woods that I never in my
life could try. It's a
feeling of how I got out
of there, 'cause that was
the quickest way out of
there. And then I found
this guy sitting on a bench,
who helped me. . . . You
know, when I didn't go unconscious and I was able to
scream, I knew I was going
to live—I thought that
going unconscious might mean
the end for me, I'd be dead.
I was feeling that maybe
these were my last few
moments. . . . I think, maybe, well, I have a dog for a
reason. She was *there*. I
mean, I hate to black out,
I'd have hated to black out
and not be able to protect
her . . . though I don't
know, I think it was probably
my own desire. To live. To
keep conscious—I think I had
a choice. There was no *reason*
for me to die. My feeling
was that if I had passed out
he would have hit me
again. I mean, there was
enough space between us and
the rest of the world of

I'm afraid when . . . I look out my window and see and hear loud, violent gatherings of people in my neighbor-hood. I imagine some sort of violent trouble and me in the middle of it. I seem afraid to go out into the "mean streets," to borrow a movie title. I also am afraid when I have to go uptown on a train. Being too far from my apart-ment leaves me feeling remote, alone. Am I really this afraid? I'm ashamed of it! I'm ashamed of myself. But I *hate* the violent world I chose to live in. Is this what I've lived for 30 years to know man's own inhumanity to man?[16]

people. Without a sound
from me he could have
bludgeoned me once on the
head, and that was it. I
was sitting on the hill and
he also saw I had nothing.
I had just a ball and a
leash. Nothing to protect
myself with. It was truly
a motiveless crime, in the
sense that there was no
robbery attached to this.
I also had dungarees on.
I mean, he was not going
to have an easy job of it
if he wanted to do a rape.
With the dog around. I
should think, in his
thinking, he was going to
take care of her, too. . . .
By calling CVCS I felt
relief. But also, I
think, anxiety. I don't know
whether the anxiety was more
than to have to take that
subway all the way into
Brooklyn, to an area that I
was not familiar with, and
to do it alone, and not
knowing anything about what
was happening except that
your voice on the telephone
is very good. It's
assuring, so it was not like

Read my short poems to the poetry therapy class. Here is one of them that I read last week.

> **Violent**
> **villainous varlets**
> **violating aged victims,**
> **vile, vicious**
> **vipers.**

The group was much struck by the hatred shown in such poems. I read them with considerable emotion, getting a little excited over the thoughts they aroused. I told the group that I got a lot of pleasure denouncing the robbers in this way.[17]

I'm afraid when . . . walking down steps (subway, building, etc.), because I am fearful that I'll be pushed from behind me. Also, when walking, I got into the habit of continually looking behind me, because I was afraid someone might push me to the ground.[18]

I had a sense of fear of
the group, it was just
dealing with the new environment. . . . I would say for
the first three weeks [after
the crime] I was really
pushing myself. I kept very
busy, and one of the reasons
that I was going to go back
to work that day was because
I was typing a paper for one
of our Ph.D. students, to
make extra bucks, and so I
had to deal with that. I
had to work after hours,
and on the following weekend,
and the following weekend,
so that that kept me calm.
And I was also trying to
show how strong I was and not
to go down. Show myself, and
others, that I was okay. But
then, by the fourth week,
then the rage, the anger,
came so ferociously that I
thought I was going cross-
eyed. I have a word
processor that I use at my
job: Sometimes it just
blurred out for me.
Because of my rage. I even
had this strange feeling
(which we talked about once,
in one of the sessions)

*The generic mental health consequences
of victimization that are of demonstrated
concern for crime victims are contained
within the diagnostic criteria for the
"post-traumatic stress disorder": (these
are the diagnostic criteria provided for
the first time in the new "diagnostic
manual" of the American Psychiatric
Association: DSM-III).*

A. *Existence of a recognizable stressor
that would evoke significant symptoms of distress in almost everyone.*

B. *Re-experiencing of the trauma as
evidenced by at least one of the
following:*
   *(1) recurrent and intrusive recol-
   lections of the event*
   (2) recurrent dreams of the event
   *(3) sudden acting or feeling as the
   traumatic event were reoccur-
   ring, because of an association
   with an environmental or ideational stimulus*

C. *Numbing of responsiveness to or
reduced involvement with the external world, beginning some time after the trauma, as shown by at least
one of the following:*
   *(1) markedly diminished interest
   in one or more significant
   activities*
   *(2) feeling of detachment or es-
   trangement from others*
   (3) constricted affect

D. *At least two of the following symptoms that were not present before
the trauma:*
   *(1) hyperalertness or exaggerated
   startle response*
   (2) sleep disturbance

that this man had touched
me like nobody else did,
so this almost gave me a
sense of caring for him
because I didn't know how,
in the beginning, before I
got to rage. . . . But how can
that be??? How could someone
that close to me harm me???
And he's changed the contour
of my body, too. He put a dent
in my head. . . . My
rage, once I got to it, was
so great that I pantomimed
about hitting him. I'd
stand in the apartment and
go box around, thinking,
"I'm going to hit him in the
groin next time, in the
stomach next time! Boy, I'm
going to punch him in the eye!
Oh, boy!" and that got the
energy moving in the body
'cause I was bouncing up and
down on my toes, and swinging
my arms up with my fists
clenched, and I needed to
do it maybe four minutes.
But, boy, that really
helped! I must have done
that for about three or
four weeks, off and on.
One time I got a little
frightened, I got so into

(3) *guilt about surviving when others have not, or about behavior required for survival*
(4) *memory impairment or trouble concentrating*
(5) *avoidance of activities that arouse recollection of the traumatic event*
(6) *intensification of symptoms by exposure to events that symbolize or resemble the traumatic event.*[19]

If the perpetrator of the crime came into this room right now . . . I would probably kill him. At least, beat him up, to see him shriveled up, to see him cringe, to see him humiliated, totally unhappy, to ask, "Why? Why me? Was it something I wore?" To scream, "I hate you," over and over again—to rip off his clothes, to claw his face—hit him in the stomach and the groin—to inflict tremendous pain, to take away his freedom—to ask how could he do such a horrendous thing, to put him away forever, to remove him off the streets, punch him in the mouth, beat up his face. I need to really make him suffer.[20]

it—I realized that I could
really hurt someone—it's
a very scary feeling. . . .
Now, I must say, I'm far more
cautious on the subway, and
I do get a little nervous
still on the subways . . .
whether that's ever going
to . . . it bothers me, and
it never did before. Even
on buses, I just don't have
that sense of security that
I used to have. In fact,
friends of mine said I
walked the city a little
too secure, which was maybe
because I was so familiar
with Central Park. We had
done that route for five
years . . . it's an invasion
of my *home*, almost. And I
also—my lord, here I am,
I've been going to school,
don't have a lot of cash,
and to have something like
this . . . to enjoy . . .
and I was sitting on that
hill, thinking that, at
that point, it was sunshiny,
it was pleasant, and then,
boom! A stranger wiped it
out for me—he took away
Central Park, yes. Now, I
don't go in unless I go

I get angry when . . . others either make like the mugging was *not much* and I should be more happy, forgiving towards the muggers, etc., *or*, that people constantly remind me of the mugging when I want *not* to be reminded at that time. I get angry when I think of that night and realize I could be dead. Perhaps stabbed, shot, or both. Who did they think they were to put two weapons to me and I could not do a thing? I get angry when I realize how much time I've lost since December 23 till now. My life came to a halt. I couldn't do what I've done before. I'm just now easing up my tensions, fears, frustrations and anger in order to cope and to regain strength to become the person most like before. But I'm not, I'm not totally the same.[21]

with a friend and usually
we're doing our dogs to-
gether, and when women come
now and tell me at eight
o'clock in the morning
they're walking across Central
Park, I freeze and I almost,
like, get on a little lecture
and I think, "Wanda, don't.
We all can make decisions for
our own." My fear extends to
your friends and other people;
my sense of trust has undergone injury, too, as a result
of this crime. I'm not sure
sometimes whether people are
sociopaths or not sociopaths.
I can't quite trust. But
what has happened is that I now
have what I call "attacks
of paranoia." One attack
was before I came (or maybe
even after). I had one
before Christmas and it
happens mostly in the office—
in fact, it happens with the
people I'm closest with. I
suddenly start turning on
them. I mean, I suddenly
feel that they are turning
on me, so I start turning on
them, and when the gals get
together and—you know how
there always seem to be

. . . in terms of addressing the critical mental health needs (short term and long term) of crime victims, several concrete, implementable *strategies that incorporate both mental health services and public police perspectives should be underscored.*

(1) Research should be undertaken on the long term consequence of criminal victimization, *the emotional problems which follow from it, and the long term disabilities of victims (although there is some understanding of the immediate emotional and psychological consequences of victimization, there needs to be more research on the long term, delayed consequences which are associated with mental illness, and related ef-*

cliques here and there? I just move around. I'm sort of friends with everybody, though I have my own friends, too. But when they get together I sort of think they are talking about me, what happened. So this attack came—my second one came, I can't remember what triggered off the first one. The second one came last week, just at my birthday— and it's been the nicest birthday of my whole life. *Everybody* was doing something. I suddenly began to think that maybe, after a bit, that I never had that many people being so nice to me and saying that many nice things. I don't know when the paranoia comes in, but suddenly in my life . . . the assault has triggered off a lot of things from childhood and from high school. I've been in therapy, and have gotten to things we could never get to. I had a block on dealing with my father, who left when I was nine. I had a block on dealing with the pain of

fects, which may continue to persist over a lifetime).

(2) Demonstration studies should be developed and implemented which are intended to reverse the syndrome of long term and delayed emotional consequences. *In this context, one needs to be concerned with physical as well as mental problems. Along with these "demonstration projects," technical assistance should be offered to service providers to increase their competence in establishing and providing these needed services.*

(3) After developing and implementing several crime victim service "prototypes", the federal government should be responsible for transferring the technology *(service packages) to community mental health centers, community programs, and other related human service providers.*

(4) Mental health services for crime victims should not be under the administration of criminal justice system, *which is, naturally, most concerned with apprehending criminals and preventing crime. (In extracting mental health services from the auspices of the criminal justice system, we are not trying to be critical of the criminal justice system. Mental health services needs are believed to be best met under separate adminstrative auspices.)*[22]

Central to the Christian vision of the purpose of life is man's relationship to a God of love and forgiveness. That relationship preempts the primary importance of life on earth.

Psychoanalysis acknowledges no God, only a prophet. But Freud's view of human behavior also encourages forgiveness, in this case by reducing personal responsibility.

The law, in distinction, is only con-

when he left. At Thanks-
giving I was with my aunt,
and she made a remark that
I didn't want to stay with
my mother, that I wanted to
live with my father, and I
realized I can be in touch
with the devastation of his
leaving me with this woman
who I did not want to be
with (I mean, she wasn't a
nice woman and he had
given signs that he was
going to take us, but then
she said no, we're going to
split you). So Dad didn't
want my sister and I to be
split. Due to the crime,
I came in touch with something, with something that
therapy never got me to. I
came in touch with real
feelings of helplessness
that therapy never really
touched in me. And the,
this paranoia, because as
a high school kid I weighed
one hundred and seventy-five
pounds. I mean, I was gross,
and the boys would be making
all sorts of wise-ass remarks,
and I remember feeling people
whispering (at least I felt
they were whispering) and

cerned with earthly matters and demands a central assumption of personal responsibility. Where Christianity and psychoanalysis, in their separate ways, are concerned with individual salvation, the law must preserve the state and the social order. Criminal justice must respect the individual but serve the common good. It assigns two champions of absolute positions: a defender who will argue nothing but innocence and a prosecutor who acknowledges only guilt. They will battle in a court of law before a jury of peers. The jury, using standards of the community at large, will decide which advocate represents "truth"—therefore, where justice lies. This is the adversarial process.[23]

If the perpetrator of the crime came into this room right now I . . . might ask why they had not asked for money—because I would have given them what I had in my bag. That would have been preferable to being hurt and possibly breaking bones and being hospitalized again. (I was just over a major operation, and had been in the hospital a month.) My attitude is "It's only money, and money can be replaced." Of course, I may be fooling myself, but I am not a violent person, and always try to avoid facing up to unpleasantness or violence.[24]

talking about me. I don't
know whether I had just put
these feelings down, repressed
them, and the blow on the
head relieved a lot of things,
or what. The result of
these feelings with my
father I decided, this
Christmas, "Let's try," and
the pain that came up! And
the realization of all this
anger that I had carried
all these years towards him
and never realizing, never
seeing his side, feeling
compassion for the situation
but just totally feeling
anger, I really felt very
sad because he really cares.
So this crime helped—
mobilize the anger for me.
I went and did something
about it for the first time,
and there was "old fright"
attached to the current
anger—when I was walking
around boxing in my apartment,
at some level, [I was] boxing
with my father as well. In
therapy, I tried it—it was
never successful. So this
blow on the head kind of
moved me in a new direction,
oddly. This is what a

I get angry when . . . I think of what effect my experience might have on the way I feel in general about things. I don't like to have to be on guard every time I get into an elevator or walk into a hallway. Maybe it's being complacent, but I just don't like the idea that I have to be on guard all the time. Then, last week, I have been riding the subway a lot. I generally drive, but this week I took the subway because I had jury duty. I found myself checking anybody that I thought looked suspicious to me. Now this was on a crowded train and here I am checking suspicious-looking characters for no reason at all.[25]

crime can do—unleash a lot of old feelings, that you didn't even know you had. The thing is, I know life could not be the same. That's one thing I know: It could not be the same— this event has drastically changed my life. I want to do things that I haven't done before—I realize I've been trying to change my career. I took a test, the other night, for a job, and walked out of that thinking, "Oh, this is ridiculous. I'm not this person that he's looking for, I couldn't have been that person. Ten years ago, but that's not where I am today." I've changed. I've changed. I've taken another direction. That made it clear. So I realize that I have to hang onto something and do it, *for me*. Life may be too short. . . . Powerlessness— that's still is there, some of that. It's that feeling that my life is not in my control. That definitely came out from the blow on the head. I really felt,

As a psychoanalyst, I am trained in a tradition that places the individual at the center of things, and that, too, is a problem. If one thinks in terms of the individual, a warp will be introduced into the concept of justice that will distort the very purposes of justice. It is not just that we are forced into a single perspective rather than a collective one—which is bad enough—but it will always be the same individual whose perspective is dominant. It is only a criminal whose sensitivities, whose unconscious, whose hopes and ambitions and aspirations will be explored. Never the victim.

A system of justice must consider the victim even though she can no longer be helped, in order to protect others who also may become victims and unhelpable. To be beyond help must not mean to be beyond thought or compassion. Otherwise we lose the focus of the very intentions of our laws. And justice demands more. A system of justice must speak to righteousness. It must not just defend the good; it must proclaim the good. It must announce our moral purposes.[26]

The victim may seek reassurance and direction from others during the impact stage. He or she may seem uncertain and ask for advice. "I can't handle this," the victim is saying. "Help me. Tell me what to do." Immediately after a crime there are usually many things that need to be taken care of—someone has to contact the police and deal with them, calls must be made to insurance and credit-card

by the fifth week, that I had no control over the situations of my life and that I had to start doing something. I used to have a fantasy, of some sort. Somebody would walk into my life and it would change. But this crime has made me more reality-oriented—I realize better that there are some things you can't control, but the things you *can* control I try to control more actively. Though I still keep thinking of what happened—it doesn't go away. Does *not* go away! It's there in the back of the head, all the time. But after going to Crime Victims' Counseling Services, so much has subsided, a tremendous amount has subsided. I felt really a tremendous relief. I hated that subway ride, three levels deep into the ground at nine-thirty at night! In fact, I was thinking about it—the university where I work has a service that you can go to, and then be referred. I had thought

companies; whatever mess the criminal has left has to be cleaned up; the victim may be asked to identify a suspect. All of these external demands can make the victim feel swamped.

The initial impact reaction may be expressed several hours or even days after the crime. Victims may seem to be all right and then suddenly become disorganized. People who are asked for help at this point sometimes feel that the victim should already have recovered; they may become moralistic and judgmental, denying the victim's appeal for aid. They seem to be saying, "You're an adult. Act like one." Even if it is not expressed in words, this attitude adds immeasurably to the victim's distress. The victim needs to have some structure provided in a suddenly chaotic world, some help in restoring order. The need for this support is temporary; it will diminish over time if it is satisfied. But if the help does not come, the victim's need for direction can become fixed; he or she may continue to seek reassurance and be unable to move to the next stage of recovery.[27]

Group Evaluation
[composite]

For each of the items below, evaluate your feelings on a scale from 1 (one) to 10 (ten), one being least helpful, ten being most helpful. Circle the number which corresponds to your feelings.

A. *counselor's interpretations*
   1 2 3 4 5 6 7 8 9 10
B. *group sharing (oral)*
   1 2 3 4 5 6 7 8 9 10
C. *group exercises (written)*
   1 2 3 4 5 6 7 8 9 10
D. *group responses to written exercises*
   1 2 3 4 5 6 7 8 9 10
E. *keeping a journal*
   1 2 3 4 5 6 7 8 9 10

about maybe using that
service, and then I thought
I would really want to work
with someone who's familiar
with the situation, who's
gone through some things.
So I realized. After that,
I had made my decision. I
was definitely helped by
CVCS. Definitely. I had
come up with a lot of ideas
about myself and what was
happening to myself and
going back to early years
of life, which was what was
triggered off for me.
Feelings from way back,
and also the interpretation
that some of the things that
were happening to me . . .
having your responses, or
just listening to what you
would say to other people's
circumstances or to mine,
verified what *I* was saying
to *me*. It gave support to
the ideas that I was coming
to, and also that I wasn't
crazy. Because, I would
say to my friends what I
thought might be triggering
off and it didn't make
sense to me . . . your
professional response was useful

F. self defense/
  prevention information
  1 2 3 4 5 6 7 8 9 10 [28]

. . . service-oriented agencies are aimed at the immediate needs of victims, and there is little attempt to help victims with long-term effects, such as suppressed and delayed stress reactions. This particular deficiency is illustrative of the broader paradox that even though more recognition is being given to the psychological effects of victimization, there are few victims programs with adequate mental health personnel qualified to deal with such complex problems as delayed stress syndromes. The small amount of counseling and ventilation that is done rarely is provided by mental health professionals, and a component for psychological counseling of victims is not integrated into the existing mental health delivery system. Moreover, few, if any, of the victim programs are sponsored by a mental health agency, nor is there any evidence of mental health leadership or even consultation in the administration of the programs. [29]

I feel powerless when . . . someone tells me I am not hurt when I was just attacked; when a perpetrator puts a gun to my head and demands my money or my life; I feel powerless when I am at a disadvantage while being held up and can't fight back. I feel hurt and angry with people who refuse to sympathize with my problems by saying, "Why were you there in the first place?" or begin to tell me what I should have done or what they would have done. I feel angry and powerless while watching TV seeing all the crimes solved. It's so unreal. [30]

and the interpretations made
me feel *less*
out of control, because my
feelings were appropriate
to the situation. . . .
Just hearing what other people
had gone through, though I
think it was kind of intro-
spective, gave me a little
bit more compassion for myself, listening to the
ordeals of other people.
Also, just the support—it
was not even verbal support
in this situation, it was
just like an energy support
that was coming. I felt
that I was very much understood by the others in the
group, and that what I was
going through triggered off
sympathy and understanding
in *others*. . . . The writing
exercises let me . . . put
down some of what I felt were
terribly "young" feelings—
the real anger of wanting to
punch and rip out [the
assailant's] eyes, tear out
his hair, punch him in the
groin, kick him in the
groin, everything. To put
that all on paper kind of
was a good release—it

The survivor's experience is evidence that the need to help is as basic as the need for help, a fact which points to the radically social nature of life in extremity and explains an unexpected but very widespread activity among survivors.[31]

If the perpetrator of the crime came into this room right now I . . . know my heart would pound and my blood would boil. I would grab each of the two and start to choke them. I'd like to pound their heads against the wall until they crack open and they scream for mercy and I would not stop. I'd keep pounding and pounding their heads against the wall. Then I'd like to stab them a million times each, to show

helped me focus; it helped me relieve my anger. Also, the group responses to these written exercises were useful, as well. But, again, it's the total, whole picture of the session. I can't particularly remember what my particular writing exercise brought out, but during the whole session it would sort of make the feelings more succinct. . . . I haven't been doing [journal-keeping] now, no. I did during the sessions and I did during December. What I did find is that by my writing down (which I should start doing again, because by writing down uncomfortable situations it moved them), I didn't hang on to them any-more. I get it out of my system. *Out!*. . . . Both the crime and CVCS have changed me, a lot. I would say that it has influenced my life, definitely. In the sense of how I look at it, and my biggest thing is to get out of fantasies and into life. This has really been a hard way to get

them how angry I am about being so frightened. How my life is now turned upside down. How I can't do the things I could have before. I'd like them to know I'm powerful now, and THEY are the helpless ones. Then I think I'd just walk away and either silently or perhaps laugh at them, now that I had the control and they were the helpless ones.[32]

Last night there was a meeting of block representatives from all the local tenant associations. They are to discuss security, which probably means patrols. I should go, but the matter doesn't seem imperative. So I don't go. Perhaps that means that I am not quite as concerned about personal safety as I was immediately after.[33]

there. It's been a "blow
of redirection." I'm
beginning to wonder whether
these feelings of feeling
powerless that come up
now—if in the past I'd
just put them aside, but
now I realize I can't put
these feelings aside, it's
something that has to be
dealt with. I think I've
aged a lot in the last six
months. My face has aged,
but I think I've aged. The
gals say I look older. So
it's been "a growing
experience," it's been a
most chastening experience,
altogether, and the Crime
Victims' Counseling Services
groups helped me change
direction, definitely. I
mean, not everybody wants to
deal with it, but if they
really do, definitely. I
would definitely recommend
that they go to Crime Victims'
and *not* to a therapist who's
never been through it, or
has never really dealt with
crime victims. I mean, they
are just not going to have
the empathy to help them,
not the way you and the

I'm afraid when . . . I have to change an activity—leave the house, return to the house, go marketing or shopping; or initiate an activity, such as coming to this group; or proceed with daily chores and routines; carry on with my work (real estate) which is my livelihood.[34]

For me, one of the most salient characteristics of action research is that it forces us "out of the pocket"; it places social problem researchers in unfamiliar and unsafe environments. It is a method that deters arrogance and contravenes the tendency to "look in the mirror," that is, to study others who are like ourselves, to make our observations under benign, comfortable and well-ordered circumstances.

Indeed, the essence of action research is anything but well-ordered. Conditions change, the unexpected happens with

group helped me.

suddenness and real control is usually out of the investigator's hands. Indeed, these are the very same conditions that are experienced by the victims of malignancy. In effect, the promise of action research is the promise of a kind of ordered disorder. . . . where action research and social malignancy are concerned, it is almost as if the method fits the madness![35]

NOTES

1. CVCS victim's journal excerpt.
2. Pileggi, p. 21.
3. Barkas, p. 6.
4. CVCS victim's journal excerpt.
5. *The New York Times*, July 21, 1982.
6. New York City Police Department, brochure.
7. The Interfaith Civilian Patrol, Inc., booklet (unpaged).
8. State of New Jersey, Department of Law and Public Safety, Violent Crimes Compensation Board, brochure.
9. CVCS victim's journal excerpt.
10. CVCS group exercise.
11. Friedman, p. 19.
12. CVCS group exercise.
13. CVCS victim's journal excerpt.
14. CVCS victim's journal excerpt.
15. CVCS group exercise.
16. CVCS group exercise.
17. CVCS victim's journal excerpt.
18. CVCS group exercise.
19. Salasin and Rich, pp. 3–4.
20. CVCS group exercise.
21. CVCS group exercise.
22. Salasin and Rich, p. 6 (emphases Salasin and Rich).
23. Gaylin, pp. 112–113.
24. CVCS group exercise.
25. CVCS group exercise.
26. Gaylin, p. 316.
27. Bard and Sangrey, pp. 35–36.
28. CVCS records.
29. Stelmachers, p. 127.
30. CVCS group exercise.
31. Des Pres, p. 160.
32. CVCS group exercise.
33. CVCS victim's journal excerpt.
34. CVCS group exercise.
35. Morton Bard, "Action Research and the Question of Social Malignancy," p. 16. Paper for the American Psychological Association Task Force on Violent Crime, 1982.

Afterword

The anguish, frustration, and pain recorded in this book represent only the most supersubmicroscopic fraction of victim trauma. Each year in the United States, millions of crimes are reported: If we tally only direct victims, the sum is staggering. If we then add to this figure the conservative estimate of one unreported crime for each one that goes on record, and include the all too frequent—but statistically absent—covictims, we then begin to develop a gross measure of the pervasiveness of what is truly a national mental health crisis.

Crime victimization, and the fear of crime victimization, are unraveling our social fabric. The delicate but threadbare cloth we call civilization may soon be in tatters if massive mental health interventions are not forthcoming. Alas, there is little evidence that the nation takes notice that its citizenry is disaffected and imperiled, both on the streets and in the home, where family violence is generally denied and hidden from public view. The tabulations, though they easily exceed the annual aggregates of the Centers for Disease Control—our barometer of epidemic and pandemic afflictions—cannot really convey the misery and terror of even a single crime victim. Statistics convey only the surface phenomena, providing a far too distanced and therefore distorted perspective on post traumatic stress.

The purposes of this volume have been twofold: To add the dimension of human suffering to the abstractions of numeration and to demonstrate that with appropriate intervention victim trauma can be reduced and normal life resumed. We must eschew hopelessness, despair, denial of possibility and embrace the art of the possible, the arts of healing. While we as a society *are* helpless to predict and therefore control crime, we do have choices about how we may acknowledge, respond to, and treat those who have been unwilling participants in an act of evil: crime victims.

Invisible wounds—emotional trauma—need not and cannot remain invisible and thereby ignored. There *is* recovery: We need only discover the wounds for healing to begin.

Crime Victims' Counseling Services, Inc., G.P.O. Box 3003, Brooklyn, New York 11202, (718) 875-5862, welcomes inquiries and support. Feel free to write or telephone.

Bibliography

Abrahamsen, David. *Crime and the Human Mind.* New York: Columbia University Press, 1944.

Albin, Rochelle Semmel. "Psychological Studies of Rape." *Signs.* Winter 1977. Vol. 3, No. 2, 423–435.

Amir, M. *Patterns of Forcible Rape.* Chicago: University of Chicago Press, 1971.

Aquilera, Donna C., and Messick, Janice M. *Crisis Intervention: Theory and Methodology.* St. Louis, MO: C.V. Mosby, 1974.

Argyris, C. *Personality and Organization.* New York: Harper and Row, 1957.

Astor, Gerald. *The Charge Is Rape.* Chicago: Playboy Press, 1974.

Baluss, Mary E. "Services for Victims of Crimes: A Developing Opportunity." *Evaluation and Change.* Special Issue, 1980.

Bard, Morton. "Action Research and the Question of Social Malignancy." Center for Social Research, The City University of New York. Unpublished paper.

_____and Diane Sangrey. *The Crime Victim's Book.* New York: Basic Books, 1979.

Barkas, J.L. *Understanding the Criminal Justice System.* Public Affairs Pamphlet #574 (381 Park Avenue South, New York 10010).

_____. *Victims.* New York: Scribners, 1978.

Berne, Eric. *Principles of Group Treatment.* New York; Grove Press, 1966.

Bion, W.R. *Experiences in Groups.* New York: Ballantine Books, 1961.

Bogdan, R., and Taylor, S. *An Introduction to Qualitative Research Methods: A Phenomenological Approach to the Social Sciences.* New York: John Wiley & Sons, 1975.

Brady, Katherine. *Fathers' Days: A True Story of Incest.* New York: Dell, 1979.

Brownmiller, Susan. *Against Our Will: Men, Women, and Rape.* New York: Simon and Schuster, 1975.

Bulman, R., and Worhman, C. "Attributions of Blame and Coping in the 'Real World:' Severe Accident Victims React to Their Lot." *Journal of Personality and Social Psychology*, 1977, *35*, 351–363.

Burgess, Ann Wolbert. "Family Reaction to Homicide." *American Journal of Orthopsychiatry*, Vol. 45 (April 1975), 391–398.

_____and Holmstrom, L. "Rape Trauma Syndrome." *American Journal of Psychiatry*, 1974, *131*, 981–986.

_____. *Rape: Victims of Crisis.* Bowie: Robert J. Brady, 1974.

The Cadman Complex, Vol. 5, No. 1, January 1982.

Cartwright, Dorwin, and Zander, Alvin. *Group Dynamics: Research and Theory*, Third Ed. New York: Harper and Row, 1968.

Chappell, Duncan, and Monahan, John, eds. *Violence and Criminal Justice.* Lexington, MA: D.C. Heath, 1975.

Citizens Action on Crime. "Pocket Facts About Crime in New York." Brochure.

Clark, Ramsey. *Crime in America.* New York: Touchstone Books, 1971.

Clark, T.P. "Counseling Victims of Rape." *American Journal of Nursing*, 1976, *76*, 1964–1966.

Collins, Carol. Letter to CVCS, September 2, 1982.

Community Service Society of New York, "Interim Report: The Elderly Crime Victim's Assistance Project." New York: May 1979.

Cook, Thomas D., and Reichardt, Charles. *Qualitative and Quantitative Methods in Evaluation Research.* Beverly Hills, CA: Sage, 1979.

"Crime Against the Elderly." *Aging* 250:5 August 1975.

Crime Victims' Counseling Services, Inc., G.P.O. Box 3003, Brooklyn, New York 11202. Brochure.

———. Crime Prevention Instruction Sheet.

———. Group Evaluations, *Passim.*

———. Group Evaluation, composite, 1982.

———. Group Exercises. *Passim.*

———. Public Service Announcement for WOR-TV.

———. Victims' Journal Excerpts. *Passim.*

Croft, Elizabeth. Victim Assistance Program: Experimental Action. University of Rochester, New York, 1975.

Denton, Allan. What They Think/What They Do: A Study of the Perceptions and Service Utilization of Victims of Violent Crime. Brochure. 1979.

Denver Anti-Crime Control. Analysis of 1972 Denver Victimization Survey. Denver, 1974.

des Pres, Terence. *Survivors.* Pocket Books, 1976.

Drapkin, Israel, ed. *Victimology.* Lexington, MA: Lexington Books, 1974.

Drapkin, Israel, and Viano, Emilio, eds. *Victimology.* Lexington, MA: Lexington Books, D.C. Heath, 1974.

———, eds. *Victimology: A New Focus.* Volume I—Theoretical Issues in Victimology. Lexington, MA: Lexington Books, D.C. Heath, 1975.

———, eds. *Victimology: A New Focus.* Volume II—Society's Reaction to Victimization. Lexington, MA: Lexington Books, D.C. Heath, 1975.

———, eds. *Victimology: A New Focus.* Volume III—Crimes, Victims, and Justice. Lexington, MA: Lexington Books, D.C. Heath, 1975.

———, eds. *Victimology: A New Focus.* Volume IV—Violence and Its Victims. Lexington, MA: Lexington Books, D.C. Heath, 1975.

———, eds. *Victimology: A New Focus.* Volume V—Exploiters and Exploited. Lexington, MA: Lexington Books, D.C. Heath, 1975.

Dyer, Wayne W. "Against All Odds: An Inspiring Story of Survival." *Family Circle*, September 1, 1981.

Editorial. *The New York Times.* March 11, 1982.

———. September 23, 1982.

———. January 10, 1983.

"Ederly and Crime." *Time* 108: 21–22, November 29, 1976.

Farley, Senator Hugh T. Letter in CVCS, March 17, 1982.

Feild, Huberts, and Bienen, Leigh B. *Jurors and Rape.* Lexington, MA: D.C. Heath, 1980.

Feinberg, Norma. "The emotional and behavioral consequences of violent crime on elderly victims." Thesis, 1978. University of Pittsburgh.

Festinger, L. *A Theory of Cognitive Dissonance.* Stanford: Stanford University Press, 1957.

Filstead, W.J. *Qualitative Methodology: Firsthand Involvement With the Social World.* Chicago: Markham, 1970.

"Forgotten Victims." *Newsweek* 92:91–92, October 2, 1978.

Forman, Bruce D. "Psychology With Rape Victims." *Psychotherapy: Theory, Research and Practice,* Vol. 17, No. 3, Fall 1980, 304–311.

Fox, S.S., and Scherl, D.J. "Crisis Intervention With Victims of Rape." *Social Work,* 1972, *17,* 37–42.

Francis, D. *People at Work: A Practical Guide to Organizational Change.* La Jolla: University Associates, 1975.

Franklin, J., and Kohout, J., eds. *Social Psychology and Everyday Life.* New York: McKay, 1973.

Freese, Arthur S. "If You're A Crime Victim." *Modern Maturity* (April–May 1981).

Friedman, Kenneth, *et al. Victims and Helpers: Reactions to Crime.* New York: Victim Services Agency, 1982.

Galaway, Burton, and Hudson, Joe, eds. *Perspectives on Crime Victims.* St. Louis: C.V. Mosby, 1981.

Garofalo, James. "Introduction to the National Crime Survey—Analytic Report." Washington, D.C.: U.S. National Criminal Justice and Statistics Service, 1977.

———. "Local Victim Surveys: A Review of the Issues." U.S. Department of Justice: LEAA, National Criminal Justice Information and Statistics Service, 1977.

———and Hindelang, Michael. "An Introduction to the National Crime Survey." U.S. Department of Justice, LEAA, National Criminal Justice Information and Statistics Service, 1977.

Gaylin, Willard. *The Killing of Bonnie Garland.* New York; Simon and Schuster, 1982.

Georges, Robert A., and Jones, M.O. *People Studying People: The Human Element in Fieldwork.* University of California Press, 1980.

Giorgi, A., Knowles, R., and Smith, D. (eds). *Duquesne Studies in Phenomenological Psychology.* Vols. I–III. Pittsburgh, PA: Duquesne University Press, 1971–1979.

Glaser, B.G., and Strauss, A.L. *The Discovery of Grounded Theory: Strategies for Qualitative Research.* Chicago: Aldine Press, 1967.

Goldfried, Marvin. "Toward the Delineation of Therapeutic Change Principles." *American Psychologist,* 1980, 35, 11, 991–999.

Grayson, Betty. "A comparison of criminal perceptions of the nonverbal behavior of potential victims of assault and a movement analysis based on lab analysis." Ph.D. thesis, New York University, 1978.

Greenberg, M.S., and Ruback, R.B. *Social Psychology of the Criminal Justice System.* Monterey, CA: Brooks/Cole, 1982.

Halmos, Paul. *The Faith of the Counselors.* New York: Schocken, 1976.

Hansen, James C., Stevic, Richard, and Warner, Richard W., Jr. *Counseling: Theory and Process.* Boston: Allyn and Bacon, 1977.

Heinz, John. "Op-Ed Page," *The New York Times,* July 20, 1982.

"Help for the Forgotten Victim." *Psychology Today* 8:15–16, March 1975.

Heppner, P.P., and Heppner, M. "Rape: Counseling the Traumatized Victim." *Personnel and Guidance Journal*, 1977, *56*, 77–80.

Hilberman, Elaine. *The Rape Victim*. Washington, D.C.: American Psychiatric Association, 1976.

Hillman, Robert. "The Psychopathology of Being Held Hostage." *American Journal of Psychiatry*, 1981 (138:9).

Holder, Maryse. *Give Sorrow Words: Maryse Holder's Letters from Mexico*. New York: Grove Press, 1979.

Horowitz, M. *Stress Response Syndromes*. New York: Jason Aronson, 1976.

———, Wilner, N., Kaltreider, N., and Alvarez, W. "Signs and Symptoms of Post-trauma Stress Disorders." *Journal of Nervous and Mental Disease*, 1980.

Houts, Marshall. *They Asked for Death*. New York: Cowles, 1970.

"How Much Crime?" *Scientific American* 237:56+, July 1977.

"How Not To Be A Victim." *Good Housekeeping* 191:247, September 1980.

Hudson, Joe, and Galaways, Burt, eds. *Considering the Victim*. Springfield, IL: Charles C Thomas, 1975.

Hunt, Morton. *The Mugging*. New York: Atheneum, 1972.

"Influence of a Victim's Suffering on an Attacker's Aggression." *USA Today* 108: 49–52, September 1979.

Institute for Local Self-Government. "Criminal Victimization in Maricopa County." Berkeley, CA, 1969.

The Interfaith Civilian Patrol, Inc., Booklet. Unpaged.

Kilpatrick, D.G., Smith, A.D., and Sippell, J.M. "On the Training of Paraprofessions for Rape Crisis Counseling." Paper, APA Annual Convention, March 1976.

Kinder, Gary. *Victim*. New York: Delacorte Press, 1982.

Klebba, A. "Mortality Trends for Homicide by Age, Color, and Sex—Statistical Profiles of the Victims during 1900–59 *and* 1973." National Center for Health Statistics, Division of Vital Statistics. Rockville, MD, 1973.

Knudten, Richard. "Victims and Witnesses: Their Experiences With Crime and the Criminal Justice System: Executive Summary," LEAA, 1977.

Kohut, H. *The Restoration of the Self*. New York: International University Press, 1977.

Krupnick, Janice L., and Horowitz, Mardi J. "Victims of Violence: Psychological Responses, Treatment Implications. *Evaluation and Change*, Special Issue, 1980.

Kutash, I., Kutash, S., and Schlesinger, L., eds. *Violence: Perspective on Murder and Aggression*. San Francisco: Jossey-Bass, 1978.

"Lack of Concern for Crime Victims." *Intellect* 106:440, May 1978.

LaPointe, Karen A., and Rimm, David C. "Cognitive, Assertive, and Insight-Oriented Group Therapies in the Treatment of Reactive Depression in Women." *Psychotherapy: Theory, Research and Practice*, 1980, 17, No. 3, 312–321.

Lawrence, P.R., and Lorsch, J.W. *Developing Organizations: Diagnosis and Action*. Reading, MA: Addison-Wesley, 1969.

Levine, Murray. "Investigative Reporting as a Research Method: An Analysis of *All the President's Men*." *American Psychologist*, Vol. 35, No. 7, 1980.

Lifton, Robert. *Death in Life: Survivors of Hiroshima*. New York: Random House, 1968.

Lindemann, E. "Symptomology and Management of Acute Grief." *Journal of Psychiatry* 101:141, 1944.

Luckman, Thomas, ed. *Phenomenology and Sociology*. New York: Penguin Books, 1978.

Lund, Sander. "How Ready Is the Mental Health System to Adopt or Expand Services for Victims?" *Evaluation and Change*. Special Issue, 1980.

Malvik, Ethel. "Society Blames the Victim of Crime." *Science Digest*, Vol. 77, March 1975, 64–69.

Maslow, Abraham. *Toward a Psychology of Being*. New York: Van Nostrand, 1968.

May, Rollo. *The Art of Counseling*. New York: Abingdon Press, 1967.

McCahill, Thomas, Meyer, Linda C., and Fischman, Arthur M. *The Aftermath of Rape*. Lexington, MA: Lexington Books, D.C. Heath, 1979.

McGillis, Daniel. "Biases and Jury Decision Making." *New Approaches to Social Problems*. Frieze, Irene Hamson, Daniel Bar-Tal, and John S. Carroll, eds. San Francisco: Jossey-Bass, 1979.

McClure, Lawrence, *et al*. "Community Psychology Concepts and Research Base." *American Psychologist*, 1980, 35, 11, 1000–1011.

McCombie, Sharon L. *The Rape Crisis Intervention Handbook: A Guide for Victim Care*. New York: Plenum, 1980.

McDonald, William, ed. *Criminal Justice and the Victim*. Beverly Hills: Sage, 1976.

———. *The Victim: A Social Psychological Study of Criminal Victimization*. Ann Arbor: University of Michigan, 1972.

McHugh, P. *Defining the Situation: The Organization of Meaning in Social Interaction*. New York: Bobbs-Merrill, 1968.

Mendelsohn, Beniamin. "Victimology and Contemporary Society's Trends." *Victimology: An International Journal*. Spring 1976.

Mischler, Elliot G. "Meaning in Context—Is There Any Other Kind?" *Harvard Educational Review*, 1979, Vol. 49, 1–19.

Mott, P.E. *Characteristics of Effective Organizations*. New York: Harper and Row, 1972.

National District Attorney's Association. Commission on Witness Assistance. Year-end report, 1976.

Newsday. August 5, 1982.

The New York City Advisory Task Force on Rape. "What You Should Know About Rape: A Guidebook For Women in New York City," 1981.

New York City Police Department. Brochure.

The New York Daily News. May 5, 1981.

———. May 23, 1981.

———. November 1, 1981.

———. April 20, 1982.

"New York Police in Service to the Elderly." *Aging* 244:6, February 1975.

The New York Sunday News. January 31, 1982.

The New York Sunday Times Magazine. January 24, 1981.

The New York Times. November 12, 1980.

———. November 17, 1980.

_____. November 22, 1980.

_____. November 23, 1980.

_____. January 4, 1981.

_____. February 2, 1981.

_____. February 25, 1981.

_____. April 6, 1981.

_____. May 5, 1981.

_____. November 15, 1981.

_____. November 17, 1981.

_____. December 14, 1981.

_____. December 18, 1981.

_____. February 7, 1982.

_____. March 8, 1982.

_____. March 16, 1982.

_____. March 23, 1982.

_____. April 4, 1982.

_____. July 21, 1982.

_____. September 20, 1982.

New York Women Against Rape. Flyer.

Nicholson, George, Candit, Thomas W., and Greenbaum, Stuart. *Forgotten Victims: An Advocate's Anthology.* Sacramento: California District Attorney's Association, 1977.

"Now We're Doing More for Victims." *Changing Times* 32:23–24, February 1978.

Ohlsen, Merle M. *Group Counseling.* New York: Holt, Rinehart and Winston, 1970.

Parsonage, W., ed. *Perspectives on Victimology.* Beverly Hills: Sage, 1979.

Pasternack, Stefan A., ed. *Violence and Victims.* New York: Spectrum Publications, 1975.

Patton, Michael A. *Alternative Evaluation Research Paradigm.* Grand Forks: University of North Dakota, 1975.

Peters, Cara, and Bronkhorst, Erin Van. *How to Stop Sexual Harassment: Strategies for Women on the Job.* Seattle: Facts for Women, P.O. Box 15113, Seattle, Washington 98115. Pamphlet.

The Phoenix. January 25, 1982.

_____. February 13, 1982.

_____. March 31, 1983.

Pileggi, Nicholas. "How To Stay Out of Trouble." *New York Magazine.* February 8, 1982.

Piliavin, J.A., Dovidio, J.F., Gaertner, S.L., and Clark, R.D. *Emergency Intervention.* New York: Academic Press, 1981.

Portland State University Urban Studies Center. "Robbery and Burglary Victimology Project. A Study Prepared for the High Impact Crime Problem." Portland, Oregon, 1972.

Progoff, Ira. *At a Journal Workshop.* New York: Dialogue House, 1973.

Rappaport, J. *Community Psychology: Values, Research, and Action.* New York: Holt, Rinehart and Winston, 1977.

Reagan, Ronald. Speech. October 14, 1982.

Rich, R., and Stenzel, S. "Mental Health Services for Victims: Policy Paradigms." *Evaluation and Change*, Spring 1980.

Rogers, Carl R. *Client-Centered Therapy*. Boston: Houghton Mifflin, 1965.

Rogers, P.C. "Rape Counseling Manual." Atlanta: Rape Crisis Center, Grady Memorial Hospital, 1978.

Rothenberg, David. "The Everybody-Talks-About-Crime-But-Nobody-Does-Anything-About-It EQ Test." *The Village Voice*. September 28, 1982.

Rush, A.J., Beck, A.T., Kovacs, M., and Hollen, S. "Comparative Efficacy of Cognitive Therapy and Pharmacotherapy in the Treatment of Depressed Outpatients." *Cognitive Therapy and Research*, 1977, *1*, 17–87.

Ryan, William. *Blaming the Victim*. New York: Random House, 1971.

Safety and Fitness Exchange. Brochure.

Salasin, Susan. "Caring for Victims: An Interview With Steven Sharfstein." *Evaluation and Change*, Special Issue, 1980.

———, ed. *Evaluating Victim Services*. Beverly Hills: Sage, 1981.

———and Rich, Robert. "Mental Health Needs for Crime Victims." Position Paper Presented to the Presidential Task Force on Victims of Crime. September 1982.

Schafer, Stephen. *Victimology: The Victim and His Criminal*. Reston, VA: Reston Publication Co., 1977.

Schatzman, Leonard, and Strauss, Anselm. *Field Research: Strategies for Natural Sociology*. Englewood Cliffs, NJ: Prentice-Hall, 1973.

Schutz, A. *On Phenomenology and Social Relations: Selected Writings*. Chicago: University of Chicago Press, 1970.

Seligman, Martin. *Helplessness: On Depression, Development and Death*. San Francisco: Freeman, 1975.

Shaffier, William, *et al*. *Fieldwork Experience: Qualitative Approaches to Social Research*. New York: St. Martin's Press, 1978.

Shellow, Jill. *Grantseekers Guide: A Directory for Social and Economic Justice Project*. Chicago: National Network of Grantmakers and The Interreligious Foundation for Community Organization, 1980.

Shorter, Edward. "On Writing the History of Rape." *Signs*. Winter 1977. Vol. 3, No. 2, 471–482.

Silberman, Charles E. *Criminal Violence, Criminal Justice*. New York: Random House, 1978.

Skogan, Wesley, ed. *Sample Surveys of the Victims of Crime*. Cambridge, MA: Ballinger, 1976.

———and Michael Maxfield. *Coping with Crime: Individual and Neighborhood Reactions*. Beverly Hills: Sage, 1981.

Smith, Robert B., and Manning, Peter. *Qualitative Methods*. Irvington, NY: Science Methods Service, 1980.

"Society Blames the Victim." *Science Digest* 77:64–69, March 1975.

Spates, Richard. "The Mental Health Needs of Victims: A Review of the Literature with Recommendations for Research." American Psychological Association Task Force on Violent Crimes, 1982.

Spradley, J.P. *The Ethnographic Interview*. New York: Holt, Rinehart and Winston, 1979.

Stang, D.J., and Wrightsman, L.S. *Dictionary of Social Behavior and Social Research Methods*. Monterey, CA: Brooks/Cole, 1981.

State of New Jersey. Department of Law and Public Safety. Violent Crimes Compensation Board. Brochure.

State of New York. 1980 Comprehensive Crime Control Plan. Office of Planning and Program Assistance, Division of Criminal Justice Services, 80 Centre Street, New York, NY 10013.

Stein, John Hollister. "Better Services for Crime Victims: A Prescriptive Package." *Evaluation and Change*. Special Issue, 1980.

Stelmachers, Zigfrids T. "Evaluation of Victim Services: Is Enough Being Done?" *Evaluation and Change*. Special Issue, 1980.

Stolorow, R., and Lachman, F. *Psychoanalysis of Developmental Arrests*. New York: International University Press, 1980.

Sutherland, S., and Scherl, D. "Patterns of Response Among Victims of Rape." *American Journal of Orthopsychiatry*, 1970, *40*, 503–511.

Symonds, Martin. "The Rape Victim: Psychological Patterns of Response." *American Journal of Psychoanalysis*, 1976, *36*, 27–34.

_____. "The 'Second Injury' to Victims." *Evaluation and Change*, Special Issue, 1980.

_____. "Victims of Senseless Violence." *Psychiatric Workview* (Lederle Laboratories), Jan./March 1977, 1.

_____. "Victims of Violence: Psychological Effects and After Effects." Paper delivered April 24, 1974.

"Thief Robbed My Family of More Than Money." *Good Housekeeping* 191:34, September 1980.

Toledo Metropolitan Area Council of Government. "Criminal Victimization Study: A Report of a Regional Survey."

United States House of Representatives. Bill S.2420. September 16, 1982.

United States Senate. "Report of the Committee on the Judiciary, to Accompany S.2420 to Protect Victims of Crime." August 19, 1982.

Viano, Emilio, ed. *Victims and Society*. Washington: Visage Press, 1976.

_____. "Victimology: The Study of the Victim." *Victimology: An International Journal*. Spring 1976.

"Victim Advocate: A New Style of Crimefighter." *Ms. Magazine*. September 1982.

The Victim's Perspective on American Criminal Justice. A report prepared by the Minnesota Department of Connections for the Governor's Commission on Crime and Prevention and Control. (Mimeo). St. Paul, MN: June 1976.

"Victims' Witness Assistance Program." *McCalls* 103:37 March 1976.

Weis, Kurt, and Borges, Sandra S. "Victimology and Rape: The Case of the Legitimate Victim." *Issues in Criminology*, Vol. 8 (Fall 1973), 71–115.

"What About Victims?" *US News and World Report*, 78:43, February 24, 1975.

"What Happened to Me Is My Fault." *Good Housekeeping* 185:44 +, October 1977.

White, Arthur H. "Coping with the Cost and Fear of Violence." *Public Relations Review*. (Vol. VIII, No. 1), Spring 1982.

"Why Violent Crime Is Now in Fashion." *US News and World Report*, 82:57–58, February 28, 1977.

Willems, E.P., and Raush, H.L. *Naturalistic Viewpoints in Psychological Research*. New York: Holt, Rinehart and Winston, 1969.

William Brill Associates. *Victimization, Fear of Crime, and Altered Behavior*. United States Department of Housing and Urban Development, 1977.

Young, Randy. "Putting a Guard on the Block." *New York Magazine*. February 8, 1982.

About the Author

Shelley Neiderbach, Ph.D., Founding President of Crime Victims' Counseling Services, Inc., is an associate professor, Counseling and Psychological Services, Jersey City State College.

Articles by and about her and her work have appeared in *The New York Times, Ms., Harper's Bazaar*, and *New York Newsday*.

In addition to numerous radio and television appearances on behalf of crime victims, she is a member of the Advisory Council Planning Committee of the New York State Crime Victims Board.

Dr. Neiderbach is a lecturer, workshop leader, consultant, and trainer, and can be reached at CVCS, G.P.O. Box 3003, Brooklyn, New York 11202 (718) 875-5862.

WRITE ME!
What were *Your* Experiences?

Have you been a crime victim? Has a family member, lover, friend, or coworker been a victim? I would like to hear of *your* experiences in preparation for a second volume of crime victim incidents and outcomes. All accounts will, if used, be acknowledged or left anonymous, as you wish. Be sure to include your address and phone number.
Write to:

Dr. Shelley Neiderbach
CVCS
G.P.O. Box 3003
Brooklyn, New York 11202